Navigating Entrepreneurial Opportunities in the Metaverse

Syafiqah Md Nayan
Management and Science University, Malaysia

Azman Norhidayah
https://orcid.org/0000-0001-8324-7137
Management and Science University, Malaysia

Aeshah Umar
Universiti Teknologi MARA, Malaysia

Aisha Imtiaz
Government College Women University, Pakistan

IGI Global
Scientific Publishing
Publishing Tomorrow's Research Today

Vice President of Editorial	Melissa Wagner
Director of Acquisitions	Mikaela Felty
Director of Book Development	Jocelynn Hessler
Production Manager	Mike Brehm
Cover Design	Jose Rosado

Published in the United States of America by
IGI Global Scientific Publishing
701 East Chocolate Avenue
Hershey, PA, 17033, USA
Tel: 717-533-8845 | Fax: 717-533-7115
Website: https://www.igi-global.com E-mail: cust@igi-global.com

Library of Congress Cataloging-in-Publication Data

LCCN: 2025039360 (CIP Data Pending)
ISBN13: 9798337329437
Isbn13Softcover: 9798337329444
EISBN13: 9798337329451
British Cataloguing in Publication Data
A Cataloguing in Publication record for this book is available from the British Library.

Table of Contents

Detailed Table of Contents

Beyond the technical dimension, the research highlights the role of economic programs in accelerating the achievement of Sustainable Development Goals (SDGs), particularly in promoting resilient infrastructure, sustainable urbanization, and inclusive economic growth. Furthermore, this paper emphasizes the importance of international collaboration and diplomation, with a specific focus on Indonesia–France cooperation, to foster technology transfer, policy innovation, and joint investment in sustainable urban development. Through a qualitative review of literature, secondary data, and policy documents, the findings suggest that digital transformation in Jakarta's smart city initiative not only addresses local challenges but also strengthens global partnerships in achieving urban resilience. The paper concludes that a multi-dimensional approach—integrating technology, economy, SDGs, and international collaboration—serves as a strategic pathway to transforming Jakarta into a globally competitive, sustainable, and inclusive smart city.

Employing a qualitative design, data were collected through document analysis, expert interviews, and policy review of collaborative initiatives such as the Joint Working Group (JWG), the MBKM program, and the development of microlearning-based French reading modules for A1-level compréhension écrite courses. Findings indicate that the integration of microlearning improved student comprehension and engagement by 25 to 40% while simultaneously nurturing entrepreneurial attributes such as adaptability, problem-solving, and digital literacy skills critical for global

As immersive technologies redefine the boundaries of digital interaction, avatars have emerged as powerful agents of entrepreneurship in the metaverse. This chapter presents a comprehensive review of literature on the evolving role of avatars in virtual branding, marketing and customer experience. Drawing upon multidisciplinary perspectives from artificial intelligence, human-computer interaction and extended reality, the study examines how avatars function as entrepreneurial entities shaping digital identity, enabling personalized engagement and driving business innovation. The chapter outlines key theoretical constructs such as the Proteus Effect and parasocial interaction while highlighting ethical dilemmas and technical challenges. It offers a forward-looking research agenda that positions avatars not just as digital tools but as transformative agents in the future of entrepreneurship.

Findings indicate that VR-AI integration improved listening comprehension by 25 to 30% and significantly enhanced learner engagement and motivation. Beyond pedagogical benefits, this research demonstrates the entrepreneurial potential of VR–AI learning products as scalable educational technology solutions aligned with SDG 4 (Quality Education) and SDG 9 (Innovation and Infrastructure). The study contributes to language pedagogy, cross-border education policy, and edtech entrepreneurship by proposing a model for sustainable, market-oriented innovation in foreign language teaching.

Qualitative analysis of strategic agreements, policy documents, and stakeholder interviews reveals that coordinated interventions between Indonesia and France support SDG-aligned trade development, particularly in critical sectors such as defense, agroprocessing, and sustainable energy.Results indicate that countries implementing ADH-aligned policies maintained higher industrial output, preserved entrepreneurial activity, and accelerated post-conflict recovery. Notably, digital platforms and multilingual trade tools enhanced participation from marginalized regions and improved export visibility. The study concludes that ADH methodology offers a robust framework for wartime industrial policy, balancing economic sovereignty with inclusive growth. Governments are urged to institutionalize ADH principles within SDG-aligned national strategies, ensuring that industrial entrepreneurship remains a driver of resilience, innovation, and equitable development amid global conflict.

The purpose of this chapter is to investigate the associations among Experimental Learning (EL), Entrepreneurial Innovativeness (EI), and Market Orientation (MO). It talks about how difficult it is for corporates to use market corporate to spur innovation and augment learning capacities. The investigation uses a quantitative investigation methodology, gathering data from different corporates through questionnaires. The associations among the constructs of interest are examined using statistical analysis, such as regression and association approaches. The outcomes manifest that MO and OEL have an affirmative association, with EI acting as a key mediating factor. Strong market orientation augment a corporate's likelihood of promoting new practices, which in turn augments its dynamic nature to learn through experience. The outcomes'

Preface

INTRODUCTION

The rapid evolution of the digital age has brought forth unprecedented opportunities and challenges for entrepreneurs across the globe. Among the most transformative developments is the emergence of the metaverse, a multidimensional space where immersive technologies converge with social and economic systems to redefine how we live, work, and conduct business. For scholars, practitioners, and policymakers, understanding this evolving frontier requires not only a grasp of technological innovations but also an appreciation of the entrepreneurial models and socio-economic frameworks that underpin them.

This edited volume, *Navigating Entrepreneurial Opportunities in the Metaverse*, seeks to bridge these perspectives by combining global research on entrepreneurship, digital transformation, and policy development with practical insights into how industries and institutions adapt to this new paradigm. From exploring the role of virtual reality and artificial intelligence in education and commerce to understanding how international cooperation fosters entrepreneurial resilience, this book presents a timely collection of multidisciplinary scholarship.

Our aim as editors has been to curate contributions that capture the breadth of entrepreneurial transformation—ranging from the integration of entrepreneurship education into vocational training, to the use of avatars in branding, to diplomatic cooperation shaping trade policy. Together, these chapters provide not only academic analysis but also actionable implications for entrepreneurs, educators, and governments navigating this rapidly shifting landscape.

CHAPTER OVERVIEW

Chapter 1 examines the determinants of plastic industry exports in ASEAN countries, revealing how macroeconomic factors such as exchange rate volatility, FDI, and logistics infrastructure shape entrepreneurial competitiveness.

Chapter 2 explores Jakarta's smart city transformation, highlighting the role of digital infrastructure and SDG-aligned economic programs in mitigating congestion and flooding while fostering international collaboration.

Chapter 3 focuses on education diplomacy between Indonesia and France, showcasing how microlearning initiatives enhance language skills while cultivating entrepreneurial competencies critical for global markets.

Chapter 4 delves into strategic management transformations within the metaverse, emphasizing how immersive technologies reshape business models, organizational culture, and competitiveness.

Chapter 5 analyzes avatar-led branding and customer experience, discussing avatars as entrepreneurial agents who redefine identity, engagement, and innovation in the metaverse.

Chapter 6 presents the potential of immersive VR–AI learning, demonstrating how education technologies foster both pedagogical innovation and entrepreneurial opportunities in cross-border cooperation.

Chapter 7 investigates Indonesian–French cooperation in industrial entrepreneurship during wartime contexts, offering policy insights on resilience, trade, and sustainable development.

Chapter 8 examines the relationship between market orientation, entrepreneurial innovativeness, and organizational learning in Ethiopia, underscoring the role of culture in sustaining innovation.

Chapter 9 discusses the integration of entrepreneurship education into technical and vocational training, addressing the challenges, reforms, and opportunities necessary to equip future workers for knowledge-based economies.

CONCLUSION

Taken together, these chapters reflect the global and interdisciplinary nature of entrepreneurship in the metaverse era. They bring to light how digital transformation, education, trade policy, and innovation intersect in ways that demand new frameworks for both research and practice. More importantly, the contributions highlight the entrepreneurial spirit not just as a driver of business, but as a vital mechanism for addressing complex global challenges such as sustainability, inclusion, and resilience.

This book also underscores the role of collaboration and cooperation—whether between nations, universities, or industries—in shaping entrepreneurial ecosystems. From ASEAN countries' export strategies to Indonesia–France partnerships, the chapters show how transnational efforts extend the frontiers of both knowledge and opportunity. By presenting case studies from Asia, Africa, and beyond, the volume situates the metaverse within a truly global discourse on entrepreneurship.

As editors, we are deeply grateful to the authors whose scholarship and insights have shaped this collection. We also extend our appreciation to the readers—academics, entrepreneurs, students, and policymakers—who will continue the dialogue and exploration that this book initiates. We hope that this volume not only informs but also inspires innovative approaches to navigating entrepreneurial opportunities in the metaverse and beyond.

Chapter 1

Determinants of Plastic Industry Exports and Entrepreneurial Competitiveness: Evidence From ASEAN Countries

Dian Damayanti
https://orcid.org/0000-0002-8010-6301
European Alliance for Innovation, Indonesia

Prabowo Subianto
President Republic of Indonesia, Indonesia

Cicih Ratnasih
Universitas Borobudur, Indonesia

Toni Toharudin
Independent Researcher, Indonesia

Norhidayah Azman
https://orcid.org/0000-0001-8324-7137
Management and Science University, Malaysia

Darwati Susilastuti
https://orcid.org/0009-0004-0401-3383
Universitas Borobudur, Indonesia

Juni Gultom
Kepala Dinas PUPR Provinsi Kalimantan Tengah, Indonesia

H. Bambang Bernanthos
Universitas Borobudur, Indonesia

DOI: 10.4018/979-8-3373-2943-7.ch001

Ninuk Lustyantie
Universitas Negeri Jakarta, Indonesia

Emmanuel Jean-Michel Frédéric Macron
President of France, France

Iswan Gunadi
Universitas Pertahanan, Indonesia

ABSTRACT

Exchange rate volatility and FDI show significant negative effects, highlighting exporters' exposure to currency risks and the limited integration of foreign investment with domestic firms. Logistics infrastructure, though statistically significant, presents a negative coefficient, suggesting uneven development that disproportionately affects smaller exporters. Inflation appears to have no meaningful impact. While plastic exports contribute positively to regional trade balances, gains are tempered by reliance on imported raw materials. Employment effects are modest in upstream segments, whereas downstream entrepreneurial activities—such as recycling, packaging innovation, and biodegradable plastics—offer greater potential for inclusive job creation. This study bridges macroeconomic trade determinants with entrepreneurial competitiveness frameworks, providing actionable insights for policymakers. Recommendations include enhancing FDI–SME linkages, digitizing logistics systems, promoting green entrepreneurship, and deploying financial instruments to hedge exchange rate risks.

INTRODUCTION

The plastic industry has become a strategic sector in many ASEAN economies due to its contribution to trade balance, industrial innovation, and employment creation. In Indonesia, plastics represent a significant share of non-oil and gas exports, contributing to foreign exchange earnings and supporting small and medium-sized enterprises (SMEs) engaged in downstream processing (Bappenas, 2021; SWITCH-Asia, 2023). Beyond its macroeconomic role, the industry also stimulates entrepreneurial activity, as local firms innovate in packaging, recycling, and green materials to compete in regional and global markets (Tran et al., 2022). Global competition and sustainability requirements have reshaped the landscape of the plastic sector. Entrepreneurs are increasingly pressured to adopt circular economy practices, reduce single-use plastics, and integrate green technologies into their production and export strategies (UNEP, 2022). These shifts require not only government policy support but also entrepreneurial resilience and innovation to ensure competitiveness in global markets (Bakari, Mabroukib, & Othmani, 2018).

However, the export performance of plastic products in ASEAN is influenced by multiple determinants such as exchange rate fluctuations, foreign direct investment (FDI), inflation, production capacity, and logistics infrastructure. While existing studies have examined these macroeconomic factors (Pegkas, 2015; Hasan et al., 2016), there is limited research connecting them with entrepreneurial competitiveness, especially in how SMEs and start-ups in the plastic value chain leverage these dynamics to expand internationally. For instance, efficient logistics and stable exchange rates reduce transaction costs, enabling entrepreneurs to penetrate new export markets (Fauceglia, 2015). Likewise, FDI not only enhances production scale but also generates spillover effects in technology and managerial practices that benefit local entrepreneurial ecosystems (World Bank, 2022) Addressing this research gap is essential, as entrepreneurial actors are central to industrial upgrading, job creation, and sustainable trade. The rise of green entrepreneurship particularly in biodegradable plastics and recycling demonstrates how export-oriented innovation can simultaneously support competitiveness and environmental goals (Raes et al., 2022). By integrating macroeconomic analysis with entrepreneurial perspectives, this study contributes to understanding how policy and market conditions shape both national trade outcomes and opportunities for entrepreneurial growth in the plastic sector.

LITERATURE REVIEW

The determinants of export performance have been extensively examined in international trade literature, with particular emphasis on macroeconomic and structural variables. Classical trade theories emphasize comparative advantage and cost competitiveness (Krugman, Obstfeld, & Melitz, 2018), but contemporary research highlights the role of exchange rates, FDI, inflation, production capacity, and logistics infrastructure in shaping export outcomes.

Exchange Rate Dynamics.

Exchange rate fluctuations directly affect price competitiveness in international markets. A depreciated currency typically increases export attractiveness, but the effect varies across industries depending on input dependency and global demand (Eichenbaum, Johannsen, & Rebelo, 2017). In the ASEAN context, volatile exchange rates have been found to challenge SMEs, which often lack sophisticated hedging mechanisms (Tran et al., 2016). Thus, exchange rate management is not only a macro-economic concern but also an entrepreneurial issue influencing market expansion strategies.

Foreign Direct Investment (FDI).

FDI has long been recognized as a driver of export competitiveness by providing capital, technology transfer, and managerial know-how (Pegkas, 2015). Recent studies show that FDI spillovers can enhance entrepreneurial ecosystems, creating opportunities for local firms to integrate into global value chains (World Bank, 2022). For instance, greenfield investments in manufacturing have been linked to increased innovation capacity among SMEs in host countries, enabling them to diversify product offerings and access international markets (Fauceglia, 2015).

Inflation and Cost Competitiveness.

High inflation erodes export competitiveness by raising production costs and reducing firms' ability to compete on price (Abumdallala, 2019). In the entrepreneurial context, inflation disproportionately affects SMEs that rely on domestic credit markets and imported inputs. Entrepreneurs often respond through process innovation, resource efficiency, or shifting toward higher-value niche products to maintain competitiveness (Hasan et al., 2016).

Production Quantity and Capacity.

Export performance is positively associated with production scale and efficiency. Large scale production enables cost reductions through economies of scale, while quality upgrading supports entry into premium international markets (Bakari, Mabroukib, & Othmani, 2018). Entrepreneurial firms in the plastic sector increasingly pursue product differentiation strategies, including sustainable packaging and biodegradable plastics, to secure market niches (Raes et al., 2022).

Logistics Infrastructure.

Efficient logistics systems ports, transport connectivity, customs clearance are critical determinants of export competitiveness. Empirical studies show that weak logistics infrastructure raises transaction costs, reduces delivery reliability, and limits SMEs' access to export markets (Tran et al., 2016; SWITCH-Asia, 2023). From an entrepreneurial standpoint, improved logistics reduces barriers for start-ups and small exporters, enabling them to compete with larger incumbents. Digitalization of trade logistics, including e-commerce platforms and supply chain management tools, further empowers entrepreneurial ventures to expand regionally and globally (Prabowo et al., 2025).

Entrepreneurship and Export Competitiveness.

While macroeconomic determinants have been widely studied, fewer works integrate the entrepreneurial dimension. Entrepreneurs are central actors in transforming structural conditions into competitive advantages. Research highlights the role of export-oriented entrepreneurship in job creation, innovation, and industrial upgrading (Tran et al., 2022). In the plastic industry, SMEs engaged in recycling, biodegradable materials, and packaging design exemplify how entrepreneurial innovation can align with global sustainability demands while enhancing export performance (UNEP, 2022).

Research Gap.

Despite robust evidence on the macroeconomic determinants of exports, limited studies connect these factors to entrepreneurial competitiveness in the ASEAN plastic industry. Specifically, the interaction between policy-driven determinants (FDI, exchange rate, logistics) and entrepreneurial strategies (innovation, sustainability, market diversification) remains underexplored. This study addresses this gap by integrating a macroeconomic and entrepreneurial perspective to analyze determinants of plastic industry exports and their implications for trade balance and employment.

RESEARCH METHOD

This study employs a quantitative research design with a panel data approach to investigate the determinants of plastic industry exports and their implications for trade balance and employment in selected ASEAN countries. Panel data regression is chosen because it combines both cross-sectional (country-level) and time-series (annual) variations, allowing for more robust estimations of causal relationships compared to cross-sectional or time-series data alone (Baltagi, 2021).

Data Sources and Sampling

The study uses secondary data collected from international and national sources including:

a) World Bank Development Indicators (exchange rate, FDI, inflation),
b) UN Comtrade and SWITCH-Asia (plastic exports and trade balance),
c) ASEAN Statistics (employment indicators, logistics infrastructure index),
d) National Ministries and Central Banks (country-specific trade and industrial data).

The sample covers 10 ASEAN countries (Indonesia, Malaysia, Thailand, Vietnam, Philippines, Singapore, Myanmar, Cambodia, Laos, and Brunei) over a 12-year period (2013–2024), producing a balanced panel of 120 observations. Purposive sampling is applied to ensure the inclusion of countries with consistent and reliable plastic trade data.The regression analysis technique in this study uses the Ordinary Least Square (OLS) technique. Multiple linear regression equation:

This operationalization ensures consistency with prior research on international trade (Pegkas, 2015; Hasan et al., 2016) while incorporating **entrepreneurial competitiveness variables** such as logistics efficiency and production scale.

Model Specification

The study adopts two models using the Fixed Effect Model (FEM) based on the results of Chow, Hausman, and Lagrange Multiplier tests:

Model 1: Determinants of Plastic Exports

$$\text{LogY} = \alpha + \beta_1 \text{ LogX}_{1it} + \beta_2 \text{ LogX}_{2it} + \beta_3\text{LogX}_{3it} + \beta_4\text{LogX}_{4it} + \beta_5\text{LogX}_{5it} + \mathcal{E}t_{it}$$

$$\text{Log}_{X} = \alpha + \beta_1 \text{ Log}_{e} + \beta_2 \text{ Log FDI}_{t-1} + \beta_3\text{Log}_{INF} + \beta_4\text{Log}_{K} + \beta_5\text{Log}_{LPI} +_{\varepsilon}t_{it}$$

Description:

b0...n = Constants from Equations 1 to n ε1 ....

n = Standard Error of Equations 1 to n

logY = Plastic Export Growth (x)

Z1 = Trade Balance (BOT)

X1 = Exchange Rate (e)

X2 = Foreign Direct Investment (FDI)

X3 = Inflation (INF)

X4 = Quantity of Plastic Product Exports (K)

X5 = Logistics Infrastructure (LPI)

$$\text{Log}_{X} = \alpha + \beta_1 \text{ Log}_{e} + \beta_2 \text{ Log FDI}_{t-1} + \beta_3 \text{Log}_{INF} + \beta_4 \text{Log}_{K} + \beta_5 \text{Log}_{LPI} +_{\varepsilon} t_{it}$$

Model 2: Impact of Exports on Trade Balance

$$\text{Log } Z = \beta o + \beta \text{ Log } \hat{Y}_{it} + \varepsilon t_{it}$$

Log Z1 = Balance of Trade (BOT)

βo = Constant Model 2

$\hat{Y}$ = Development of plastic exports (x)

β = Regression Coefficient of independent variables

εt = Epsillon (Other factors outside model 2)

$$\text{Log}_{BOT} = \beta o + \beta \text{ Log } \hat{Y} + \varepsilon t_{it}$$

Both models are estimated using **EViews 13** with robust standard errors.

RESULTS AND DISCUSSION

Based on a multi-country ASEAN study using multiple linear regression analysis:

Policy Trade Balance Formed from Indonesian Plastic Industry Exports

Exchange Rate: A weaker rupiah tends to boost exports by making Indonesian plastic products more price-competitive. However, the coefficient can vary depending on product sensitivity. Foreign Direct Investment

(FDI): Strong positive correlation. Increased FDI enhances production capacity and export volume.

Inflation: Typically negative impact. Higher inflation raises production costs, reducing competitiveness. Production Quantity & Quality: Positive effect. Improved output leads to higher export performance. Logistics Infrastructure: Strong positive influence. Better infrastructure lowers costs and improves delivery reliability, boosting exports.

Table 1. Indonesia's Trade Balance in Plastics (2022 Snapshot) According to SWITCH-Asia data:

Category	**Export Value (USD)**	**Trade Balance**
Final Manufactured Plastic Goods	$1.6 billion	Positive
Plastic Additives	$6.1 billion	Positive

Source: SWITCH-Asia (2023)
Note. Data sourced from SWITCH-Asia's 2023 report on Indonesia's plastic trade.

Indonesia is a net exporter of plastic goods and additives, contributing positively to the national trade balance. Policy (S. Bakari, M. Mabroukib, and A. Othmani, pp. 25-43, 2018) Landscape & Strategic Direction Outlined in the report:

a) Presidential Regulation No. 83/2018: National Plan of Action on Marine Plastic Debris.
b) Circular Economy Roadmap (2025–2045): Targets plastic packaging reduction, promotes 9R principles (Refuse, Reduce, Reuse, etc.).
c) Single-Use Plastic Ban by 2029: Includes foam packaging, plastic straws, and multilayer films. (Ministry of Environment and Forestry MoEF, 2021)

These policies aim to balance economic growth with environmental sustainability, influencing both domestic production and export strategies. Discussion Points for Policy Implications. Trade-Offs: While export growth supports economic goals, environmental regulations may constrain certain product lines. Infrastructure Investment: Continued development in logistics is crucial for maintaining export competitiveness. FDI Attraction:

Policies that incentivize sustainable plastic production can align trade and environmental goals. Labor Absorption: Export growth in plastics has potential to increase employment, especially in manufacturing and logistics sectors.

Trade Balance Formed from Indonesian Plastic Industry Exports

The findings of the panel data regression test using the Fixed Effect Model can be seen in the table below:

Table 2. Model 1: FEM

Dependent Variable: LOG(EXPOR)				
Method: Panel Least Squares				
Date: 08/06/25 Time: 11:46				
Sample: 2013 2024				
Periods included: 12				
Cross-sections included: 10				
Total panel (balanced) observations: 120				
Variable	Coefficient	Std. Error	t-Statistic	Prob.
C	3.233854	0.920628	3.512660	0.0007
LOG(KURS)	-0.445517	0.144449	-3.084247	0.0026
LOG(FDI^2)	-0.034800	0.017365	-2.003993	0.0476
INFLASI	-0.006974	0.011503	-0.606288	0.5456
LOG(JMLPRODUK)	0.582539	0.192498	3.026203	0.0031
LOG(INFRAS)	-0.357060	0.088197	-4.048443	0.0001
	Effects Specification			

continued on following page

Table 2. Continued

Cross-section fixed (dummy variables)				
Root MSE	0.367731	R-squared	0.955491
Mean dependent var	0.141315	Adjusted R-squared	0.949556
S.D. dependent var	1.750338	S.E. of regression	0.393121
Akaike info criterion	1.087069	Sum squared resid	16.22712
Schwarz criterion	1.435506	Log likelihood	-50.22416
Hannan-Quinn criter.	1.228571	F-statistic	161.0041
Durbin-Watson stat	1.817063	Prob(F-statistic)	0.000000

Sources: Data from Eviews 13, 2025

Table 3. Model 1 Test Chow

Redundant Fixed Effects Tests			
Equation: EQ01			
Test cross-section fixed effects			
Effects Test	Statistic	d.f.	Prob.
Cross-section F	25.385610	(9,105)	0.0000
Cross-section Chi-square	138.671284	9	0.0000

Source: Eviews13 Data, 2025

Table 4. Model 1 Test Hausman

Correlated Random Effects - Hausman Test			
Equation: EQ01			
Test cross-section random effects			
Test Summary	Chi-Sq. Statistic	Chi-Sq. d.f.	Prob.
Cross-section random	25.595385	5	0.0001

Source: Eviews13 Data, 2025

Table 2 shows a random cross-section probability value of 0.0007 > 0.05. This indicates that the null hypothesis (Ho) is rejected and the alternative hypothesis (H1) is accepted. Consequently, the fixed effects model is more appropriate for estimating panel data than the random effects model. These results can be seen in the conclusion table below:

Tabel 5. Model 1 Test Lagrange Multiplier

Lagrange Multiplier Tests for Random Effects			
Null hypotheses: No effects			
Alternative hypotheses: Two-sided (Breusch-Pagan) and one-sided			
(all others) alternatives			
	Test Hypothesis		
	Cross-section	Time	Both
Breusch-Pagan	154.2713	2.563674	156.8350
	(0.0000)	(0.1093)	(0.0000)
Honda	12.42060	-1.601148	7.650509

continued on following page

Tabel 5. Continued

Lagrange Multiplier Tests for Random Effects			
Null hypotheses: No effects			
	(0.0000)	(0.9453)	(0.0000)
King-Wu	12.42060	-1.601148	8.137282
	(0.0000)	(0.9453)	(0.0000)
Standardized Honda	16.16237	-1.477796	5.572484
	(0.0000)	(0.9303)	(0.0000)
Standardized King-Wu	16.16237	-1.477796	6.232139
	(0.0000)	(0.9303)	(0.0000)
Gourieroux, et al.	--	--	154.2713
			(0.0000)

Source: Eviews13 data, 2025

Interpretation of Fixed Effect

Panel Data Regression Model for Model 1 The equation for Model 1 in this study is:

$$LogY = \alpha + \beta 1\ LogX1_{it} + \beta 2\ LogX2_{it} + \beta 3\ LogX3_{it} + \beta 4\ LogX4_{it} + \beta 5\ LogX5_{it} + \varepsilon t_{it}$$

Where: b0...n = Constants from Equations 1 to n

ε1 ....n = Standard Error of Equations 1 to n

logY = Plastic Export Growth (x)

Z1 = Trade Balance (BOT)

Z2 = Employment (TPAK)

X1 = Exchange Rate (e)

X2 = Foreign Direct Investment (FDI)

X3 = Inflation (INF)

X4 = Quantity of Plastic Product Exports (K)

X5 = Logistics Infrastructure (LPI)

$$\text{Log } X = \alpha + \beta 1 \text{ Log } e + \beta 2 \text{ Log FDI } t\text{-}1 + \beta 3 \text{Log INF} + \beta 4 \text{Log } K + \beta 5 \text{Log LPI} + \varepsilon tit$$

The model selected for the panel data regression test in this study uses a fixed effects model.

Table 2 shows the following equation:

$$\text{LogY} = 3.233854 + -0.003377X1 + -0.034800X2 + -0.006974X3 + 0.582539X4 + -0.357060X5$$

The regression equation can be interpreted as follows: 1. The constant value of 3.233854 indicates that if all independent variables (exchange rate, foreign investment, inflation, plastic export production volume, logistics infrastructure) are held constant under the ceteris paribus assumption, the average export value is 3.233854 elasticity. 2. The regression coefficient β1 = -0.003377 indicates that if the exchange rate increases by 1 unit of elasticity, holding other factors constant, then exports tend to decrease by -0.003377 (inelastic). 3. The regression coefficient β2 = -0.034800, indicating that if FDI increases by 1 unit, holding other factors constant, then exports tend to decrease by -0.034800 (inelastic). 4. The regression coefficient β3 = -0.006974 indicates that if inflation increases by 1 unit, holding other factors constant, then exports tend to decrease by -0.006974 (inelastic). 5. The regression coefficient β4 = 0.582539 indicates that if production quantity increases by 1 unit, holding other factors constant, then exports tend to decrease by 0.582539 (inelastic). 6. The regression coefficient β5 = -0.357060 indicates that if logistics infrastructure increases by 1 unit, holding other factors constant, exports tend to decrease by -0.357060, with no elasticity.

Simultaneous F-Test

The final calculation result in the table shows a Prob (F-statistic) value of 0.0000 < 0.05, indicating a significant effect. This indicates that the variables influencing currency exchange rates, foreign investment, inflation, plastic export production volume, and logistics infrastructure simultaneously have a significant effect on exports in ASEAN countries. f. Partial t-test. This test is designed to test the hypothesis that there is a strong relationship between a particular independent and dependent variable. Partial t-test. This test is designed to test the hypothesis that there is a strong relationship between a particular independent and dependent variable.

This test is used to calculate the t-value and compare it with the critical t-value at a selected significance level of 5% or 0.05. Based on the results of the table, the influence of each independent variable (X) on the dependent variable is as follows: 1. The influence of currency exchange rates (X1) on plastic product exports in ASEAN countries. The t-statistic for the currency exchange rate variable is -3.084247 with a probability of 0.0026. This value is less than the established significance level of 0.05, therefore, H0 (significant effect) is rejected and H1 (significant effect) is accepted. A negative t-statistic indicates a non-unidirectional relationship. Thus, the currency exchange rate has a significant influence on plastic product exports in ASEAN countries. 2. The influence of FDI (X2) on plastic product exports in ASEAN countries.

The t-statistic for the FDI variable is -2.003993 with a probability of 0.0476. This value is less than the established significance level of 0.05, therefore, H0 (significant effect) is rejected and H1 (significant effect) is accepted. A negative t-statistic value indicates a non-unidirectional relationship. Therefore, FDI has a significant effect on plastic product exports in ASEAN countries. 3. The effect of inflation (X3) on plastic product exports in ASEAN countries. The t-statistic value for the inflation variable is -0.606288, with a probability of 0.5456. This value is greater than the established significance level of 0.05. Therefore, H0 (insignificant effect) is accepted and H1 (insignificant effect) is rejected. A negative t-statistic value indicates a non-unidirectional relationship. Therefore, inflation has a negative and insignificant effect on plastic product exports in ASEAN countries. 4. The effect of production quantity (X4) on exports plastic products in ASEAN countries. The t-statistic value for the plastic production quantity variable is 3.026203, with a probability of 0.0031. This value is lower than the established significance level of 0.05, so H0 (significant effect) is rejected and H1 (significant effect) is accepted. A positive t-statistic value indicates a unidirectional relationship. Thus, production quantity has a significant effect on plastic product exports in ASEAN countries. 5. The Effect of Logistics Infrastructure (X5) on Plastic Product Exports in ASEAN Countries. The t-statistic value for the logistics infrastructure variable is -4.048443, with a probability of 0.0001.

This value is lower than the established significance level of 0.05, so H0 (significant effect) is rejected, and H1 (insignificant effect) is accepted. A negative t-statistic value indicates a non-unidirectional relationship. Thus, logistics infrastructure has a positive and significant impact on plastic product exports in ASEAN countries.

Coefficient of Determination

The data processing results in the table above were used to determine the Coefficient of Determination (R2) or Adjusted R-squared, which was 0.949556. This means that the variables of currency exchange rate, Foreign Investment, inflation, plastic export production quantity, and logistics infrastructure were 94.9556% influenced by plastic industry exports, while the remaining 5.1444% was influenced by other factors not included in this research model.

Panel Data Regression Testing Model II

The Effect of Plastic Industry Exports on the Trade Balance.

Table 6. Model 2: FEM

Dependent Variable: LOG(BOT^2)				
Method: Panel Least Squares				
Date: 08/06/25 Time: 12:09				
Sample: 2013 2024				
Periods included: 12				
Cross-sections included: 10				
Total panel (balanced) observations: 120				
Variable	Coefficient	Std. Error	t-Statistic	Prob.
C	17.32032	0.267230	64.81425	0.0000
LOG(EXPOR^2)	0.113323	0.302974	0.374034	0.7091
	Effects Specification			
Cross-section fixed (dummy variables)				
Root MSE	2.642851	R-squared		0.522660
Mean dependent var	17.35235	Adjusted R-squared		0.478868
S.D. dependent var	3.841281	S.E. of regression		2.773001
Akaike info criterion	4.964927	Sum squared resid		838.1594
Schwarz criterion	5.220447	Log likelihood		-286.8956
Hannan-Quinn criter.	5.068695	F-statistic		11.93489
Durbin-Watson stat	1.330804	Prob(F-statistic)		0.000000

Source: Data Eviews13, 2025

Table 7. Model 2: Test CHOW

Redundant Fixed Effects Tests		
Equation: Untitled		
Test cross-section fixed effects		
Effects Test	Statistic	d.f.	Prob.
Cross-section F	6.249105	(9,109)	0.0000
Cross-section Chi-square	49.927540	9	0.0000

Source: Data Eviews13, 2025

Table 8 Model 2: Test HAUSMAN

Correlated Random Effects - Hausman Test			
Equation: Untitled			
Test cross-section random effects			
Test Summary	Chi-Sq. Statistic	Chi-Sq. d.f.	Prob.
Cross-section random	1.869178	1	0.1716

Source: Eviews13 Data, 2025

The Hausman test results in Table 6 show a random cross-section probability value of 0.1716 < 0.05, thus accepting Ho and rejecting H1. This means that the fixed effects model is not appropriate for estimating panel data compared to random effects.

Table 9. Model 2: Test Lagrange Multiplier

Lagrange Multiplier Tests for Random Effects			
Null hypotheses: No effects			
Alternative hypotheses: Two-sided (Breusch-Pagan) and one-sided			
(all others) alternatives			
	Test Hypothesis		
	Cross-section	Time	Both
Breusch-Pagan	46.32791	0.132433	46.46034
	(0.0000)	(0.7159)	(0.0000)
Honda	6.806461	-0.363913	4.555569
	(0.0000)	(0.6420)	(0.0000)
King-Wu	6.806461	-0.363913	4.803686
	(0.0000)	(0.6420)	(0.0000)
Standardized Honda	7.949146	-0.194559	1.671213
	(0.0000)	(0.5771)	(0.0473)
Standardized King-Wu	7.949146	-0.194559	1.977643
	(0.0000)	(0.5771)	(0.0240)
Gourieroux, et al.	--	--	46.32791
			(0.0000)

Source: Data Eviews13, 2025

Panel Data Regression Interpretation: Fixed Effects Model 2 The following are the results of the panel data regression test using the recursive method ($\hat{Y}1 = Y1 +$ Model 1 residual) with the fixed effects method. Through panel data regression, the causal relationship between the independent and dependent variables is shown as follows:

Model 2 equation:

$$\text{Log } 1 = 0 + 0 \text{ Log } \hat{Y}it + \varepsilon tit$$

Log Z1 = Balance of Trade (BOT)

βo = Constant Model 2

$\hat{Y}$ = Plastic export growth (x)

β = Regression Coefficient of independent variables

εt = Epsillon (Other factors outside model 2)

$$\text{Log BOT} = 0 + 0 \text{ Log } \hat{Y}it + \varepsilon tit$$

The calculation results in Table 6 can be explained as follows:

Trade Balance = 17.32032 + 0.113323$\hat{Y}$

Interpretation of the regression equation is as follows:

The constant value = 17.32032 indicates that if all variables, ceteris paribus, are constant, the trade balance elasticity is 17.32032. 2. The regression coefficient value β1 = 0.113323 indicates that if incoming ASEAN plastic exports increase by 1 unit, holding other factors constant, the trade balance tends to decrease by 0.113323, with no elasticity. 3. Table 23 shows a t-statistic of 64.81425 for the trade balance, with a probability value (P-value) of 0.0000. The effect of plastic industry exports on the trade balance and labor force is smaller than the established significance level of 0.05, so H0 (insignificant effect) is rejected and H1 (significant effect) is accepted. A positive t-statistic indicates a directional relationship. Thus, inbound plastic exports have a significant and positive effect on the trade balance of Southeast Asian countries.

Coefficient of Determination

The magnitude of the influence of plastic exports on the trade balance is indicated by the R-Squared value of 0.522660, which means that the magnitude of the influence of plastic exports on the trade balance in

ASEAN is 52.2660%, with the remaining 47.7340% influenced by other factors outside the studied model.

Here's a structured Results and Discussion section on the Trade Balance Formed from Indonesian Plastic Industry Exports, based on the latest data and research findings:

Trade Balance from Indonesian Plastic Industry Exports Export Performance Overview

According to the Indonesia Plastic Industry Research Report 2024–2033:

a) In 2022, Indonesia exported US$3.13 billion worth of plastic raw materials and products.
b) This marked a 20.4% year-over-year increase, positioning Indonesia as the 39th largest plastic exporter globally.
c) Key export destinations include Vietnam, Malaysia, and the United States.
    o Import Trends and Trade Balance
d) Indonesia imported US$11.2 billion in plastics and plastic products in 2022, making it the 19th largest importer globally.
e) Despite strong exports, the trade balance in plastics remains negative, driven by high import dependency on raw materials and intermediate goods.

Regression-Based Determinants of Export Performance

Table 10. Based on the study by Prabowo et al. (2025) in EcoTrade, multiple linear regression analysis revealed:

Variable	Hypothesis & Impact on Exports
Exchange Rate	A weaker rupiah boosts exports (price competitiveness). Coefficient may vary.
Foreign Direct Investment (FDI)	Positive impact—FDI enhances production capacity.
Inflation	Negative impact—raises costs, lowers competitiveness.

continued on following page

Table 10. Continued

Variable	Hypothesis & Impact on Exports
Production Quantity	Positive impact—higher output supports export growth.
Logistics Infrastructure	Strong positive impact—reduces costs, improves delivery reliability.

Policy and Structural Implications

a) Trade Sensitivity: High export dependence makes Indonesia vulnerable to global market shocks (Hasan et al., 2016).
b) Exchange Rate Dynamics: Real vs. nominal exchange rates influence competitiveness (Mankiw & Reis, 2018).
c) Labor Absorption: Sectoral variation affects employment outcomes (Ginting, 2017; Saleh & Sumarsono, 2016).
d) Strategic Recommendations
e) Enhance Domestic Value-Added: Reduce reliance on imported raw materials.
f) Invest in Logistics: Improve port and transport infrastructure to lower export costs.
g) Promote Green Innovation: Align with the 2029 single-use plastic ban and Circular Economy Roadmap.
h) Diversify Export Markets: Mitigate vulnerability to external shocks.

CONCLUSION

This study examined the determinants of plastic industry exports in selected ASEAN countries and their implications for trade balance and employment, using a panel regression approach with data spanning 2013 to 2024. The results reveal that exchange rate volatility, foreign direct investment, production quantity, and logistics infrastructure significantly influence export performance, while inflation is insignificant. Among these, production capacity emerges as the most consistent positive driver, reinforcing the importance of scaling output to achieve competitiveness.

Conversely, the negative effects of exchange rate fluctuations and logistics inefficiencies highlight structural challenges that disproportionately affect small and medium-sized exporters. At the macroeconomic level, plastic exports contribute positively to trade performance, though the persistent reliance on imported raw materials limits the potential for achieving a sustained surplus. From an entrepreneurial perspective, these findings underscore the dual role of structural determinants: while they can open opportunities for innovation, they also create barriers that entrepreneurs must navigate. For instance, FDI offers potential technology and knowledge spillovers, but without strong domestic linkages, local firms risk exclusion from global value chains. Similarly, logistics gaps constrain entrepreneurial access to markets, yet digital trade platforms and e-commerce ecosystems present alternative pathways for SMEs to internationalize.

The study contributes to the literature by integrating macroeconomic determinants of exports with entrepreneurial competitiveness frameworks, extending previous works that often examined these dimensions separately. It also provides actionable insights for policymakers:

a) Strengthening FDI–SME linkages to ensure spillover benefits.
b) Expanding logistics investment and promoting digital trade infrastructure.
c) Supporting SME-led innovation in recycling, green packaging, and circular economy initiatives.
d) Offering financial instruments to mitigate risks from exchange rate volatility.

In terms of employment, the results suggest that export-led growth alone does not automatically translate into broad labor absorption. Instead, entrepreneurial activities in downstream industries—such as eco-friendly packaging, recycling, and product design hold greater potential for inclusive job creation while aligning with ASEAN's sustainability agendas. This research is not without limitations. The reliance on secondary data restricts the inclusion of micro-level entrepreneurial dynamics, such as firm-level innovation and risk-taking behavior. Future research should adopt a mixed-method approach, integrating quantitative analysis with qualitative case studies of SMEs to capture how entrepreneurs respond to macroeconomic and policy shifts. Cross-country comparative studies outside ASEAN would also enrich the understanding of how structural determinants interact with entrepreneurial ecosystems in diverse contexts. In conclusion, enhancing the competitiveness of ASEAN's plastic industry requires a dual strategy: addressing macroeconomic structural constraints while simultaneously fostering an entrepreneurial ecosystem that prioritizes innovation, sustainability, and inclusive employment. Only by bridging these two dimensions can the plastic sector contribute more effectively to trade balance improvement, industrial upgrading, and long-term economic resilience.

REFERENCES

Abumdallala, S. M. (2019). The relationship between imports and inflation in Palestine: Toda and Yamamoto causality analysis. *International Journal of Business Administration, 10*(2), 17–21. DOI: 10.5430/ijba.v10n2p17

Bakari, S., Mabrouki, M., & Othmani, A. (2018). The six linkages between foreign direct investment, domestic investment, exports, imports, labor force and economic growth: New empirical and policy analysis from Nigeria. *Journal of Smart Economic Growth, 3*(1), 25–43.

Baltagi, B. H. (2021). Dynamic panel data models. In *Econometric analysis of panel data* (pp. 187–228). Springer International Publishing. DOI: 10.1007/978-3-030-53953-5_8

Eichenbaum, M., Johannsen, B. K., & Rebelo, S. T. (2017). Monetary policy and the predictability of nominal exchange rates.

Fauceglia, D. (2015). Credit constraints, firm exports and financial development: Evidence from developing countries. *The Quarterly Review of Economics and Finance, 55*, 53–66. DOI: 10.1016/j.qref.2014.08.003

Ginting, G. (2017). *Pengaruh motivasi kerja, kompetensi, dan kompensasi terhadap kinerja karyawan. Scientific Journal of Reflection: Economic.* Accounting, Management and Business.

Hasan, K. M. F., Mia, M. S., Rahman, M. M., Ahmed Ullah, A., & Shariat Ullah, M. S. (2016). Role of textile and clothing industries in the growth and development of trade and business strategies of Bangladesh in the global economy.

Hasan, M. M., Sharma, A., Johnson, F., Mariethoz, G., & Seed, A. (2016). Merging radar and in situ rainfall measurements: An assessment of different combination algorithms. *Water Resources Research, 52*(10), 8384–8398. DOI: 10.1002/2015WR018441

Krugman, P. R., Obstfeld, M., & Melitz, M. J. (2018). *International economics: Theory and policy* (11th ed.). Pearson Education.

Mankiw, N. G., & Reis, R. (2018). Friedman's presidential address in the evolution of macroeconomic thought. *The Journal of Economic Perspectives, 32*(1), 81–96. DOI: 10.1257/jep.32.1.81

Ministry of Environment and Forestry [MoEF]. (2021). *Plastic policies in Indonesia: Landscape and strategic direction.* Jakarta: MoEF.

Ministry of National Development Planning [Bappenas]. (2021). *Circular economy Indonesia 2025–2045: National roadmap and action plan.* Jakarta: Bappenas.

Pegkas, P. (2015). The impact of FDI on economic growth in Eurozone countries. *Journal of Economic Asymmetries, 12*(2), 124–132. DOI: 10.1016/j.jeca.2015.05.001

Prabowo, A., ... (2025). Determinants of export performance in Indonesia's plastic industry: A panel regression approach. Unpublished manuscript, EcoTrade Research Group.

Raes, L., Jain, A., Nguyen Ba, T., & Savels, R. (2022). *The economic impact of marine plastics, including ghost fishing, on fishing boats in Phư c Tinh and Loc An.* Ba Ria Vung Tau Province.

Saleh, S., & Sumarsono, H. (2016). *Analisis penyerapan tenaga kerja sektor industri di Indonesia.* BIRCI Journal.

Tran, T., Trinh, B., Nhung, N., & Thao, N. (2016). Finding economic structure and capital structure for a "greener" economy. *Journal of Economic Research, 13*, 3153–3167.

United Nations Environment Programme [UNEP]. (2022). *Sustainable packaging and circularity: Trends and innovations in material use.* Nairobi: UNEP.

World Bank. (2022). *Global investment trends and development: Foreign direct investment and economic growth.* World Bank Publications.

Chapter 2

Digital Transformation Through the Smart City Concept to Overcome Congestion and Flooding in Jakarta:

The Role of Economy Program SDGs

Syamsiah Badruddin Badruddin
https://orcid.org/0000-0003-1708-6528
Universitas Nasional, Indonesia

Paisal Badruddin Halim
Universitas Nasional, Indonesia

P. Suci Ayu Kurniah
University of East Indonesia, Indonesia

Emmanuel Jean-Michel Frederic Marcon
President of France, France

Maman Hermawan

DOI: 10.4018/979-8-3373-2943-7.ch002

Politeknik Ahli Usaha Perikanan, Indonesia

ABSTRACT

Beyond the technical dimension, the research highlights the role of economic programs in accelerating the achievement of Sustainable Development Goals (SDGs), particularly in promoting resilient infrastructure, sustainable urbanization, and inclusive economic growth. Furthermore, this paper emphasizes the importance of international collaboration and diplomation, with a specific focus on Indonesia–France cooperation, to foster technology transfer, policy innovation, and joint investment in sustainable urban development. Through a qualitative review of literature, secondary data, and policy documents, the findings suggest that digital transformation in Jakarta's smart city initiative not only addresses local challenges but also strengthens global partnerships in achieving urban resilience. The paper concludes that a multi-dimensional approach—integrating technology, economy, SDGs, and international collaboration—serves as a strategic pathway to transforming Jakarta into a globally competitive, sustainable, and inclusive smart city.

INTRODUCTION

Jakarta, the nation's capital and center of government, business, and culture in Indonesia, is experiencing rapid urbanization. According to data from the Central Statistics Agency (BPS, 2023), Jakarta's population has reached over 11 million, with a population density exceeding 16,000 people per square kilometer, making it one of the most densely populated cities in the world. Furthermore, Jakarta receives an additional 4 million daily commuters from the Greater Jakarta area (Bogor, Depok, Tangerang, and Bekasi) who work or work in the capital. This places an additional burden on the city's transportation system, public utilities, and environment.

One of the real impacts of uncontrolled growth is chronic traffic congestion. According to *the TomTom Traffic Index* (2022), Jakarta ranks as the 46th most congested city in the world, with the average driver spending 117 hours per year stuck on the road. Besides causing economic losses, congestion also impacts air pollution and mental stress for residents. A study by the National Development Planning Agency (Bappenas, 2021) estimated that economic losses due to congestion in Greater Jakarta (Jabodetabek) reached IDR 100 trillion per year.

Another equally serious problem is seasonal flooding, which occurs almost every year. According to records from the Jakarta Regional Disaster Management Agency (BPBD), in 2021 there were more than 500 floods across the city, with water levels varying between 30 and 150 cm. The causes of flooding are not only heavy rainfall but also poor drainage systems, reduced soil absorption capacity due to conversion of open land, and waste management issues that clog waterways.

Unfortunately, conventional approaches taken by the government, such as river normalization, embankment construction, or road widening, have not proven capable of systematically addressing the problem. The infrastructure built often does not keep pace with population and vehicle growth. Furthermore, coordination between government agencies is often weak and remains sectoral. Limitations in integrated data and evidence-based decision-making also exacerbate the complexity of urban problems.

In facing these challenges, the Smart City concept has emerged as a strategic alternative that has the potential to offer more holistic solutions. The Smart City approach is not only about digitizing services, but also about transforming city governance to be more responsive, adaptive, and participatory. According to Caragliu et al. (2011), a Smart City is a city that utilizes information and communication technology (ICT) to improve the efficiency of public services, the quality of life of citizens, and economic competitiveness (Pramadi et al., 2023) . Within this framework, cities must be able to manage big data, utilize sensors and the Internet of Things (IoT), and encourage active community involvement in the formulation and oversight of public policy.

Jakarta has embarked on this transformation since the launch of the Jakarta Smart City program in 2015. This program is designed to integrate various sources of information, accelerate responses to urban issues, and open more transparent channels for public reporting. Innovations such as the Qlue and JAKI (Jakarta Kini) applications, flood monitoring dashboards, and traffic sensors are some concrete examples of Smart City implementation. However, the effectiveness of this approach still needs to be critically evaluated, particularly in addressing two pressing issues: congestion and flooding.

Therefore, this study aims to describe how the Jakarta Smart City program was designed and implemented, systematically analyze the contribution of digital solutions in addressing congestion and flooding, and evaluate the effectiveness of this approach from the perspective of public services, citizen participation, and inclusive governance. Therefore, the results of this study are expected to contribute to the formulation of future urban policies, not only in Jakarta, but also in other major cities in Indonesia facing similar challenges.

Indonesia and France have established a long-standing diplomatic relationship that extends across culture, defense, education, and the economy. In the era of global transformation and sustainable development, economic collaboration has become a crucial pillar for both countries. France, as one of the leading economies in the European Union, offers expertise in technology, renewable energy, and industrial innovation. Indonesia, on the other hand, represents one of the fastest-growing economies in Southeast Asia, with a large market potential, abundant natural resources, and a strategic geographical position. Strengthening economic diplomacy and collaboration between the two nations can accelerate growth, foster innovation, and support sustainable development goals (SDGs).

Policy Issues

1. **Investment and Trade**: Enhancing market access and expanding sustainable investment, particularly in infrastructure, renewable energy, and digital technology.
2. **Technology Transfer**: Addressing Indonesia's technological gaps through joint research, innovation hubs, and knowledge exchange with French partners.
3. **Economic Diplomacy**: Strengthening bilateral diplomacy and city-to-city diplomacy to connect governments, businesses, and research institutions.
4. **Green Economy and SDGs**: Aligning economic collaboration with SDGs, especially SDG 7 (Affordable and Clean Energy), SDG 9

(Industry, Innovation, and Infrastructure), and SDG 13 (Climate Action) (SDGs Bappenas, 2023).

Policy Options

- **Joint Investment Schemes**: Developing public–private partnerships for sustainable urban infrastructure, smart city programs, and climate-resilient projects.
- **Technology and Knowledge Transfer**: Establishing joint innovation centers focused on digital economy, Industry 4.0, and renewable energy.
- **City Diplomacy**: Promoting city-to-city collaboration between Jakarta, Bandung, Surabaya and French smart cities such as Paris, Lyon, and Nice to share best practices in sustainable urban management.
- **Cultural-Economic Diplomacy**: Linking economic cooperation with cultural diplomacy, including vocational education, student exchanges, and creative industry promotion.

Policy Recommendations

1. **The Indonesian government** should strengthen economic diplomacy strategies by establishing a bilateral economic forum with France, emphasizing green investment and digital innovation.
2. **The French government** should be encouraged to expand direct foreign investment (FDI) in Indonesia, especially in renewable energy, smart transportation, and environmentally friendly industries.
3. **Private sector collaboration** should be facilitated through business-to-business partnerships supported by favorable regulations and fiscal incentives.
4. **Academic and research diplomacy** should be prioritized to enhance Indonesia's human capital competitiveness in the global economy.

Studies on the implementation of the Smart City concept in various cities have shown varying results, depending on the readiness of infrastructure, institutions, and levels of public participation. Some relevant previous research can be summarized as follows:

1. Putra, A., & Nugroho, Y. (2019) Their study, *"Smart Cities and the Challenges of Their Implementation in Indonesia,"* states that major cities in Indonesia still face system interoperability issues and minimal public involvement in decision-making. They emphasize that the success of Smart Cities lies not only in technology but also in governance and citizen participation (Mursalim, 2017) .
2. Rahmawati, N., & Sarwono, J. (2020) Examining the effectiveness of the Qlue application in Jakarta in accelerating public services. The study found that the public reporting channel improved government response times, but still faced limitations in data processing and disparities in digital access.
3. Nugroho et al. (2022) In *"Digital Infrastructure and Urban Resilience: A Case Study of Jakarta,"* they highlight the importance of spatial data integration and AI-based flood predictions in mitigating the impact of urban disasters. They also advocate the importance of real-time dashboards and interagency collaboration.
4. Setiawan, D. & Salamah, L. (2023) emphasized that the smart mobility approach developed through the integration of transportation modes in Jakarta is still hampered by sectoral policies and a suboptimal ERP (Electronic Road Pricing) system.

These studies reinforce the urgency of the need for system integration, data strengthening, and adaptive and inclusive cross-sectoral approaches in technology-based urban governance.

This research is supported by several main theories which form the conceptual basis for analyzing the implementation of Smart City in overcoming congestion and flooding:

1. Public Management Information System (PMIS) Theory

PMIS refers to the use of information technology to manage public information efficiently, in real-time, and accountably (Khaidar et al., 2024) . In the context of Smart Cities, PMIS includes flood monitoring dashboards, reporting systems, and the Smart City Theory (Caragliu, Del Bo, & Nijkamp, 2011) . A Smart City is defined as a city that utilizes information and communication technology (ICT) to improve the quality of life, efficiency of public services, and economic competitiveness. This theory emphasizes six main pillars: Smart Economy, Smart Society, Smart Governance, Smart Mobility, Smart Environment, and Smart Living. The success of a Smart City depends not only on technology, but also on collaboration between stakeholders and institutional capacity (Zefti Sulfatul Qoida, 2024). (Nirwono Joga, 2017) .

2. Urbanization Theory by Louis Wirth (1938)

Wirth explained that urbanization causes a dense, impersonal, and complex social life. Uncontrolled urbanization will put pressure on infrastructure and social systems, including transportation and environmental management, which is particularly relevant in the context of Jakarta (Harahap, 2013) .

3. Public Management Information System (SIMP) Theory

PMIS refers to the use of information technology to manage public information efficiently, in real-time, and accountably. (Fathony et al., 2021; Santoso Puji Ahmad, 2025) . In the context of Smart Cities, PMIS includes a flood monitoring dashboard, a citizen reporting system, and the use of sensors for data-driven decision-making. PMIS strengthens the concept of digital government (e-government) and data-driven public services.

4. The Theory of Sustainable Urban Development

Urban development must consider the balance between social, economic and environmental aspects. (Pertiwi, 2021; Ui, 2010) . Smart cities can only be successful if they support the principles of inclusion, spatial equity, and resilience to climate change and disasters. In the context of Jakarta, flooding and congestion must be addressed systematically through a sustainable and integrated approach. (Ribeiro & Jardim Gonçalves, 2019; Son et al., 2023).

5. The Theory of Technological Innovation in Government (Digital Innovation in Governance) (Alputra & Saidin, 2025; Budijaya & Situmeang, 2025; MUKHLIS et al., 2023).

This theory explains that digital innovation in government is not only related to technology adoption, but also changes in bureaucratic culture, work patterns, and institutional structures. The successful implementation of applications such as JAKI, Qlue, and the use of IoT in Jakarta depends on the readiness of human resources, organizational structure, and policy support.

This research is based on the understanding that traffic congestion and flooding in Jakarta are multidimensional problems that require a cross-sectoral approach. Smart Cities, as a technology-based approach and digital governance, have the potential to provide a systemic solution. To this end, a conceptual framework is developed by mapping the relationships between urbanization, urban problems, and Smart City digital solutions, and the impact of digital transformation on urban governance and the quality of life of citizens. Urbanization is the main trigger for the emergence of urban problems such as traffic jams and flood.

1. To address this problem, Smart City-based interventions are implemented, which utilizes digital technology.
2. This intervention resulted in a positive impact in the form of faster, more participatory and transparent services.
3. However, its effectiveness is greatly influenced by supporting and inhibiting factors. such as digital infrastructure, technological literacy, and policy coordination.

RESEARCH METHODS

1. Research Approach

This research uses a descriptive qualitative approach. with case study method This approach was chosen because it allows for an in-depth description of the dynamics of *Smart City program implementation in*

Jakarta, particularly in addressing congestion and flooding issues. This case study allows researchers to contextually explore the relationships between digital policy, governance, citizen participation, and their impact on public services.

2. Location and Coverage

The research focused on DKI Jakarta Province, the implementing area of the Jakarta Smart City program. The scope of the study includes:

a. Digital intervention program : Qlue application, JAKI, Smart City Lounge dashboard
b. Related public services: transportation, drainage, flood mitigation
c. Institution: Communication and Information Service, Transportation Service, BPBD, and residents who use the application
   1. Documentation: Content analysis of annual reports, system dashboards, online media, and related public policies.
   2. Literature Study: Literature review of related theories (Smart City, urbanization, SIMP, sustainable development).
   3. Interviews and observations: If necessary, carried out deliberately with parties directly involved in program design and implementation.

3. Data Analysis Techniques

Data analysis was performed hematologically through stages:

a. Data Reduction: Filtering data relevant to the research focus.
b. Categorization and Coding: Grouping of findings based on main themes: traffic congestion, flooding, digital technology, citizen participation, service effectiveness.
c. Interactive Analysis (Miles and Huberman, 1994):
   1) Data is reviewed continuously
   2) Compared with previous theories and findings
   3) Concluded in narrative and visual form

4. Data Validity

Validity was strengthened through triangulation of sources and techniques. Where available, data from official reports was validated through interviews, observations, and media. Additionally, member checking was conducted . And Peer review can be done to test the consistency of the analysis results.

RESULTS AND DISCUSSION

1. Implementation of Smart City Technology in Handling Traffic Congestion

Jakarta has integrated digital technology through various applications and infrastructure to address traffic congestion. Here are some of them:

a. Traffic monitoring based on CCTV and IoT sensors Thousands of CCTV cameras are installed at strategic points along Jakarta's main roads. This visual data is integrated into the Smart City Lounge . for real-time monitoring and prediction of congestion patterns.
b. Integration of transportation modes through digital applications . JakLingko And Trafi Application Facilitating intermodal integration (MRT, LRT, TransJakarta, and microtransit) and simplifying the payment system.

   According to Jakarta Smart City (2022), the use of this digital application has reduced private vehicle use by 6% in the past two years.
c. Electronic Road Pricing (ERP) Implementation Plan The ERP is designed to control vehicle volumes in densely populated areas. The system will utilize road user data and RFID technology.
d. This finding is in line with the theory of Intelligent Mobility. (Caragliu et al., 2011), which states that transportation efficiency can be achieved through the integration of technology, traffic information systems, and citizen participation in travel decision-making.

2. Digital Innovation in Flood Mitigation

Flooding issues are addressed through a combination of predictive technology and citizen engagement, including:

a. IoT and flood monitoring dashboard Sensor systems are placed in rivers and major drainage channels, connected to the Smart City Lounge dashboard. This allows for a rapid response from the Regional Disaster Management Agency (BPBD) when water levels exceed the threshold.
b. JAKI (Jakarta Kini) application. The JakWaspada feature *provides real-time weather, water level, and floodgate status information* . The app also receives reports from residents regarding flooding, breached embankments, and clogged drains .
c. The use of drones and GIS for mapping affected areas In several major flood incidents, the DKI Jakarta Provincial Government utilized drones to map flood points with high accuracy, then integrated the data into a Geographic Information System (GIS) for long-term planning.

This implementation is in line with the SIMP (Public Management Information System) approach which emphasizes the importance of real-time data management in emergency decision-making.

3. Social Impact of Smart Cities

Digital transformation not only has technical impacts, but also social and cultural impacts:

a. Response times to citizen reports have been drastically reduced, from 8 hours to 2.5 hours (JSC, 2022). This demonstrates an increased bureaucratic responsiveness to citizen needs.
b. digital citizen participation Reporting through Qlue and JAKI has increased sharply, especially among the younger age group (20–40 years old). This engagement strengthens the bond between citizens and the government and fosters a sense of ownership in the city.

c. Cultural shift from passive to active. Communities are no longer just objects of development, but active subjects involved in environmental monitoring and public services.

This phenomenon is in line with the Smart Governance framework which emphasizes the collaborative role of citizens in digital city governance (Mergel et al., 2019).

4. Challenges of Smart City Implementation

Although digital innovation shows positive results, structural and social challenges remain:

a. Digital infrastructure inequality: Densely populated and impoverished areas still experience limited internet access and digital devices. This creates *a digital divide* that hinders equal participation.
b. inter-agency system Several cross-agency digital systems are not yet fully integrated, resulting in data duplication and slow coordination.
c. Digital literacy is low among marginalized groups . The elderly and those with low education struggle to access digital applications, despite their significant benefits.

These findings indicate that the success of Smart Cities does not only depend on technology, but also requires an integrated inclusive development strategy and bureaucratic reform (UN-Habitat, 2020).

Illustration of the Impact of Smart City Implementation

To clarify the results, the following graph shows the increase in public service efficiency after the implementation of the digital system:

DISCUSSION

1. Smart Cities as a Form of Paradigm Change in Governance

Jakarta's digital transformation through *the Jakarta Smart City program* reflects a paradigm shift in urban governance from a closed bureaucratic model to a more open and participatory e-governance system. This approach aligns with the views of Mergel et al. (2019). *digital governance*, where technology is not just a technical tool, but a transformational instrument that drives change in the structures, processes and culture of government.

The implementation of applications like **Qlue** and **JAKI** creates a two-way channel of interaction between the government and citizens. This encourages the emergence of *co-production* in public services, where citizens become not only recipients of services but also providers of information and oversight. This aligns with the Smart People concept. and the concept of Smart Governance in the model of Caragliu et al. (2011).

2. Access Inequality: The Challenge of Digital Inclusivity

While digital systems offer many benefits, the study also found a significant digital divide., *especially in densely populated areas, informal settlements, and low-income communities.* These groups face challenges in accessing Smart City applications due to limited devices, internet connections, and technological literacy.

This shows that the success of a Smart City is not only measured by the existence of digital systems, but also by the extent to which these systems are inclusive and accessible to all citizens., as emphasized in the sustainable urbanization approach. (UN-Habitat, 2020) . In other words, digital development that does not consider equality has the potential to perpetuate new inequalities.

3. Interoperability and Data Fragmentation Between Institutions

One of the main challenges in implementing Jakarta Smart City is limited interoperability between information systems. Each agency or department tends to build its own digital platform without data integration and a common system architecture. This leads to information duplication and data inconsistencies ., and delays in cross-sector decision-making.

This condition is contrary to the principles of SIMP (Public Management Information System). which emphasizes the importance of connected, integrated, and real-time data-driven systems. In line with the critique expressed by Scholl (2015) , system fragmentation in government is a form of structural resistance to digital transformation that requires digital governance and bureaucratic reform.

4. Citizen Participation and Urban Cultural Change

One of the positive achievements of the Smart City approach in Jakarta is the emergence of a participatory culture among residents . Citizen reports on traffic congestion, flooding, and infrastructure damage through Qlue and JAKI have increased significantly each year. According to JSC data (2022), more than 1.5 million reports have been received and followed up since the program's launch.

This change reflects a shift in citizen culture from passive to active., from mere consumers of services to partners in city management. Citizens become more concerned about their surroundings and feel responsible for maintaining order and the sustainability of the city. This supports Wirth's (1938) thesis that urbanization creates social tensions that can only be alleviated through active participation and collective social control.

5. Evaluation of Program Effectiveness within a Sustainability Framework

In general, Smart Cities have made a positive contribution to reducing the structural burden of congestion and flooding. However, the program has not yet fully demonstrated sustainability from the following perspectives:

a. Sustainability of technology: some systems still rely on short-term projects and are not supported by long-term policies.
b. Social sustainability: digital exclusion still exists that hinders equal access.
c. Institutional sustainability: not all bureaucracies are ready to undertake comprehensive digital transformation.

For comparison, Seoul And Singapore The results demonstrate that the success of Smart Cities requires strong political support, integrated policies, and cross-sector participation (public-private partnerships). Jakarta needs to learn from these practices to ensure its transformation is not merely symbolic, but also substantive and sustainable.

6. Comparison: Google Maps vs. Smart City in Solving Traffic Congestion

Table 1. Google Maps vs. Smart City in Solving Traffic Congestion

Aspect	Google Maps	Jakarta Smart City System
Scale and Access	Global applications used individually by smartphone users.	An integrated city system used by governments and citizens for planning and public decision-making.
Main Function	Real-time traffic navigation and fastest route alternatives.	Collective and policy-based traffic monitoring, analysis and management.
Data source	Bulk data collection of Android and Waze user movements.	Data from CCTV sensors, citizen reporting applications (Qlue, JAKI), and public transportation systems.

continued on following page

Table 1. Continued

Aspect	Google Maps	Jakarta Smart City System
Purpose of Use	Helps users avoid traffic jams.	Manage traffic volume systematically and reduce city congestion.
Intervention Response	Only providing passive information. No direct intervention.	This could trigger active policy interventions such as traffic diversion, ERP, or increased public transport frequency.
Citizen Participation	Limited to reporting via Google or Waze (where available).	Active through issue reporting, monitoring, and public policy feedback.

In the context of urban digitalization, Google Maps has become an important tool for individuals facing traffic congestion. However, when compared to Smart City systems, as implemented in Jakarta, there are fundamental differences in terms of function, scale, and policy orientation.

Google Maps is very useful for individual responses to avoid traffic jams, but lacks the authority to regulate city traffic at a macro level. Meanwhile, Smart Cities have the mandate and capacity to intervene in the city's traffic system through route planning, vehicle volume control (ERP), or public transportation integration. In this regard, Google Maps is reactive-individual , while Smart City is proactive-collective. .

However, collaboration between the two has great potential. Data from Google Maps could be integrated as an additional crowdsourced data source. for Smart City systems to enrich predictive analytics. Several major cities worldwide have developed shared APIs between their city transportation systems and Google Transit.

Comparison conclusion : Google Maps is efficient as a micro solution for individual users, while Smart City Jakarta excels on a macro scale because it has policy capacity, intermodal integration, and real-time data-driven decision-making.

Key Findings and Research Novelties

1. Key Findings
   a. Digital transformation through Smart City Jakarta has proven to accelerate the government's response to citizen complaints, partic-

ularly regarding traffic congestion and flooding. Response times have decreased from 8 hours to 2.5 hours, demonstrating improved public governance efficiency.

b. Citizens' digital participation has increased significantly, especially in the productive age group (20–40 years), which shows that the application of digital technology encourages the growth of a participatory and collaborative city culture.

c. Jakarta's Smart City system is not yet fully inclusive and sustainable . *The digital divide* persists in densely populated and low-income areas, and there is fragmentation between agencies regarding data interoperability.

d. The Smart City approach has systemic advantages over global platforms like Google Maps in addressing congestion. Smart Cities provide not only navigation but also active intervention policies (e.g., ERP, traffic management, intermodal integration).

e. Digital technology is a catalyst for cultural change in urban bureaucracies and communities . Citizens are becoming active reporters and participants in app-based social monitoring systems, creating a model of *digital citizen engagement* that has not been widely studied in the context of developing cities like Jakarta.

2. Novel Research (Scientific Novelty)

   a. Integrating theoretical analysis of Smart City with local case studies based on actual data and digital applications (Qlue, JAKI, Smart City Lounge) in Jakarta , which have so far been studied more from a normative or macro perspective.

   b. Comparing two digital approaches (Smart City vs Google Maps) in the context of congestion management, showing the difference in orientation between individual (private) and public (collective) solutions, and highlighting the need for integration between platforms.

   c. Offers a new conceptual framework on the relationship between technology, government responsiveness, and citizen cultural change, by positioning Smart Cities not only as digital systems, but also as ecosystems of social transformation.

   d. Highlights digital literacy and inclusivity challenges as key barriers to the sustainability of Smart Cities in developing countries , and provides initial strategies for building equitable, participatory, and crisis-resilient Smart City models.

e. Providing practical contributions to the formulation of urban digital policies in Indonesia , particularly for pioneering cities of digital transformation such as Bandung, Makassar, and Surabaya, by making Jakarta a policy learning laboratory.

7. The Role of Economy, Program SDGs, Collaboration and Diplomation between Indonesia and France

The 21st century has witnessed a growing interdependence between nations, where diplomacy and international collaboration are increasingly intertwined with sustainable economic development. Indonesia and France, as strategic partners, are expanding their cooperation beyond traditional political and cultural ties into broader economic and sustainability programs. This collaboration aligns with the global agenda of the United Nations Sustainable Development Goals (SDGs), emphasizing inclusive growth, green economy, and climate resilience.

THE ROLE OF ECONOMY IN BILATERAL DIPLOMACY

The economy is not only a driver of national development but also a bridge of diplomacy. For Indonesia, collaboration with France provides access to advanced technology, renewable energy innovation, and high-value investments. For France, Indonesia offers a large emerging market, strategic maritime position, and growing digital economy. Economic diplomacy between the two countries thus plays a dual role: (1) strengthening bilateral trade and investment flows, and (2) creating a platform for sustainable development cooperation.

SDGs as a Framework for Collaboration

The SDGs serve as a global framework that shapes Indonesia–France collaboration. Three goals in particular stand out:

- **SDG 7 (Affordable and Clean Energy)** – cooperation in renewable energy projects such as solar, wind, and hydropower.
- **SDG 9 (Industry, Innovation, and Infrastructure)** – joint investment in smart city infrastructure, digital transformation, and Industry 4.0 initiatives.
- **SDG 13 (Climate Action)** – partnerships to address climate change through sustainable urban planning and low-carbon development.

By aligning economic programs with SDGs, Indonesia and France can ensure that cooperation is not only profitable but also environmentally and socially sustainable.

Collaboration and Diplomation: Strategic Dimensions

Collaboration between Indonesia and France extends into multidimensional diplomacy:

- **Economic Diplomacy**: Fostering trade and investment partnerships in key sectors such as digital economy, renewable energy, and creative industries.
- **City Diplomacy**: Linking Jakarta, Bandung, and Surabaya with French cities like Paris, Lyon, and Marseille to exchange best practices in smart city and climate adaptation.
- **Academic and Cultural Diplomacy**: Strengthening human capital through scholarships, joint research, and vocational training programs that connect economic development with education and innovation.
- **Green Diplomacy**: Jointly advocating for sustainable economic practices and climate responsibility at multilateral forums such as G20, COP climate summits, and ASEAN–EU partnerships.

Policy Implications

1. **For Indonesia**: Economic collaboration with France enhances its capacity for technological innovation, helps accelerate SDG achieve-

ments, and strengthens Indonesia's position as a leader in Southeast Asia.

2. **For France**: Partnership with Indonesia secures market access in Asia, supports its global climate diplomacy agenda, and expands influence in the Indo-Pacific.
3. **For Global Governance**: Indonesia–France cooperation represents a model of how bilateral partnerships can be integrated into global sustainable development and diplomacy frameworks.

CONCLUSION

This study shows that the implementation of the Smart City concept in Jakarta has had a positive impact. in addressing two crucial urban issues: traffic congestion and seasonal flooding. The application of digital technologies such as IoT, big data, the Qlue and JAKI applications, and real-time monitoring dashboards has significantly improved the efficiency of public services, accelerated government response, and strengthened citizen participation in city governance .

This digital transformation also drives a shift in bureaucratic and citizen culture. from a passive model to an active, collaborative, and open model. However, this study also highlights a number of fundamental challenges still faced, such as limited digital infrastructure, low digital literacy among marginalized groups, and lack of optimal cross-institutional system integration.

In terms of scientific contribution, this study confirms that Smart Cities are not simply digitalization projects , but rather systemic transformations that require institutional reform, equal access, and cross-sector participation. By comparing the role of Google Maps as an individual navigation system, this study emphasizes the importance of public orientation and data-driven policy. in collective traffic management.

The role of economy, SDGs, collaboration, and diplomation in Indonesia–France relations highlights the growing significance of economic diplomacy as a tool for achieving sustainable development. By embedding SDGs into bilateral programs, both countries ensure that cooperation produces mutual benefits that are resilient, inclusive, and globally relevant. This multidimensional approach positions Indonesia and France not only as partners in trade but also as co-creators of a sustainable global future.

Recommendation

Based on the findings and critical reflections of this research, here are some strategic recommendations:

1. Strengthening Fair Digital Infrastructure

The Jakarta government needs to expand digital infrastructure coverage to suburban and densely populated areas. This includes public internet networks, sensor devices, and access to affordable and convenient mobile devices.

2. Improving Digital Literacy and Inclusion

Community-based digital training programs (digital literacy training) need to be promoted massively, especially for the elderly, housewives, and low-income communities so that they are not left behind by the flow of urban digitalization.

3. Inter-Agency System Integration and Open Data

It is essential to build an integrated digital system architecture. Cross-agency and departmental coordination within the DKI Jakarta Provincial Government to avoid data fragmentation and overlapping policies. The principles of interoperability and openness of government data must be prioritized.

4. Strengthening Citizen Participatory Role in Urban Planning

Apps like Qlue and JAKI need to be developed not only as problem-reporting tools but also as platforms for accumulating citizen aspirations and feedback on government policies. This will strengthen community-based digital democracy.

5. Developing a Long-Term Smart City Roadmap Based on the SDGs

The Jakarta Provincial Government needs to develop and communicate a Smart City roadmap that aligns with the Sustainable Development Goals (SDGs), particularly point 11 (*Sustainable Cities and Communities*). This roadmap should include a balance of social, economic, and environmental targets.

6. Replicating Jakarta's Smart City Model for Other Cities in Indonesia

By refining existing approaches, Jakarta can become a national digital policy laboratory, whose models and practices can be emulated by other cities such as Bandung, Makassar, Surabaya, and Medan.

REFERENCES

Alputra, F., & Saidin, S. (2025). *E-government: Digital transformation in government governance*. Cv. Eureka Media Aksara.

Budijaya, M., & Situmeang, M. (2025). Digital transformation in governance: Analysis of the effectiveness of application-based public services in the Society 5.0 era. *All Fields of Science Journal Liaison Academia and Society*, *5*, 1–13. DOI: 10.58939/afosj-las.v5i2.1024

Caragliu, A., Del Bo, C., & Nijkamp, P. (2011). Smart cities in Europe. *Journal of Urban Technology*, *18*(2), 65–82. DOI: 10.1080/10630732.2011.601117

Central Statistics Agency. (2023). *DKI Jakarta in figures 2023*. https://jakarta.bps.go.id

Fathony, R., Muradi, M., & Sagita, N. I. (2021). Utilization of information technology in the provision of public services within the Bandung city government. *Jurnal Aggregasi: Action for Government Reform in Democracy*, *9*(2), 1–12. DOI: 10.34010/agregasi.v9i2.5581

Harahap, F. R. (2013). The impact of urbanization on city development in Indonesia. *Society*, *1*(1), 35–45. DOI: 10.33019/society.v1i1.40

Jakarta Regional Disaster Management Agency. (2021). *Annual report on flood management in Jakarta*. https://bpbd.jakarta.go.id

Jakarta Smart City. (2022). *Citizen digital services performance and statistics report*. https://smartcity.jakarta.go.id

Khaidar, M. F., Ardiansyah, M. N., & Permatasari, I. (2024). Development of a project management information system (PMIS) for monitoring and controlling systems at PT Telkom Indonesia. *Technologia: Scientific Journal*, *15*(4), 843. DOI: 10.31602/tji.v15i4.16401

Mergel, I., Edelmann, N., & Haug, N. (2019). Defining digital transformation: Results of expert interviews. *Government Information Quarterly*, *36*(4), 101385. DOI: 10.1016/j.giq.2019.06.002

Miles, M. B., & Huberman, A. M. (1994). *Qualitative data analysis: An expanded sourcebook* (2nd ed.). Sage Publications.

Mukhlis, S., Awaliah, F., Usman Siam, N., & Karim, Z. A. (2023). Implementation of governance. *Journal of Social and Political Sciences, 4*(2), 1069–1078.

Mursalim, S. W. (2017). Implementation of smart city policy in Bandung City. *Journal of Administrative Science: Media for the Development of Administrative Science and Practice, 14*(1), 126–138. DOI: 10.31113/jia.v14i1.1

National Development Planning Agency. (2021). *Study of the economic impact of traffic congestion in Greater Jakarta.* Ministry of National Development Planning/Bappenas.

Nirwono Joga, D. (2017). *Sustainable smart cities.* November Issue.

Nugroho, A., Putri, R. N., & Wicaksono, A. (2022). Digital infrastructure and urban resilience: A case study of Jakarta. *Indonesian Journal of Urban and Regional Planning, 33*(1), 45–61.

Pertiwi, N. (2021). *Implementation of sustainable development in Indonesia.* Pustaka Ramadhan.

Pramadi, Y., Fathy, R., & Arifa, S. H. (2023). Smart city based on smart communities in Bandung City: A social innovation. *Journal of Regional and Urban Development, 19*(3), 336–354. DOI: 10.14710/pwk.v19i3.43856

Putra, A., & Nugroho, Y. (2019). Smart cities and the challenges of their implementation in Indonesia. *Journal of Public Administration, 13*(2), 125–138.

Rahmawati, N., & Sarwono, J. (2020). The effectiveness of digital public reporting through the Qlue application in Jakarta. *Journal of Communication and Digital Society, 8*(1), 70–82.

Ribeiro, P., & Jardim Gonçalves, L. A. (2019). Urban resilience: A conceptual framework. *Sustainable Cities and Society, 50*, 101625. DOI: 10.1016/j.scs.2019.101625

Santoso Puji Ahmad, I. (2025). The role of digitalization in increasing government transparency and accountability. *Indonesian Journal of Public Administration Review*, *2*(3), 1–10.

Scholl, H. J. (2015). *E-government: Information, technology, and transformation*. Routledge. DOI: 10.4324/9781315704906

SDGs Bappenas. (2023). *Roadmap SDGs 2023–2030*. https://sdgs.bappenas.go.id/product/roadmap-sdgs-2023-2030-eng/

Setiawan, D., & Salamah, L. (2023). Interconnection of transportation modes in Jakarta's smart mobility system. *Journal of Transportation and Urban Studies*, *5*(1), 12–26.

Son, T. H., Weedon, Z., Yigitcanlar, T., Sanchez, T., Corchado, J. M., & Mehmood, R. (2023). Algorithmic urban planning for smart and sustainable development: Systematic review of the literature. *Sustainable Cities and Society*, *94*, 104562. DOI: 10.1016/j.scs.2023.104562

TomTom. (2022). *Traffic index: Measuring congestion around the world*. https://www.tomtom.com/en_gb/traffic-index

Ui, F. E. (2010). *Evaluation of the policy*. Carolina Vivien Christianti, FE UI, 31–57.

UN-Habitat. (2020). *World cities report 2020: The value of sustainable urbanization*. United Nations Human Settlements Programme. https://unhabitat.org/wcr/

Wirth, L. (1938). Urbanism as a way of life. *American Journal of Sociology*, *44*(1), 1–24. DOI: 10.1086/217913

Zefti Sulfatul Qoida, A. (2024). Regional development through smart city implementation in Sumenep Regency. *Journal of Public Sector Innovation*, *4*(3), 94–105.

Chapter 3

Education Diplomacy and Microlearning Indonesia and France Cooperation for Advancing:
Quality Education Entrepreneurship and the SDGs

Ninuk Lustyantie
https://orcid.org/0000-0002-7528-6846
Universitas Negeri Jakarta Indonesia, Indonesia

Iwan
Kementerian Dalam Negeri Republik Indonesia, Indonesia

Hafida Kies
https://orcid.org/0009-0001-8630-4528
Faculte des Langues Etrangères, Université d'Oran, Algeria

Benmostefa Harig Fatima Zohra

Fatima Zohra
Faculte des Langues Etrangères, Université d'Oran, Algeria

Ratna
Universitas Negeri Jakarta, Indonesia

Wahyu Tri Widyastuti
Universitas Negeri Jakarta, Indonesia

Salman Al Farisi
Universitas Negeri Jakarta, Indonesia

DOI: 10.4018/979-8-3373-2943-7.ch003

ABSTRACT

Employing a qualitative design, data were collected through document analysis, expert interviews, and policy review of collaborative initiatives such as the Joint Working Group (JWG), the MBKM program, and the development of microlearning-based French reading modules for A1-level compréhension écrite courses. Findings indicate that the integration of microlearning improved student comprehension and engagement by 25 to 40% while simultaneously nurturing entrepreneurial attributes such as adaptability, problem-solving, and digital literacy skills critical for global labor markets and innovation-driven economies. From a policy perspective, the cooperation illustrates how education diplomacy can serve as a form of soft power, aligning national strategies like Indonesia's Golden Indonesia 2045 vision with France's multilingual education policy. The study contributes to the literature by bridging the domains of education diplomacy, entrepreneurial learning, and digital transformation, offering a scalable model for transnational cooperation in the Global South.

INTRODUCTION

Education is increasingly recognized as a strategic driver of sustainable development, innovation, and entrepreneurial capacity in the 21st century. The United Nations 2030 Agenda emphasizes that quality education (SDG 4) is not only a human right but also a foundation for economic growth (SDG 8) and international partnerships (SDG 17) (United Nations, 2015). For emerging economies such as Indonesia, strengthening educational quality and global linkages has become a national priority under the RPJMN 2025 to 2029 and the long-term vision of Golden Indonesia 2045, which positions human capital and entrepreneurial skills as key enablers of competitiveness. At the same time, France has placed multilingual education and cultural diplomacy at the core of its foreign policy, making bilateral academic cooperation an important pillar of its soft power strategy. Despite growing recognition of the value of education diplomacy, most studies have focused on traditional forms of exchange such as scholarships and cultural programs, while limited attention has been given to how digital pedagogy and entrepreneurial learning can be embedded within bilateral cooperation frameworks. Recent technological innovations, particularly microlearning and machine learning, have created new opportunities for personalized and scalable education delivery (Thomas & Gardiner, 2020; Singh et al., 2023). However, their integration into transnational education initiatives, particularly in the Global South, remains underexplored. The case of Indonesia and France education cooperation provides an important lens to examine this intersection. Through initiatives such as the Joint Working Group (JWG), the Merdeka Belajar Kampus Merdeka (MBKM) program, and collaborative curriculum development, both countries have sought to enhance foreign language competencies, promote academic mobility, and align educational outcomes with labor market needs. A notable example is the co-development of microlearning-based French reading modules for A1-level comprehension courses, which not only improved linguistic proficiency but also cultivated entrepreneurial attributes such as adaptability, problem-solving, and digital literacy skills crucial for navigating uncertain global markets. Accordingly, this study addresses two key research gaps where the lack of empirical analysis connecting education diplomacy and digital pedagogy with SDG-aligned outcomes, and the limited discussion on how bilateral cooperation can foster entrepreneurial learning and innovation-driven growth in developing contexts. By adopting a qualitative approach, the paper examines how education diplomacy between Indonesia and France contributes to quality education, entrepreneurial capacity building, and sustainable development. The study's novelty lies in its integration of education diplomacy, entrepreneurial learning, and digital transformation, offering a scalable model for international collaboration in higher education.

LITERATURE REVIEW

Education Diplomacy and Soft Power

Education diplomacy has emerged as a strategic tool for fostering international cooperation, cultural exchange, and sustainable development. Rooted in Nye's (2008) concept of soft power, education serves as a vehicle for building long-term influence through people to people connections, academic mobility, and collaborative research. Public diplomacy literature highlights education as a "human dimension" of foreign policy, strengthening relationships beyond state-level negotiations (Cull, 2008; Metzgar, 2016). Recent studies emphasize that education diplomacy contributes not only to cultural exchange but also to capacity-building for innovation and entrepreneurship, particularly when aligned with national development agendas (Byrne & Hall, 2013; Golan, 2013). In this context, bilateral education cooperation between Indonesia and France reflects a strategic alignment of interests: Indonesia seeks to enhance human capital and global competitiveness under the Golden Indonesia 2045 vision, while France leverages multilingual education as part of its cultural diplomacy. Such partnerships represent a form of academic soft power, where the exchange of knowledge and pedagogical innovation reinforces broader socio-economic ties.

Microlearning and Digital Pedagogy

Digital transformation has redefined teaching and learning practices, with microlearning gaining prominence as a pedagogical innovation for digital-native learners. Defined as the delivery of learning in concise, focused modules, microlearning enhances retention, reduces cognitive load, and improves learner engagement (Thomas & Gardiner, 2020). Studies demonstrate that microlearning particularly when supported by artificial intelligence (AI) and machine learning (ML) facilitates personalized, adaptive learning pathways (Chen et al., 2021; Singh et al., 2023). For foreign language education, microlearning has proven effective in addressing barriers such as limited vocabulary, unfamiliar grammar structures, and low learner motivation (Ellis, 2020). Furthermore, the integration of mobile platforms and offline-compatible solutions enables accessibility for geographically dispersed learners (Nasution et al., 2024). Importantly, microlearning is increasingly linked to entrepreneurial skill development, as it encourages self-directed learning, digital literacy, and adaptability competencies essential for the innovation-driven economy (García et al., 2020).

Entrepreneurial Learning and Innovation Capacity

Entrepreneurial learning extends beyond business creation; it encompasses the development of competencies such as creativity, problem-solving, adaptability, and resilience skills vital for success in uncertain labor markets (Fayolle & Linan, 2020). Higher education institutions play a central role in embedding entrepreneurial skills across curricula, particularly through experiential and technology-enhanced learning (Devi, 2024). Scholars argue that entrepreneurial education is increasingly tied to digital skills, as innovation in the Fourth Industrial Revolution requires graduates to navigate both technological and entrepreneurial ecosystems (Volery & Müller, 2023). In bilateral cooperation contexts, entrepreneurial learning emerges as both a policy objective and an outcome of transnational partnerships. Programs such as student mobility, joint curriculum design, and microlearning initiatives foster entrepreneurial mindsets, enabling learners to operate in multicultural environments, leverage digital tools, and co-create innovative solutions. This aligns with SDG 8, which emphasizes skills development for decent work and economic growth.

Education and the Sustainable Development Goals (SDGs)

Education is positioned as a cornerstone of the 2030 Agenda, with SDG 4 calling for inclusive and equitable quality education and lifelong learning opportunities for all. Beyond access and equity, quality education is increasingly framed as a driver of sustainable entrepreneurship, innovation, and social mobility (García et al., 2020). Integrating sustainability principles into education equips learners with competencies to contribute to green economies, inclusive growth, and global citizenship (Grobler & Dittrich, 2024). Bilateral education cooperation contributes directly to multiple SDGs:

a) SDG 4 (Quality Education): Enhancing teaching and learning practices through digital innovation.
b) SDG 8 (Decent Work & Economic Growth): Strengthening entrepreneurial and employability skills.

c) SDG 17 (Partnerships for the Goals): Expanding international collaboration in research, pedagogy, and policy.

Research Gap

While there is extensive scholarship on education diplomacy and growing research on microlearning, limited studies have examined how bilateral cooperation can integrate digital pedagogy with entrepreneurial learning outcomes in pursuit of the SDGs. Moreover, empirical studies from the Global South remain scarce, particularly in contexts where education cooperation is leveraged to address both linguistic and economic development goals. This study addresses this gap by analyzing the Indonesia–France partnership, focusing on how microlearning based French language modules contribute to entrepreneurial competencies and sustainable development.

RESEARCH METHODOLOGY

Research Design

This study employed a qualitative exploratory design to examine how bilateral education cooperation between Indonesia and France contributes to quality education, entrepreneurial learning, and the achievement of SDGs. A qualitative approach was chosen to capture the complexity of policy implementation, institutional collaboration, and stakeholder perspectives (Creswell, 2013).

Case Selection

The research focused on the Indonesia and France bilateral cooperation framework, particularly the development of microlearning-based French reading modules for A1-level compréhension écrite courses. This case was selected because it represents a convergence of education diplomacy, digital pedagogy, and entrepreneurial skill-building within the SDG framework.

Data Collection

Three complementary data sources were utilized:

1. Document Analysis
    a) Policy documents: RPJMN 2025–2029, Golden Indonesia 2045 strategy, Joint Working Group (JWG) agreements.
    b) Institutional reports: Universitas Negeri Jakarta (UNJ), Universitas Negeri Medan (UNIMED), Centre National de la Recherche Scientifique (CNRS), French Embassy in Jakarta.
    c) International references: UNESCO, EU, and World Bank reports on higher education and SDGs.
2. Semi-Structured Interviews
    a) Conducted with 15 key informants using purposive sampling:
    b) Indonesian government officials (Kemdiktisaintek, BRIN, Kemlu).
    c) French counterparts (CNRS, Embassy of France).
    d) University lecturers and program coordinators (UNJ, UNIMED).
    e) Interviews explored perceptions of cooperation effectiveness, digital pedagogy integration, and entrepreneurial outcomes.
3. Pilot Study Observation
    a) Classroom observations of microlearning module implementation at UNJ and UNIMED.
    b) Focused on student engagement, learning challenges, and evidence of entrepreneurial attributes (e.g., problem-solving, adaptability).

Data Analysis

Data were analyzed using thematic analysis (Braun & Clarke, 2006). The process included:

a) Familiarization with data (reading transcripts and documents).
b) Initial coding of recurring concepts (e.g., "policy alignment," "digital learning," "entrepreneurial skills").
c) Development of themes aligned with research objectives (e.g., Education Diplomacy as Soft Power, Microlearning for Entrepreneurial Competence).

d) Cross-case comparison between Indonesian and French contexts.
e) NVivo 12 software was used to support coding and ensure transparency in data management.
f) Validity and Reliability
g) Several strategies were adopted to ensure trustworthiness:
h) Triangulation of data sources (documents, interviews, observations).
i) Member checking with selected informants to validate interpretations.
j) Peer debriefing with academic colleagues for critical review.
k) Audit trail of coding decisions to enhance dependability.

Ethical Considerations

Informed consent was obtained from all interviewees. Institutional clearance was granted by Universitas Negeri Jakarta's Research and Community Service Board (LPPM). To maintain confidentiality, participant identities are anonymized.

FINDING AND DISCUSSION

Improved Student Outcomes Through Microlearning

The implementation of microlearning-based modules in the compréhension écrite A1 course significantly enhanced students' reading comprehension, with scores improving between 25 to 40% compared to traditional textbook-based approaches (Lustyantie et al., 2025). Beyond academic performance, students reported higher levels of motivation and self-confidence, particularly when engaging with short, interactive digital tasks. This finding supports prior studies that highlight the effectiveness of microlearning in reducing cognitive overload and increasing learner engagement (Thomas & Gardiner, 2020; Ellis, 2020). Importantly, the modules nurtured entrepreneurial attributes, such as adaptability (navigating unfamiliar grammar), problem-solving (deciphering meaning with limited vocabulary), and digital literacy (using online platforms for independent learning). These competencies align with research that positions foreign language learning as a platform for entrepreneurial skill development in globalized economies (Fayolle & Linan, 2020; Volery & Müller, 2023).

Education Diplomacy as Soft Power

The Indonesia and France collaboration demonstrates how education diplomacy functions as a form of soft power. Through joint curriculum design, faculty exchanges, and digital innovation, both nations leveraged academic cooperation to strengthen bilateral ties. This finding is consistent with Nye's (2008) argument that education enhances cultural influence and global standing. For Indonesia, the initiative supports the Golden Indonesia 2045 vision, which prioritizes human capital and international competitiveness. For France, it reinforces the role of multilingual education as part of its foreign policy. In line with Byrne & Hall (2013), this study shows that education diplomacy not only facilitates cultural exchange but also enhances entrepreneurial ecosystems by equipping students with globally relevant skills.

Policy Alignment and SDG Contribution

The cooperation directly supports:

a) SDG 4.3 – Expanding access to quality tertiary education through inclusive language instruction.
b) SDG 8.6 – Enhancing youth skills for employability, entrepreneurship, and innovation.
c) SDG 17.6 – Strengthening international partnerships in science, education, and technology.

By integrating microlearning with bilateral policy frameworks such as Indonesia's RPJMN 2025 to 2029 and France's multilingualism strategy, the initiative demonstrates how education diplomacy can translate into tangible SDG outcomes. This aligns with García et al. (2020) and Grobler & Dittrich (2024), who emphasize the role of education in fostering sustainability and inclusive growth.

Challenges and Limitations

Despite promising results, several challenges emerged:

a) Technological disparities ; Unequal digital infrastructure in Indonesia limits scalability, echoing Nasution et al. (2024).
b) Funding constraints ; Lack of permanent bilateral funding schemes hinders long-term sustainability.
c) Mobility barriers ; Visa restrictions and limited scholarship schemes reduce physical exchanges, making cooperation overly dependent on online platforms.
d) Curriculum differences; Divergent national standards required extensive harmonization, delaying implementation.

These barriers reflect broader structural issues in cross-border education projects (Metzgar, 2016) and highlight the need for policy coherence, infrastructural investment, and sustained financing.

Theoretical and Practical Implications

The findings extend education diplomacy theory by showing that digital pedagogy (microlearning) can function not only as a teaching innovation but also as a diplomatic instrument that nurtures entrepreneurial learning. This suggests a shift from education diplomacy as cultural exchange to education diplomacy as a driver of innovation ecosystems. Practically, the Indonesia and France case provides a replicable model for other Global South countries seeking to internationalize higher education while simultaneously building entrepreneurial human capital. Embedding microlearning into bilateral cooperation offers a scalable, culturally responsive, and cost-effective approach to advancing SDGs and preparing students for the digital economy.

CONCLUSION

This study demonstrates that bilateral education cooperation between Indonesia and France, anchored in microlearning-based French language modules, serves not only as a pedagogical innovation but also as a strategic instrument of education diplomacy. The findings show that microlearning improved students' reading comprehension by 25 to 40%, while simultaneously cultivating entrepreneurial attributes such as adaptability, problem-solving, and digital literacy. These outcomes reinforce the argument that quality education is a foundation for innovation, employability, and sustainable growth, thereby advancing SDG 4 (Quality Education), SDG 8 (Decent Work and Economic Growth), and SDG 17 (Partnerships for the Goals). Theoretically, the study extends the literature on education diplomacy by positioning digital pedagogy as a tool of soft power that fosters both cultural exchange and entrepreneurial learning. It bridges three domains often studied separately for education diplomacy, microlearning, and entrepreneurial capacity offering an integrated framework for transnational education in the Global South. Practically, the cooperation between Indonesia and France provides a replicable model for other bilateral or regional partnerships. Embedding microlearning into higher education curricula can enhance foreign language proficiency, support entrepreneurial competencies, and strengthen international collaboration. However, challenges such as funding limitations, digital disparities, and mobility barriers must be addressed through policy coherence, sustained investment, and inclusive infrastructure development. Looking forward, future research should examine how microlearning-based cooperation can be scaled across disciplines beyond language learning for example, entrepreneurship education, vocational training, and STEM fields. Comparative studies across multiple country partnerships would also enrich understanding of how education diplomacy can accelerate progress toward the SDGs. In doing so, education cooperation can evolve into a catalyst for entrepreneurial ecosystems, preparing graduates not only as competent professionals but also as innovative global citizens.

REFERENCES

Byrne, C., & Hall, R. A. (2013). Realising Australia's international education as public diplomacy. *Australian Journal of International Affairs, 67*(4), 419–438. DOI: 10.1080/10357718.2013.806019

Chen, Y., Zhang, M., & Yu, S. (2021). Personalized learning pathways supported by artificial intelligence: A review of microlearning in higher education. *Computers & Education, 172*, 104251. DOI: 10.1016/j.compedu.2021.104251

Cull, N. J. (2008). Public diplomacy: Taxonomies and histories. *The Annals of the American Academy of Political and Social Science, 616*(1), 31–54. DOI: 10.1177/0002716207311952

Devi, G. A. (2024). Role of quality education for sustainable development goals (SDGs). *International Journal of Creative Research Thoughts, 12*(6), 217–224. https://ijcrt.org/papers/IJCRT2506217.pdf

Ellis, J. L. (2020). Microlearning in second language acquisition: Theories, design, and practice. *Journal of Language Teaching and Research, 11*(3), 345–356. DOI: 10.17507/jltr.1103.03

Fayolle, A., & Linan, F. (2020). The future of research on entrepreneurial intentions. *Journal of Business Research, 110*, 402–407. DOI: 10.1016/j.jbusres.2019.09.045

García, E. G., Magaña, E. C., & Ariza, A. C. (2020). Quality education as a Sustainable Development Goal in the context of the 2030 Agenda: A bibliometric approach. *Sustainability (Basel), 12*(15), 5884. DOI: 10.3390/su12155884

Golan, G. J. (2013). An integrated approach to public diplomacy. *The American Behavioral Scientist, 57*(9), 1251–1255. DOI: 10.1177/0002764213487711

Grobler, S., & Dittrich, A. K. (2024). Envisioning quality education for sustainability transformation in teacher education: Perspectives from an international dialogue on SDG 4. *International Journal of Comparative Education and Development*, *26*(3), 175–192. DOI: 10.1108/IJCED-06-2023-0048

Kementerian Pendidikan Tinggi. Sains, dan Teknologi Republik Indonesia. (2025). Laporan implementasi program riset dan pengabdian masyarakat 2025. https://kemdiktisaintek.go.id

Metzgar, E. T. (2016). Institutions of higher education as public diplomacy tools: China-based university programs for the 21st century. *Journal of Studies in International Education*, *20*(3), 223–241. DOI: 10.1177/1028315315604718

Nasution, R. A., Lubis, F. R., & Hidayat, T. (2024). Overcoming digital divide in microlearning adoption: Evidence from Indonesian higher education. *Education and Information Technologies*, *29*(2), 1805–1823. DOI: 10.1007/s10639-023-12015-6

Nye, J. S.Jr. (2008). Public diplomacy and soft power. *The Annals of the American Academy of Political and Social Science*, *616*(1), 94–109. DOI: 10.1177/0002716207311699

Sekretariat Negara Republik Indonesia. (2025). RPJMN 2025–2029: Fondasi awal mewujudkan visi Indonesia Emas 2045. https://setneg.go.id

Singh, A., Kumar, V., & Sharma, P. (2023). Artificial intelligence in microlearning: Enhancing engagement and adaptive learning for Generation Z students. *Education and Information Technologies*, *28*(6), 7895–7912. DOI: 10.1007/s10639-023-11867-2

Thomas, M., & Gardiner, C. (2020). *Digital learning and teaching: Microlearning in foreign language education*. Routledge., DOI: 10.4324/9780429341903

United Nations. (2015). Transforming our world: The 2030 Agenda for Sustainable Development. https://sdgs.un.org/2030agenda

Volery, T., & Müller, S. (2023). Digital skills, entrepreneurship education, and employability in the Fourth Industrial Revolution. *Journal of Small Business Management, 61*(2), 345–367. DOI: 10.1080/00472778.2022.2041831

World Bank. (2020). The promise of education in Indonesia. https://www.worldbank.org/en/country/indonesia/publication/the-promise-of-education-in-indonesia

Chapter 4

Entrepreneurship and Business Transformations in the Metaverse for Strategy Management

Jose De Jesus Reyes Sanchez
https://orcid.org/0000-0002-3866-2363
Instituto Tecnologico Superior de Fresnillo, Mexico

Johana Paola Reyes Davalos
https://orcid.org/0009-0005-0330-635X
Instituto Tecnologico Superior de Fresnillo, Mexico

Ayme Carolina Reyes Davalos
https://orcid.org/0009-0003-9659-2978
Universidad Autónoma de Durango Campus Zacatecas, Mexico

Claudia Guadalupe Lara Torres
https://orcid.org/0000-0002-3066-2967
Universidad Politécnica de Zacatecas, Mexico

Selene Castañeda-Burciaga

DOI: 10.4018/979-8-3373-2943-7.ch004

https://orcid.org/0000-0002-2436-308X

Universidad Politécnica de Zacatecas, Mexico

ABSTRACT

This study explores how the metaverse is redefining entrepreneurship and strategic management in contemporary business environments. Through a meta-analytical approach, academic research and case studies are analyzed that highlight the convergence between emerging technologies, such as virtual reality, artificial intelligence and blockchain, with organizational dynamics oriented towards innovation and co-creation of value. The results reveal that the metaverse not only facilitates new business models, but also drives cultural, organizational and communicative transformations, configuring an ecosystem where the active participation of the user becomes a strategic resource. Key challenges related to cybersecurity, regulation and digital inclusion are identified, highlighting the need for ethical and sustainable frameworks. This virtual environment is thus consolidated as a key platform for rethinking competitiveness strategies in the digital age.

INTRODUCTION

The metaverse has become a concept that transcends mere scientific fiction to be at the epicenter of academic and business discussions. Its definition refers to virtual spaces in which interaction, immersion and the integration of multiple technologies converge in experiences that transform the way we work, consume and socialize. Since the first virtual worlds attracted the attention of the technology community, there has been a move towards increasingly sophisticated environments, in which virtual reality and augmented reality are added to data analytics, artificial intelligence and global connectivity to provide scenarios whose purpose goes beyond the sphere of entertainment. In these environments, it is possible to carry out activities that range from academic training and cultural socialization, to the creation of economic value through the offer of original products and services. This paradigm shift invites us to reflect on the way in which organizations conceive innovation and competitiveness in an intensely volatile market.

The incursion of the metaverse into corporate dynamics arouses the interest of those looking for opportunities to expand their business horizons. Rather than being limited to transactions in physical environments, entrepreneurs value the possibility of offering immersive experiences that connect with geographically dispersed customers, harness collective creativity, and foster the construction of value networks capable of redefining the concept of competitiveness. These initiatives usually go beyond the simple purchase and sale of digital items, as they involve real-time interaction with other participants, the co-creation of content and the creation of virtual communities that give life to collaborative projects. In this way, each actor can play an active role in the evolution of products and in shaping strategies that in turn enable long-term sustainable growth.

Although the metaverse is emerging as a new scenario of opportunities, its adoption also entails complex challenges that require the attention of executives and managers. Among them, the need to carry out cultural and organizational transformations in companies stands out, so that decision-making structures are compatible with the speed and flexibility that characterize virtual ecosystems. Investments in technology and specialized training are also needed to ensure that teams have the necessary skills in areas such as programming, cybersecurity, big data analytics, and immersive experience management. To successfully meet these challenges, it is essential not only to have a strategic vision and an innovative culture, but also an openness to change and continuous experimentation.

The growing relevance of this topic is reinforced by the impact that the COVID-19 pandemic has had on consumption patterns and the way work is carried out. Many organizations were forced to move large percentages of their operations to digital platforms, thus accelerating the adoption of collaborative tools and the introduction of virtual solutions across multiple industries. Consequently, the metaverse is presented as a space where interactions can be sustained by immersion, three-dimensional realism and the integration of artificial intelligence, so that not only are the limitations imposed by physical distance overcome, but also experiences capable of awakening the motivation and loyalty of users are offered. This phenomenon has prompted various academic institutions and research centers to direct their efforts towards the analysis of the economic, social and cultural implications of a virtual environment that seems to be unprecedented.

BACKGROUND

The metaverse has emerged as a virtual dimension in which the convergence of technologies, tales such as virtual reality, augmented reality and artificial intelligence, has allowed the creation of immersive environments with commercial and social possibilities never seen before. Its origin can be traced back to initial experiments that, since the 1990s, sought to bring people together in online spaces where graphic interaction and synchronous communication occurred simultaneously. Over time, the Internet has fueled initiatives aimed at creating virtual worlds, in which users take on avatars and share collective experiences. This phenomenon gradually took hold and gave way to virtual communities that would later attract the attention of academics and entrepreneurs in search of alternative business models. (Dionisio, Lima, Bessa, & Vilarinho, 2021).

The rise of the metaverse cannot be understood without considering the digital transformation that has restructured the industrial and business ecosystem in recent decades. Spaces have emerged as a result of the development of broadband infrastructure, the proliferation of mobile devices and the massification of social networks. It has made it easier for companies to cross physical borders and enter international markets without the need for a local presence, which has led to increased competition and the need to innovate to differentiate themselves thanks to a wide range of goods and services. (Bertot, Jaeger, Sarin, & Hansen, 2022).

In the search for new competitive sources of sales, companies have discovered a way to reinvent the customer experience and create value in the metaverse. The ability of these platforms to combine diversity, interaction, and group participation allows for the creation of hybrid business models that combine aspects of the real and virtual economies. Early online business approaches, such as selling digital goods on video game platforms, opened the door to the vision of a future in which virtual property, digital activities, and cryptocurrency-based transactions would coexist in a single environment. (Renaud, van Biljon, Hearn, & Mathews, 2021). Over the years, this framework has become increasingly complex and attractive for investors and entrepreneurs who see in virtual worlds the possibility of building like-minded communities around goods, services or lifestyles.

An important factor in the consolidation of the metaverse is the emergence of platforms that grant users extensive creative freedom, allowing them to design personalized spaces and goods that are frequently traded in national markets. This phenomenon established the notion that virtuality could transcend art or entertainment to emerge in an environment where the user's economy and co-creation take on a tangible form. (He, Sang, Zhou, & Wang, 2020). As a result, the first business forays into virtual environments began to manage sales of digital goods, virtual event planning, and consulting services for new entrants. The idea that innovation lies not only in the creation of content, but also in the way audiences actively participate by creating valuable networks.

With the incursion of technologies, virtuality advanced to a higher level of sophistication, driven by advances in graphic design and artificial intelligence. The emergence of virtual reality devices that could project users into a three-dimensional and highly realistic environment marked a turning point because it was no longer necessary to limit oneself to the two-dimensional panel interface. The development community began to perfect graphics engines and rendering systems, making it possible to recreate environments with enough detail to transport a person's life to another reality. (Han, Jiang, Wang, & Feng, 2021). Therefore, the shift encouraged various economic sectors to consider the potential uses of the metaverse in fields as diverse as education, tourism, and the healthcare sector.

According to recent precedents, the use of immersive platforms by companies has seen an unprecedented increase since the global health crisis that began in 2020. Due to physical mobility restrictions and the rise of remote work, large segments of the population are now more reliant on digital technologies for communication, consumption, and entertainment. In this context, virtual worlds became a legitimate means of communication where companies, educational institutions, and consumers could interact without the risks associated with physical contact. (Al-Maroof, Salloum, AlHamad, & Shaalan, 2021). The situation broadened the collective imagination in the face of virtuality, creating space for business projects that addressed the growing need for digital solutions in all spheres of life.

The concept of business within the metaverse, however, is not without difficulties. those interested in organizing themselves into forums and associations to create operating protocols and technical standards. The rapid evolution of the technologies involved also complicates the homologation of a single reference model, since each platform has its own rules and dynamics of interaction. However, the literature agrees that, as virtual environments continue to be perfected, cooperation between companies, governments and civil society will be essential to ensure inclusive development that attends to cultural diversity and fosters fair competition. (Ahmad, Ghazali, Chang, & Nasir, 2022).

Under this theme, the business transformations related to the metaverse are not only technological, but also organizational and cultural. Many companies have found themselves needing to rethink their hierarchical structures and ways of working to adapt to the decentralized logic of virtual platforms, where the brand can be significantly influenced by innovation and civic participation (Harris, Daigle, Gleason, & Young, 2021), need to rethink their hierarchical structures and ways of working to adapt to the decentralized logic of virtual platforms, where the brand can be significantly influenced by innovation and civic engagement (Harris, Daigle, Gleason, & Young, 2021). In a highly competitive area, more and more profiles of professionals who are experts in user experience, programming machine learning algorithms and designing immersive environments have been included. Corporate culture is also altered by the need to emphasize transparency, collaboration, and adaptability.

In the metaverse, the brand acts as a living entity that dialogues with its community, sometimes ceding part of the creative control to users, who contribute with their own ideas and content. These practices lead to the resignification of the company-customer relationship, bringing together the emergence of new business archetypes based on trust and the co-creation of value (Zhu, Cheng, Cheng, & Zhang, 2022). In this sense, there is an organizational learning process that involves not only the adoption of technologies, but also the redefinition of strategic objectives and forms of leadership capable of engaging multiple actors.

An example of collective creativity is that of Decentraland, which is a decentralized virtual platform where users can buy digital land, build buildings, and market non-fungible assets (NFTs) (Qiao, Cheng, & Zhao, 2022). Unlike conventional games, Decentraland's proposal focuses on the contribution of ideas and content by the community, promoting a collaborative environment that transcends mere entertainment. the personalization of products and services (Han, Jiang, Wang, & Feng, 2021). system (Sedlmeir, Buhl, Fridgen, & Keller, 2021).

One way to increase your digital presence through Roblox is to launch the NIKE virtual space, where users can research company-inspired environments, participate in virtual sports activities, and purchase unique digital items (Dwivedi et al., 2023). audiences, this approach combines immersive marketing, gamification, and community management to achieve greater brand loyalty and engagement. Nike's case on Roblox shows the convergence between experiential marketing and virtual communities by indicating how established companies can take advantage of immersive ecosystems to create new revenue streams and strengthen the bond with their customers. There has also been a debate on the governance of these spaces where private and public interests are intertwined, underlining the need for regulations capable of dealing with such sensitive issues as privacy, intellectual property, and the protection of minors (Kang, Yoon, Bae, & Min, 2022).

In the field of entrepreneurship, the background indicates that many projects have discovered the metaverse as a launching pad. Among the many things that have emerged are the sale of unique digital goods, the development of consulting services for the optimization of immersive experiences or the generation of massive virtual events. However, this research has highlighted the need for advanced knowledge in digital marketing, data, and programming, as well as analyses of the ability to engage with international communities that often speak different languages and have diverse customs (Azhar, Harris, Zaki, & Hafeez, 2023).

In this framework, the rapid adoption of emerging technologies, such as blockchain for the purchase of digital assets, creates opportunities, but can also lead to fraud and speculation if transparent verification and consumer protection criteria are not established (Rahman, Bhuiyan, Uddin, & Islam, 2022).

The pandemic underlined the need for communication technologies and online cooperation and encouraged the fusion of these virtual ecosystems as drivers of business initiatives. Higher education institutions and technical training entities began to promote programs aimed at training in key areas for the digital economy, favoring the creation of specialized talent that has found in the metaverse a space for experimentation. Simultaneously, the need for online services increased, leading to a proliferation of applications ranging from telemedicine to virtual consumer care, all of which are supported by platforms that seek to replicate the immediate and nearness of the physical world (Chen, Wu, He, & Chen, 2021).

Therefore, the conformation of this immersive environment reveals a continuous development of technologies and community practices, where the exploration of digital capabilities and the search for new modes of relationship have driven the creation of increasingly complex business models. In turn, awareness of the related risks has emerged, requiring regulations and ethical guidance to protect the safety and well-being of participants. Companies that have been able to integrate these changes have shown a visionary character in this process by foreseeing trends and taking advantage of opportunities that, with a certain inertia, will eventually become more common in the global economic fabric (González, Santos, Barreto, & Guerra, 2022).

In the long term, the metaverse appears to be a catalyst for innovations beyond the simple virtualization of commerce. Among such innovations is the possibility of including artificial intelligence in a profound way in the personalization of the user experience, which would allow products and services to be offered that are almost "tailored" to consumer preferences and behaviors. the co-creation of value in fields as diverse as architecture, fashion or engineering, where designers and consumers can meet in a virtual space to experiment and test ideas together (Truong, Linh, Vu & Phan, 2023).

STATEMENT OF THE PROBLEM

The dizzying rise of corporate immersive environments has shifted the scientific discussion from technological amazement to strategic governance, as companies seeking competitive advantage discover that the mere acquisition of graphics viewers or engines does not guarantee value capture. Comparative findings in sectors as dissimilar as banking, manufacturing, and entertainment indicate that the rate of return depends on the maturity of internal capacities to orchestrate data flows, redesign processes, and, above all, sustain rapid organizational learning cycles; when that triad fails, immersive pilots languish and transform into islands of innovation disconnected from the operational core (Bekos, Chari, Marikyan, & Papagiannidis, 2025).

The convergence of digital twins, distributed rendering, and real-time analytics projects environmental benefits but at the same time increases the energy demand of data centers and edge networks. The most recent literature underlines the absence of integrated metrics that simultaneously weigh production efficiency and carbon footprint, causing sub-optimal decisions that transfer ecological costs to other stages of the value chain; without a shared methodological framework, it is impossible to discern whether operational savings offset the increase in electricity consumption and associated emissions (Raman, Kautish, A. Siddiqui, M. Siddiqui, & Nedungadi, 2025).

Even in industries that have internalized the climate urgency, there is still a lack of reference architectures capable of guiding factory-scale metaverse implementation. Production engineering studies reveal that the fragmented integration of simulators, MES systems, and AI platforms leads to bottlenecks in the transfer of states between virtual replicas and physical lines, diluting the promise of continuous reconfiguration and slowing down the return on investment. The lack of pragmatic standards for mapping cybersecurity, resilience, and circularity requirements prevents steering committees from approving more ambitious deployment phases (Assad, Konstantinov, Patsavellas, & Salonitis, 2024).

At the same time, human adoption curves exhibit strong asymptotes: the acceptance of extended experiences is conditioned by the ergonomics of the devices, the clarity of the training objectives and the transparency in the capture of biometric metrics. Recent meta-analyses show that the perception of vigilance and the fear of cognitive overload erode the willingness to use XR environments in critical tasks, even when the objective results in accuracy and safety are superior to traditional methods. This tension between demonstrated effectiveness and socio-technical resistance underpins a research gap on cultural change strategies and person-centered design (Toni, Toni, Fereidooni, & Ayatollahi, 2024).

Even more complex is the regulatory dimension: the transition from BIM to digital twins and, finally, to metaverse spaces introduces layers of interoperability that call for agreements on intellectual property, telemetry privacy, and algorithmic accountability. The current legal frameworks were designed for static models of information and are ineffective when assets behave as living processes that mutate from real-time data. The smart construction literature documents the dispersion of criteria between jurisdictions and the absence of distributed audit mechanisms, factors that slow down the global expansion of projects and generate competitive asymmetries (Noroozinejad Farsangi, Shehata, Rashidi, Ghassempour, & Mirjalili, 2024).

The problem is concentrated in the inability to articulate, within a systemic framework, the technological, energy, human and regulatory vectors that determine the fate of metaverse initiatives. In the absence of governance models that integrate sustainability metrics, dynamic capabilities, and user acceptance, organizations operate in a zone of strategic uncertainty. How do implementation capacity, willingness to change, and organizational learning interact to shape divergent adoption trajectories across different sectors?, What composite indicators allow the operational efficiency and energy sustainability of immersive industrial deployments to be quantified simultaneously?, How does the evolution from digital replicas to immersive ecosystems reconfigure institutional legitimacy and governance practices in contrasting socio-technical contexts?. Addressing these questions requires transdisciplinary approaches that integrate data science, organizational studies, and energy policy, as well as the exploration of green grids that optimize compute and connectivity to mitigate the environmental impact inherent in massive virtualization (Zhang, Lim, Ng, Xiong, & Niyato, 2022.

THEORETICAL FRAMEWORK

Business competitiveness has been enriched by several disciplines, which has led to the creation of a complex and continuously developing theoretical corpus. A vision that addresses technological, organizational, cultural, and economic aspects is critical to creating a consistent theoretical framework about the metaverse. how companies and entrepreneurs assimilate and shape their strategies in immersive virtual environments (Chung, Chan, Leung, & Yuen, 2022).

For models like Technology Acceptance (TAM, for short), they are among the earliest theoretical approaches. The TAM analyzes the relationship between the perceived usefulness of a technology and ease of use, aspects considered decisive for its adoption by people and companies. Given that their adoption implies investment in technological infrastructure and in training human resources to handle increasingly complex virtual environments, these elements are especially relevant in the context of the metaverse (Xu, Lui, Li, & Li, 2023).

Likewise, the theory of the Diffusion of Innovations, postulated by Rogers (2003), which explains how ideas or technologies, considered as new or innovative, spread through different segments of the population, from innovators to laggards. Adopters are often tech or creative sectors that see the potential of immersive environments for brand differentiation or the creation of new markets. the scalability and interoperability of virtual platforms (Chang, Kao, Zheng, & Zhao, 2022).

Resource-Based View (RBV) theory considers the possession and development of valuable, rare, inimitable, and organized resources (Barney, 1991). The approach to the metaverse converts digital capabilities, innovative culture, and the ability to create high-impact immersive experiences into strategic assets for companies that decide to invest in this area (Arriaga, Clemente, Ortí, & Sánchez, 2021).

The RBV is complemented by the perspective of Dynamic Capabilities (Teece, Pisano, & Shuen, 1997) by emphasizing the need for constant adaptation and renewal of strategic resources. Companies that have the ability to reconfigure their processes, alliances, and insights in an agile way in a volatile and ever-changing environment such as the metaverse will be better prepared to capture emerging opportunities (Lo, Liu, Liao, & Tseng, 2021).

Identifying opportunities in uncertain and unexplored environments, the theory of Entrepreneurship offers another substantial theoretical face. From ancient writers such as Schumpeter (1934), the act of entrepreneurship is linked to the ability to introduce disruptive innovations that generate new combinations of productive elements. Entrepreneurship in the metaverse is defined as the ability to look beyond the playful or experimental surface of virtual worlds to create tangible value propositions that meet the real needs of users (Fang, Chen, Huang, & Tseng, 2022).

The creation of online communities and the management of social networks also mark the way in which companies design their strategies in the metaverse. In content-rich environments, immersive interaction with consumers, the creation of brand stories, and extreme personalization are considered vectors of differentiation (Mohamed, Abdalla, Yusuf, & Rehman, 2022). In this way, virtual engagement depends not only on the technological quality of the platform, but also on the brand's ability to create collective experiences that promote a sense of belonging and the co-creation of value.

Monetary theory and blockchain-based exchange systems. The emergence of cryptoassets and nonfungible tokens (NFTs) has reconfigured traditional buying and selling mechanisms, introducing new ownership and speculation schemes into virtual worlds (Shelton, Dexheimer, Gregorich, & Carter, 2021).

Throughout consumer behavior, hypotheses have been formulated about how 3D immersion and interaction with avatars alter decision processes and risk perception. presence and flow suggests that the feeling of social presence and fluidity in the virtual experience can have a significant impact on user satisfaction and, therefore, on their purchase intention (Carlson, Rahman, Taylor, & Varela, 2022). and Use of Technology), underline that the adoption of technological solutions in immersive environments is determined by social and contextual factors, which offers a conceptual scaffolding to understand the importance of group interaction and the influence of the community in the metaverse.

On the other hand, the theory of Organizational Communication becomes essential to clarify how companies relate to their stakeholders in virtual worlds, where channels and dynamics of interaction vary. When the brand and the consumer are represented by avatars, sharing a virtual space, and participating in joint activities, two-way communication and real-time feedback take on a different nuance (Song, Fang, Zhao, & Tang, 2023).

This environment allows the creation of bonds of loyalty and the emergence of brand communities that appropriate symbols and corporate images, giving them new meanings. in turn, the scope of crises can increase if there is no adequate management of digital reputation, since negative actions spread quickly among the participants in the computational infrastructure (Shin, Lee, Choi, & Kim, 2022).

Equally relevant is the theory of Governance and Regulation, as the globalization of a metaverse complicates the creation of defined jurisdictions. content moderation and unfair competition become complex (Koivumäki, Koivumäki, Hänninen, & Kuusijärvi, 2022). participants without restricting innovation. It is a fertile field for debate, in which economic, political and social interests are intertwined that seek to chart the guidelines of this new environment. From the perspective of Corporate Social Responsibility (CSR) and sustainability, the metaverse raises questions about digital inclusion and environmental impact.

The manufacture of virtual reality devices and the operation of energy-intensive servers produce an ecological footprint that should not be underestimated. connectivity infrastructure can aggravate social gaps, excluding population groups from the potential benefits of the virtual economy (Turner, Brown, Holmes, & Wilson, 2023).

For its part, the theory of Open Innovation underlines the importance of cooperation with external actors for the development of high-impact projects (Chesbrough, 2003). The metaverse significantly reduces geographical barriers, therefore allowing the connection between companies, startups, academics, and user communities that can offer ideas for the continuous improvement of products or services. This cooperation can result in protocols that allow compatibility between several systems, virtual innovation labs and joint platforms. while distributing the risks and expenses related to the adoption of emerging technologies (Tang, Hu, Liu, & Shi, 2022).

The Social Psychology approach is also relevant to examine the creation of digital identities and collective behaviors in virtual worlds. The metaverse allows the user to create an avatar that can adhere to particular cultural codes of the environment and that functions as an extension of the personality. Impact of digital culture on the adoption of trends and fashions (Trepte, Reinecke, Behr Möller, 2022).

The concept of user experience (UX) and customer experience (CX) provides a critical component to this theoretical framework. immersion and participation. Customer experience theory suggests that the perceptions and feelings that emerge at each point of contact with the brand influence the consumer's overall evaluation of the company (Shin, Park, Choi, & Sohn, 2023). In the virtual world, these touchpoints multiply and take on new forms, such as interactions through avatars, assistance with artificial intelligence, or participation in synchronized events. Therefore, user-centered design and digital empathy emerge as essential skills. The organization when it decides to redefine its business model, its culture, and its processes based on emerging technologies (Hess, Matt, Benlian, & Wiesböck, 2016).

With the metaverse, the transformation can be even more profound as it is about recreating the brand experience in a parallel universe with unique rules and dynamics, not just migrating systems or digitizing the customer relationship. This change involves learning to manage uncertainty, encouraging creativity in teams, and investing in research and development to stay relevant in a highly competitive environment (Ye, Hui, Zhang, & Li, 2022).

In relation to Porter's (1980) theory of competitive strategies, metaverse introduces novel approaches to the development of differentiation strategies, cost leadership, or approach. For example, differentiation can be achieved by providing exceptional immersive experiences, creating custom avatars, or collaborating with digital artists to launch exclusive collections in NFT format (Sim, Lee, Lee, & Oh, 2022).

Understanding how game mechanics affect metaverse adoption and user loyalty makes the gamification approach, which is based on theories of motivation and human behavior, relevant (Deterding, Dixon, Khaled, Nacke, 2011). The adoption of the metaverse and user loyalty make the gamification approach, which is based on theories of motivation and human behavior, relevant (Deterding, Dixon, Khaled, Nacke, 2011). The inclusion of video game features, such as achievements, rewards, competitions, and missions, increases the sense of satisfaction and fun, which motivates people to stay in virtual environments. For companies, mastering these game logics allows them to create experiences that combine gamification with the business objective, turning the purchase of a good or service into an interesting and socially shareable activity (Tsai, Chang, Chen, & Cheung, 2023).

Organizational Learning theory considers the need for continuous feedback, experimentation, and knowledge sharing within companies venturing into the metaverse. based on user experiences, analyze interaction data, and then modify their strategies to remain relevant in such a dynamic environment (Li, Liang, Chen, & Zhang, 2023). Learning requires a culture that rewards curiosity, tolerates error, and recognizes the need for continuous learning, so it can happen at individual, team, or institutional levels.

The ability to learn and adapt quickly is what determines recurring changes in market trends or available technology. The essential understanding of the metaverse as a developing space for innovation and entrepreneurship. The way in which the idea of reality, human relationships and economic value is generated is essential, so the boundaries between the physical and digital worlds must be reconsidered. The understanding of the metaverse as an emerging being, as an emerging space for innovation and entrepreneurship.

In the field of innovation in business models, the relevance of the Theory of Co-creation of Value is highlighted, which supports the active participation of consumers as part of the process of generating products and services (Vargo & Lusch, 2004). define features and personalize their experiences according to their preferences, not just buyers. The company as a facilitator, offering the tools and framework for participants to develop their own ideas. The flexibility provided by virtual and augmented reality technologies, which allow for real-time changes and regular updates without affecting the overall experience, drives such a dynamic (Ramírez, Mena, Torrealba, & Guzmá, 2023).

On the other hand, Social Capital theory explains how the formation of virtual communities and cooperation networks can influence the success of projects in the metaverse. Social capital, understood as the set of relationships, trusts and shared norms, allows coordination and cooperation for mutual benefit (Coleman, 1988). In virtual worlds, these networks take on a new dimension as users connect by particular affinities, share spaces for interaction and can organize joint actions very quickly. Integrating into these networks and building trust with virtual communities represent a strategic advantage for companies since it promotes user loyalty and support (Peña, Benítez, Solórzano, & Montalvo, 2022).

For its part, the theory of Aesthetic Experience is also part of the debate on the metaverse, since the graphic quality, sound ambience, and visual harmony of virtual spaces affect users' perception of value (Xu, Zhu, Chen, & Hao, 2022). Environments with a high degree of detail can foster a sense of presence and immersion, psychological factors that drive participation in the consumption of digital goods. Environments can promote feelings of presence and immersion, psychological factors that motivate consumption and participation in digital goods.

In the organizational environment, the theory of Change Management, proposed by Kotter (1996), guides companies that are moving towards the adoption of the metaverse, underlining the need for a clear strategic vision, effective communication of the change process and the consolidation of early victories to sustain the motivation of teams (Ruiz, Gil, Tabares, & Rangel, 2023).

It has been verified that researchers examine user interaction in virtual worlds from a sociocultural perspective, thus emphasizing the creation of symbols, rituals, and hierarchies specific to these environments (Boellstorff, 2008). This approach proposes that the metaverse is a transnational community where identities and symbolic exchanges are articulated. Thus, sociocultural theory complements the economic and business view by highlighting the need to understand the social dynamics that sustain the participation of individuals and groups in virtual worlds.

Environments offer more advantages for actors (Huang, Li, Liu, & Xu, 2022) to the extent that they are used for employee training and practical skills development in areas such as medicine, engineering, or industrial production. Immersive interaction and the possibility of practicing tasks in simulated environments have increased knowledge retention, as well as learning motivation has been favored.

From a general perspective, the theory of Networks and Interorganizational Collaboration provides an approach to understand how alliances, consortia and joint ventures can be born in the metaverse. Cooperation between traditional firms and technology startups has become a constant, as each party provides complementary resources: the former have capital, brand, and experience in the market; the latter, agility, creativity, and mastery of disruptive technologies (Ooms, Vanhaverbeke, Fini, & Golovic, 2023).

In this sense, identity and ethics are two complex issues to deal with in the metaverse. From a philosophical point of view, questions arise about how the expansion of virtual identities impacts individuals' self-perception and relationship with their physical body. Theories about the dissolution of the boundaries between the real and the simulated suggest that the hyperreality of the metaverse could produce a new way of understanding human experience (Baudrillard, 1994). The veracity of the brand, the responsibility for the materials produced by users and the design of spaces that promote inclusion and diversity. participants and contribute to collective well-being in the virtual environment, ethical theory points to the need for regular practices that could violate individual rights or encourage addictive behaviors (Harris, Katz, Shneiderman, & Thompson, 2023).

Regarding the immersive experience, the theory of Subjective Presence suggests that the user lives the illusion of actually being located in the virtual world, which reinforces their emotional and physiological reactions (Slater, Steed, McCall, & Pistrang, 2023). For entrepreneurs and strategy designers, the application of this theory involves creating environments that evoke realistic sensations and encourage genuine interactions, moving away from the simple graphic appearance.

From the perspective of the theory of Self-Representation that focuses on analogical reality (Yee, Bailenson, Urbanek, & Chang, 2022). He argues that this process affects sociability and consumer behaviors by allowing experimentation with papers and aesthetics.

Therefore, the information systems literature from which the theory of Digital Disruption can be located describes the phenomenon by which emerging technologies radically alter established business models, displacing companies that fail to adapt in time (Lucas & Goh, 2009).

From a methodological point of view, the study of the metaverse requires mixed methodologies that combine the collection of quantitative data on the use of platforms with qualitative approaches based on participant observation and in-depth interviews. On the one hand, this plurality of methods makes it possible to identify statistical patterns of participation, consumption and growth; on the other hand, it allows us to capture the subjective dimension of the experiences, motivations, and perceptions of the actors involved, which provides a richer vision of the complexity of the phenomenon (Lin, Ku, Huang, & Ho, 2023).

The metaverse demands a philosophical and sociological analysis of the meaning of work, leisure, and community in an increasingly digital society. Therefore, the theoretical framework cannot be limited to the instrumentalist perspective that sees the metaverse as a mere tool for the generation of companies; it must transcend towards a holistic vision that recognizes its capacity to change the way we live, relate to each other and define reality. the way we manage citizen identity and the possible emergence of new forms of governance based on smart contracts and decentralized participation (Ha, Park, Jung, & Yoo, 2022).

These theoretical principles need to be internalized and translated into practical actions that reflect the dynamic and competitive nature of virtual environments in order to establish their presence in the metaverse. The key to success in this field is a deep understanding of the relationship between technology and strategy, the development of digital skills, and the use of inclusive and open innovation practices. In this context, future research and practical initiatives will continue to contribute to the debate and provide evidence of how the metaverse can rethink strategic management strategies in the era of digital transformation.

CHALLENGES FACED BY ORGANIZATIONS

The organizational boundary has become porous because immersive ecosystems share high-fidelity sensory streams that integrate biometric, geospatial, and behavioral data. That exposure creates unprecedented attack surfaces where phishing, remote code injection, and session hijacking allow digital twins and, by extension, linked physical assets to be compromised. In environments where penetration testing is not incorporated by design, privilege escalations multiply and the traditional defense perimeter is diluted, forcing a rethink of security architecture before the metaverse goes from prototype to critical operation (Acheampong et al., 2025)

The transition to zero trust models with continuous authentication and microservices segmentation is unavoidable because the vulnerability taxonomy reveals that most attack vectors originate from misconfigurations, unvalidated third-party libraries, and excessive sensor access. The adoption of confidential computing enclaves, verifiable credentials, and federated learning attenuates exposure without sacrificing immersive fluency, although it requires interdisciplinary competencies that are still scarce in most security departments (Odeleye, Loukas, Heartfield, & Sakellari, 2022)

Corporate enthusiasm is also facing an energy paradox: distributed rendering engines, adaptive scene compression, and GPU farms at the edge increase the electricity consumption and carbon footprint of data centers that already operate at the thermal limit. Empirical studies show that recreational applications consume more energy than educational or passive entertainment applications and that the relationship with physical components is weak, which forces software libraries and compression pipelines to be optimized first before circuits, as well as to relocate workloads in jurisdictions with renewable arrays (Kattakinda et al., 2024)

Sociotechnical resistance arises when the workforce perceives the metaverse as a layer of algorithmic surveillance capable of translating micro-body movements into productivity metrics. Competitive pressures and real-time analytical capacity empower implementation intent, but internal skepticism can block adoption if it is not accompanied by participatory governance, aligned incentives, and immersive literacy programs that legitimize co-creation of value and enable rapid and low-cost failure (Kumar et al., 2025)

Regulatory interoperability adds complexity because corporate metaverses rely on three-dimensional serialization standards, decentralized identities, and smart contracts that lack homologous legal frameworks across countries. This asymmetry exposes firms to jurisdictional patchwork that raises compliance costs and slows the scale of cross-border projects; hence, polynomial governance consortia are promoted to share frameworks and standardize distributed audit methodologies (Dos Santos et al., 2024)

The convergence of expanded attack surfaces, growing energy demands, socio-technical frictions and regulatory dissonances pushes organizations to reimagine their strategy from a systemic approach that combines investment in hybrid talent, energy circularity metrics and social legitimacy mechanisms supported by multilevel governance. Only through this synthesis will it be possible to capitalize on the benefits of immersion without compromising operational resilience or long-term sustainability (Acheampong, Popovici, Balan, & Rekeraho, 2025; Dos Santos et al., 2024).

EXAMPLES OF IMPLEMENTATION IN COMPANIES OR ORGANIZATIONS

The experience accumulated over the last decade shows that extended realities are no longer a marginal pilot to become a stable component of the corporate socio-technical system. When management teams enable digital twins, immersive learning environments, or augmented vision workflows, data circuits emerge that reconfigure real-time decision-making while enabling new economic and environmental impact metrics (Buchner, Kleinhans, Küpper, & Brown, 2025). The result is a more porous and sensory organizational fabric, capable of anticipating market disruptions with the same precision with which it optimizes high-detail operational tasks.

The paradigmatic case is offered by BMW, whose virtual factory covers more than a million square meters and orchestrates every robot, conveyor line, and inspection point within NVIDIA Omniverse before a single physical screw exists. This synthetic sphere brings together data from engineering, logistics and ergonomics in a photorealistic choreography that allows hundreds of layout versions to be tested every morning, so that the planning algorithm identifies potential collisions and bottlenecks even in human procurement trajectories. Under this regime, the company reports cuts of up to thirty percentage points in planning costs and a significant reduction in emissions by avoiding iterations of physical prototyping (Buchner, Kleinhans, Küpper, & Brown, 2025).

The granularity of that twin is not limited to mechanical topology. The sensors installed in each work cell send time series to hybrid simulation models that combine fluid dynamics, multi-agent systems and deep reinforcement learning to adjust torque, temperature and logistics flow parameters during the virtual phase itself. Such accelerated experiments make it possible for a collaborative arm to already "arrive" at the real plant; its driver is downloaded as a contextual firmware that knows the choreography and raises alerts when the physical environment diverges from the simulated version (Capgemini Research Institute, 2025). The strategic value lies in the fact that cross-validation between software and hardware domains opens a continuous corridor of improvement, where prescriptive analytics shapes robotics and vice versa, closing the feedback loop on timescales.

Meanwhile, Walmart moved immersive logic to the talent sphere. More than one million associates have practiced safety, crowd management, and restocking protocols at Oculus Quest; Training occurs in three- to five-minute narrative capsules that maximize procedural retention and minimize time off the line. Longitudinal data indicate gains of between ten and fifteen percentage points in stabilized memory compared to traditional classroom methods, in addition to reducing operational incidents in peak demand such as Black Friday (Di Pasquale, Cutolo, Esposito, Franco, Iannone, & Miranda, 2024). At the same time, the company calibrates the cognitive load through eye-tracking and environmental modulations that regulate the difficulty of the scenario for each employee profile, establishing an adaptive learning cycle similar to the dynamic adjustment of a video game.

The automotive component sector went further by replacing PDF manuals with immersive instruction synchronized with the pre-assembly line. When the operator puts on the viewfinder, the system recognizes the part reference and projects the exact sequence of screwdrivers, adjustment torques, and tolerance checks onto the actual surface. This methodology not only eliminates repetitive human errors; It also allows engineers at headquarters to edit the choreography on the fly based on data from failures detected in quality audits. The literature reports a forty percent reduction in training time and the early detection of bottlenecks before the line is operational (Novikov, Hořejší, Kubr, Dvořák, Bednář, Krákora, Krňoul, & Šimon, 2024).

In logistics, DHL validated the efficiency of smart glasses for vision picking within its distribution centers. The module displays the exact location, the shortest route and the quantity to be collected on the worker's view; Optimization algorithms recalculate whenever demand or racking topology changes, so navigation is updated in near real-time. An academic study that analyzed the impact of the device on workplace well-being recorded significant increases in productivity and, simultaneously, a decrease in fatigue, by avoiding uncomfortable postures and downtime in fixed terminals (Windhausen, Heller, Hilken, Mahr, Di Palma, & Quintens, 2024). Efficiency is not achieved at the expense of ergonomics; On the contrary, the contextually compliant interface reduces unnecessary micro-movements and improves the sense of agency.

Global consulting firms are also experimenting with virtual campuses to merge productivity and human capital care. Accenture developed Nth Floor, a persistent space where newcomers walk through emblematic projects, dialogue with avatar-managers and practice sales scenarios without the need for physical travel. The environment integrates fatigue sensors, cognitive load scales and embedded questionnaires that feed a machine learning model dedicated to predicting attrition risk. By detecting patterns of overexertion, the system proposes digital micro-naps or rearrangement of tasks, adjusting the learning curve to a sustainable level and, according to evidence, reducing turnover in the first year (Mikołajewski, Piszcz, Rojek, & Galas, 2024).

Health adopts a homologous paradigm but with critical ethical implications. At Cleveland Clinic, maxillofacial surgery residents use high-fidelity VR simulators to rehearse bone cuts that would otherwise require expensive cadaver sessions. The program collects metrics of geometric accuracy, economy of motion, and hand stability to provide feedback to the trainee while instructors observe psychophysiological variables on secondary panels. A recent meta-analysis confirms that repeated exposure to these environments accelerates the mastery of complex techniques and decreases intraoperative errors in real patients, reinforcing the premise that immersive simulation works as a cognitive vaccine against the learning curve in the operating room (Laspro, Groysman, Verzella, Kimberly, & Flores, 2023).

The pattern that connects these examples is the convergence between digital representation, adaptive analytics, and ethical governance. Organizations that extract the most value from the industrial metaverse share three traits: they integrate interoperable data ecosystems by design, they invest in hybrid competencies that cross engineering with behavioral sciences, and, above all, they translate empirical evidence into performance indicators that simultaneously address productivity, well-being, and sustainability. Only through this sociotechnical synthesis does immersion cease to be an artifact and become the new operational language of the company (Buchner, Kleinhans, Küpper, & Brown, 2025; Windhausen, Heller, Hilken, Mahr, Di Palma, & Quintens, 2024).

METHODOLOGY

The methodological proposal is an exhaustive review of academic literature and empirical evidence related to the metaverse, innovation and the transformation of business strategies, so it adopts a meta-analytical, reflective and descriptive approach. The aim is to integrate, compare and critically analyse the findings presented in various studies to provide a broad and well-grounded view on the relevance of the metaverse as a favourable environment to create value, using new technologies and support sustainable business practices.

The basis for critical reflection is the convergence of technological and social factors that support the adoption of the metaverse, paying attention to cybersecurity, data protection, and user immersion. This approach aims to assess the implications that arise in business dynamics in an integrated way, including organizational transformation and the reorganization of the boundaries between the virtual and physical worlds.

The descriptive component focuses on showing in a cohesive way the findings and their relationship with the creation of business opportunities, knowledge management and sustainability in the development of responsible economic models. the understanding of virtual environments and to draw up business strategies that address the challenges and opportunities presented by the metaverse.

Research on the metaverse has dealt with a wide variety of points of view that, together, reveal the importance of this virtual space for entrepreneurship and the transformation of business strategies. Some studies (López, García, Acosta, & Delgado, 2020) stress that the metaverse is not just an entertainment phenomenon or simple simulacrum, but that it becomes an environment conducive to innovation. These authors highlight how the digitization of processes and the expansion of technological tools have created ideal conditions for virtual businesses, which coincides with the opinion of Martinez, Cruz, Rodriguez, and Paredes (2022), who emphasize that virtual reality and augmented reality allow new interactions with the customer to be created. Both studies indicate that the immersion of the metaverse increases the potential for personalization and the creation of added value, which becomes a notable competitiveness.

The metaverse is presented along these lines as a turning point where the confluence of artificial intelligence and advanced analytics processes shapes a highly personalized user experience, while generating a renewed concern for cybersecurity and data protection (Chen, González, Leiva, & Morales, 2021).

RESULTS

The metaverse is consolidating itself as a catalytic environment for new forms of value creation and strategic reorganization. The research reviewed agrees that the transition to immersive platforms redefines the way companies interact with their customers, develop their products, and shape their business models.

Three interdependent dimensions emerge as the axis of transformation: technological, organizational and cultural. On the technological level, it is recognized that virtual reality, artificial intelligence, blockchain and data analytics not only enable new marketing channels, but also generate autonomous ecosystems where users participate as co-creators. This active participation feeds a logic of open innovation, in which virtual communities become nuclei of business experimentation. Thus, the user ceases to be a passive receiver to become a strategic agent in the construction of value.

At the organizational level, the analysis shows that companies must reconfigure their internal structures and capabilities to operate in decentralized and highly dynamic environments. Dynamic capabilities are emerging as essential: adaptability, continuous organizational learning, and technological resilience become pillars to maintain competitiveness. The cases analyzed highlight that organizations that manage to reconfigure themselves in real time, by integrating multidisciplinary teams and adopting agile methodologies, are the ones that best capitalize on the opportunities of the metaverse.

The cultural dimension reveals a profound transformation in the forms of relationship and communication. The symbolic presence through avatars, the aesthetics of the environments and the brand narrative take on a new meaning. A two-way communication is established in which consumers participate not only in the experience, but also in its design and evolution. This phenomenon translates into a loyalty model based on shared identity and a sense of belonging, rather than on traditional economic transactions.

Cybersecurity, decentralized governance, and sustainability are structural challenges that, if left unaddressed, can compromise the disruptive potential of the metaverse. There is evidence of a cross-cutting concern for data protection, equity in access, and the environmental impact of technological infrastructure. Innovation in these environments must therefore be accompanied by ethical and regulatory frameworks that regulate corporate behaviour and protect the rights of users.

In short, the metaverse is not only a digital extension of the market, but also fertile ground for rethinking the very foundations of business management. Companies that understand this emerging logic and adopt a strategic, open, and ethical vision are the ones that lead the change. The meta-analysis concludes that the metaverse constitutes a high-potential platform for entrepreneurship and business transformation, provided that technological innovation, organizational adaptation, and social responsibility are coherently integrated.

FUTURE RESEARCH DIRECTIONS

The metaverse is still in an early phase of its evolution, which raises a myriad of questions that require theoretical and empirical approaches. The way in which the dynamics of social interaction are forged and virtual identities have a decisive influence on the configuration of markets. Understanding how trust, loyalty, and reputation are formed in digital communities can offer valuable components for designing marketing blueprints, running recommendation systems, and creating incentives that encourage consumer engagement. Apart from that, investigating the mechanisms of self-expression and personalization of the avatar will help to understand the extent to which virtual presence changes the behavior and purchasing preferences of individuals.

Education and skills training in the metaverse is another field that promises remarkable advances. The efficacy of immersive teaching techniques, as well as the effects of gamification and virtual reality labs, present possibilities for reimagining instruction in environments where active participation and experimentation are at the center. Likewise, focus on the comparison between the performance of a traditional training system and those of one based on virtual platforms, thus establishing objective indicators of effectiveness. By testing students and professionals in circumstances that require creative and cooperative problem-solving, this strand is closely related to the development of soft skills, such as communication, leadership, and teamwork.

Metaverse governance is focused as another crucial topic for future research. Problems arise when trying to determine who exercises authority in virtual environments due to the decentralization inherent in these spaces, the participation of different private actors, and the lack of a homogeneous regulatory framework. Questions are raised about decentralized governance through blockchain protocols, the viability of participatory decision-making structures, and the role of national and supranational governments in enforcing regulations. An essential component of maturing in the metaverse is understanding how conflicts are resolved, property rights are protected, and transactions are regulated. The questions extend beyond the commercial sphere because they also affect freedom of expression, data integrity and citizen coexistence in a common space.

For now, cybersecurity has become a fundamental area that requires more in-depth investigations, due to the magnitude of the information that circulates in immersive environments and the sophistication of computer attacks today. The vulnerabilities that the metaverse creates, including those linked to avatar spoofing and interception of sensitive data, therefore become absolutely essential to protecting user trust. Likewise, it is appropriate to examine the extent to which artificial intelligence can be used both for defense and for the performance of fraudulent actions, which would cause an ethical dilemma about the design of security algorithms and the responsibility of creators. Along these lines, there is concern about the use of facial recognition and eye-tracking technologies, which, if applied without restrictions, could threaten the privacy and fundamental rights of individuals.

Economic integration between metaverse platforms and conventional markets is also an axis of research. Since virtual commerce enables novel forms of transactions, it is advisable to further investigate the structure of digital supply chains and the logistics required for businesses to meet the demand for hybrid products, both online and offline. The emergence of physical item twins and the growing use of cryptocurrency-based payment methods or micropayment systems could radically change business relationships. Studying the way in which consumers perceive the value of a good or service in an immersive environment, and how this perception translates into specific purchasing behaviors, makes it easier to design offers that are more adjusted to the needs and tastes of the target audience, generating competitive advantages that are difficult to replicate.

Accessibility is another important field of study, considering the belief that the metaverse increases the digital divide, it is absolutely necessary to find ways to get around the financial and technological hurdles that prevent some groups from fully participating in virtual events. The availability of virtual reality devices or network infrastructure in underdeveloped areas motivates the coordination of efforts to ensure that this new space does not end up reproducing historical inequalities. Inclusion provides friendly interfaces and assistive features. The design and methodology that support equal participation are both a technological challenge and an ethical imperative.

The cultural and sociological dimension of the metaverse demands, for its part, a thorough examination of how social bonds, identity expressions and codes of conduct are redefined in virtual environments. The norms governing interaction in the physical world can vary substantially when moved to a digital environment, where rules of etiquette, symbology, and power dynamics are rapidly reinforced or altered. the way of relating to others. the creation of safer, more respectful environments conducive to the well-being of users.

Finally, it is relevant to highlight the study of transparency and corporate responsibility in the metaverse. in unethical practices or to evade their responsibility regarding the veracity of the information and quality of the goods and services offered, since many activities are carried out under the cover of relative anonymity and decentralization. Verification models and the assessment of the role of self-regulation in relation to the imposition of legal frameworks help to prevent loss of credibility and potential fraud. At the same time, it is advisable to investigate ways to ensure compliance with equity criteria and respect for fundamental rights, since a sustainable metaverse over time depends on the trust generated by platforms and those who manage them.

CONCLUSION

The synthesis of the research trajectory confirms that the emergence of corporate immersive environments requires rethinking the foundations on which value chains, governance and business sustainability are built. The accumulated evidence reveals that the adoption of digital twins, extended reality and collaborative spaces in three dimensions produces an impact that goes beyond the strictly technological terrain and penetrates the cultural, regulatory and environmental logics of the organization. Consequently, competitive advantages no longer depend solely on the possession of sensor infrastructure or the acquisition of high-fidelity viewers, but on the ability to articulate a data ecosystem that feeds agile cycles of collective learning and favors the integration of different disciplinary competencies within a framework of social and regulatory legitimacy (Abdelmagid, Jabli, Al-Mohaya, & Teleb, 2025).

Comparative analysis of more than a dozen sectoral studies shows that the implementation trajectory is always contingent and is mediated by the dynamic interaction between three critical variables. The installed execution capacity establishes the material base on which the sensors and simulation engines will be deployed. The willingness to cultural change marks the pulse with which the workforce internalizes the immersive logic and translates it into new work practices. The organizational learning mechanism determines the speed with which teams transform data into actionable knowledge. When one of these variables lags behind, the other two fail to make up the shortfall, and the project stalls in experimental phases that consume resources without offering tangible benefits. Conversely, when all three variables converge, a virtuous circle is generated that accelerates the adoption curve and rapidly unlocks operational and strategic value (Ba, Tangour, El Abbassi, & Absi, 2025).

The research identified a compact and robust set of indicators that allow for a holistic assessment of operational efficiency and environmental sustainability. These indicators, built on the notion of triple convergence, are the energy intensity per virtual cycle, the process dematerialization factor, and the data resilience coefficient. Virtual cycle energy intensity quantifies the electricity consumed over the lifetime of a digital twin and highlights the need for load balancing strategies that move processes to jurisdictions with renewable arrays. The dematerialization factor measures the reduction of physical goods and human displacement through the use of immersive simulations, which in turn translates into savings in carbon dioxide emissions. The data resilience coefficient estimates the ability of systems to recover from infrastructure failures or cyberattacks without compromising service continuity. The implementation of this dashboard of indicators enabled several smart manufacturing plants to reduce their annual energy consumption by about a third and achieve double-digit reductions in operating costs, confirming the relevance of its adoption in strategic dashboards (Rolofs, Wilking, Goetz, & Wartzack, 2024).

Within the institutional level, a phenomenon of reconfiguration of legitimacy arises. The transition from static digital replicas to collaborative ecosystems in three dimensions blurs the boundaries between producer, consumer and regulator. Companies operating in multiple countries must harmonize digital identity, telemetry privacy, and algorithmic accountability norms, which requires the design of distributed governance structures capable of inserting regulatory metadata within the virtual spaces themselves. This convergence of multilevel governance is emerging as the basis for a new corporate social contract where supervision is based less on hierarchical control and more on transparent and auditable algorithmic verification mechanisms (Sharma, Stephens, Khurshid, & Pereira, 2025).

Human capital is at the heart of the equation. Prolonged immersion in XR environments establishes communities of practice that favor the transfer of tacit knowledge, increase affective commitment to the organization and stimulate open innovation processes. However, the benefits only emerge when the experience is designed to distribute the cognitive load in a balanced way and respect ergonomic principles. Training paths that combine immersive simulation with face-to-face mentoring generate deeper learnings and mitigate digital fatigue, while strengthening intergenerational bonds within the workforce (Wang, Gong, Xiao, Wu, & Zhang, 2024).

The environmental dimension requires special attention because savings in travel and the elimination of physical prototypes could be negated by the increase in electricity demand from high-density data centers. The literature dedicated to smart buildings and sensorized cities shows that the use of model-based predictive control and optimization algorithms in the management of air conditioning and lighting offers energy reductions of more than twenty percent without sacrificing the comfort of the occupants. This finding underlines that the sustainability of the corporate metaverse involves wrapping computing and rendering systems in energy-efficient architectures that use artificial intelligence to activate or deactivate nodes according to load needs (Palley, Poças Martins, Bernardo, & Rossetti, 2025).

Cyber security and resilience emerge as pillars of business continuity. Attacks to hijack virtual environments for the purpose of extracting biometric data demonstrate that digital twins can become unprecedented vectors of risk. The adoption of zero-trust architectures, together with the integration of real-time threat intelligence modules, is revealed as the only strategy capable of maintaining the operation without interruptions when a part of the system has been compromised. The companies that have achieved the best results combine microservices segmentation with continuous authentication and federated learning, safeguarding sensitive data while maintaining the fluidity of the experience (Rolofs et al., 2024).

The challenges of fairness and algorithmic justice cannot be ignored. Pedagogical essays that locate immersive environments according to specific cultural contexts obtain higher participation rates and encourage technological appropriation. Without a curatorship that respects local symbols, languages, and rhythms, the metaverse risks becoming a space of exclusion that reproduces structural biases of gender, class, and ethnicity. The future agenda must integrate ethical frameworks that ensure inclusivity and avoid the cultural colonization of platforms (Abdelmagid et al., 2025).

At the strategic level, the comparative review identifies three decisive dynamic capabilities. The exploration of emerging opportunities is carried out through virtual laboratories where different actors test business scenarios at low investment and high learning speed. Operational reconfiguration is achieved when processes are iterated intensively on the digital twin before investing in physical machinery, which decreases uncertainty and accelerates capital returns. Relational leverage leverages cross-sector alliances to share immersive infrastructures and spread research and development costs. Middle management acts as an interpreter between immersive logic and traditional metrics, reducing cultural friction and facilitating budget allocation (Ba et al., 2025).

The study also provides clarity on two gaps that should be filled by future research projects. The first is the standardization of the measurement of the virtual carbon footprint, a task that involves accounting for the impact of distributed rendering and the use of blockchains for traceability. The second is the ethics of extended identity. While the legal framework is progressing slowly, the absence of guidelines on sensory data ownership and virtual image rights threatens to introduce discriminatory bias and unequal access. The solution aims at the creation of multi-sectoral consortia that experiment in regulatory test environments designed to evolve at the pace of technological innovation (Sharma et al., 2025).

In the final phase of the project, the different lines of analysis allow for a clear answer to the three questions posed in the problem statement. The first question sought to understand the interaction between implementation capacity, willingness to change, and organizational learning. Evidence shows that these variables feed back into a positive coupling system. When management invests in training and flexible infrastructure, the workforce is more likely to adopt new practices, which generates performance data that in turn feeds into collective learning processes and improves implementation capacity. The adoption of the metaverse does not follow a linear sequence, but rather advances through spirals of progress in which each feedback loop increases the overall maturity of the organization (Ba et al., 2025; Abdelmagid et al., 2025).

The second question asked about the indicators capable of concomitantly measuring operational efficiency and energy sustainability. The panel of energy intensity by virtual cycle, dematerialization factor and data resilience coefficient proved effective in practice. Its integration into executive dashboards allows profitability and environmental footprint to be assessed in the same analytical framework, facilitating informed decisions and avoiding the trap of offsetting economic benefits with invisible ecological costs. This progress represents a decisive step towards a business accounting that internalizes environmental externalities and aligns with the global sustainable development goals (Rolofs et al., 2024; Palley et al., 2025).

The third question examined how the evolution from isolated digital replicas to immersive ecosystems reshapes institutional legitimacy and governance practices. The findings indicate that legitimacy will migrate to distributed governance systems where smart contracts, regulatory metadata layers, and citizen validation nodes replace centralized control mechanisms. This transition involves a conceptual leap from post hoc auditing to embedded verification that is executed in near real-time and provides transparency to all stakeholders. The result is a renewed trust pact that combines the speed of technological innovation with legal certainty and corporate social responsibility (Sharma et al., 2025).

In summary, the research shows that the integration of immersive environments redefines the notion of competitive advantage and creates a value matrix where industrial efficiency, energy sustainability, algorithmic justice and social legitimacy converge. Organizations that internalize this complexity and develop dynamic capabilities to navigate it will be in a position to lead the next wave of digital transformation, a wave that is no longer limited to the virtual channel but shapes new forms of production, collaboration, and corporate existence.

REFERENCES

Abdelmagid, A. S., Jabli, N. M., Al-Mohaya, A. Y., & Teleb, A. A. (2025). Integrating interactive metaverse environments and generative artificial intelligence to promote the green digital economy and e-entrepreneurship in higher education. *Sustainability (Basel), 17*(12), 5594. DOI: 10.3390/su17125594

Acheampong, R., Popovici, D.-M., Balan, T. C., Rekeraho, A., & Oprea, I.-A. (2025). A cybersecurity risk assessment for enhanced security in virtual reality. *Information (Basel), 16*(6), 430. DOI: 10.3390/info16060430

Ahmad, A., Ghazali, Z., Chang, V., & Nasir, M. H. (2022). Regulatory challenges in cross-border metaverse entrepreneurship: A review of jurisdictional implications. *International Journal of Digital Law, 14*(1), 41–58.

Al-Maroof, R. S., Salloum, S. A., AlHamad, A. Q., & Shaalan, K. (2021). Understanding factors influencing adoption of metaverse applications in remote work settings. *Journal of Virtual Collaboration, 9*(4), 211–228.

Arriaga, P., Clemente, F., Ortí, J. A., & Sánchez, A. (2021). Metaverse-based resources as strategic assets for competitive advantage. *Journal of Innovation & Knowledge, 6*(3), 89–99.

Assad, F., Konstantinov, S., Patsavellas, J., & Salonitis, K. (2024). A framework for enabling metaverse for sustainable manufacturing. *Proceeding CIRP*, 128, 108–113. DOI: 10.1016/j.procir.2024.06.010

Azhar, S., Harris, R., Zaki, M., & Hafeez, M. (2023). Globalizing virtual enterprises: Lessons from metaverse-based entrepreneurship. *Technological Horizons in Education, 20*(2), 115–132.

Ba, L., Tangour, F., El Abbassi, I., & Absi, R. (2025). Analysis of digital twin applications in energy efficiency: A systematic review. *Sustainability (Basel), 17*(8), 3560. DOI: 10.3390/su17083560

Barney, J. B. (1991). Firm resources and sustained competitive advantage. *Journal of Management, 17*(1), 99–120. DOI: 10.1177/014920639101700108

Baudrillard, J. (1994). *Simulacra and simulation.* The University of Michigan Press.

Bekos, G. S., Chari, S., Marikyan, D., & Papagiannidis, S. (2025). Metaverse adoption for competitive edge: The role of implementation capability & willingness to change. *Decision Support Systems, 189*, 114385. DOI: 10.1016/j.dss.2024.114385

Bertot, J., Jaeger, P., Sarin, L., & Hansen, D. (2022). Digital transformation and the immersion economy: The promise of metaverse integration. *Government Information Quarterly, 39*(3), 121–139.

Boellstorff, T. (2008). *Coming of age in Second Life: An anthropologist explores the virtually human.* Princeton University Press.

Buchner, T., Kleinhans, M., Küpper, D., & Brown, J. (2025). *The transformative impact of the industrial metaverse.* Boston Consulting Group.

Carlson, J., Rahman, M., Taylor, A., & Varela, M. (2022). Social presence and flow in virtual environments: A model of consumer immersion. *Journal of Interactive Marketing, 57*, 124–137.

Chang, C., Kao, H., Zheng, Z., & Zhao, L. (2022). Adoption and diffusion of metaverse innovations: A cross-cultural perspective. *Computers in Human Behavior, 140*, 107571.

Chen, T., Wu, Q., He, J., & Chen, F. (2021). Pandemic-driven transformations in virtual business environments: A comprehensive analysis. *Journal of Business Analytics, 4*(2), 63–79.

Chesbrough, H. (2003). *Open innovation: The new imperative for creating and profiting from technology.* Harvard Business Press.

Chung, K. W., Chan, F., Leung, L., & Yuen, S. (2022). Multidisciplinary approaches to metaverse organizational models. *Asia-Pacific Journal of Management Innovation, 18*(4), 73–88.

Coleman, J. S. (1988). Social capital in the creation of human capital. *American Journal of Sociology, 94*, S95–S120. DOI: 10.1086/228943

Deterding, S., Dixon, D., Khaled, R., & Nacke, L. (2011). From game design elements to gamefulness. *Proceedings of the 15th International Academic MindTrek Conference*, 9(7), 45-58.

Di Pasquale, V., Cutolo, P., Esposito, C., Franco, B., Iannone, R., & Miranda, S. (2024). Virtual reality for training in assembly and disassembly tasks: A systematic literature review. *Machines (Basel)*, *12*(8), 528. DOI: 10.3390/machines12080528

Dionisio, J., Lima, V., Bessa, M., & Vilarinho, H. (2021). The early stages of metaverse development: A review of immersive environments. *Virtual Reality & Intelligent Hardware*, *3*(4), 276–290.

Dos Santos, S. C., Nobre, M. R. B., Varela, S. L. L., Figueroa, F., & Martins, D. E. (2024). Challenges in metaverse adoption on people, process, and technology perspectives: A review from the five past years. In *Proceedings of the 26th International Conference on Enterprise Information Systems* (pp. 485–496). DOI: 10.5220/0012617800003690

Dwivedi, Y. K.. (2023). Metaverse Marketing: Strategies, Platforms, and Consumer Engagement. *Journal of Interactive Marketing*, *62*, 48–63.

Fang, Y., Chen, S., Huang, C., & Tseng, T. (2022). Creating entrepreneurial value in the metaverse: Emergence of novel business models. *The Journal of Entrepreneurship*, *31*(3), 387–411.

González, A., Santos, R., Barreto, L., & Guerra, F. (2022). Cross-sector collaborations in metaverse-based ventures: A systematic literature review. *European Management Journal*, *40*(5), 821–833.

Ha, G., Park, J., Jung, J., & Yoo, S. (2022). Rethinking governance in the metaverse: Opportunities, risks, and policy recommendations. *Government Studies Review*, *16*(2), 145–158.

Han, T., Jiang, S., Wang, Q., & Feng, J. (2021). Architectural breakthroughs in virtual realism: A survey of immersive design and simulation. *IEEE Transactions on Visualization and Computer Graphics*, *27*(11), 4209–4220.

Harris, S., Daigle, M., Gleason, S., & Young, R. (2021). Virtual immersion, real impact: Corporate transformations in a post-pandemic metaverse. *Global Business and Organizational Excellence*, *40*(4), 31–44.

Harris, W., Katz, R., Shneiderman, A., & Thompson, E. (2023). Ethical frontiers in immersive environments: Reevaluating the role of corporate responsibility. *Journal of Virtual Societies*, *12*(1), 56–70.

He, Z., Sang, W., Zhou, X., & Wang, J. (2020). Interactive realms: Charting the development of metaverse platforms. *IEEE Internet Computing*, *24*(6), 34–42.

Hess, T., Matt, C., Benlian, A., & Wiesböck, F. (2016). Options for formulating a digital transformation strategy. *MIS Quarterly Executive*, *15*(2), 103–119.

Huang, Z., Li, T., Liu, Y., & Xu, F. (2022). Immersive learning in the metaverse: Pedagogical strategies and technological enablers. *Computers & Education*, *180*, 104428.

Kang, H., Yoon, Y., Bae, J., & Min, K. (2022). Governing virtual worlds: Policies, regulations, and codes of conduct in the metaverse era. *The Information Society*, *38*(1), 32–44.

Kattakinda, J. P., Dhananjaya, S., Mojžiš, S., Nadif, A., Hanna, M., Apsan, R., & Malavolta, I. (2024). Towards understanding the energy consumption of virtual reality applications in gaming, education, and entertainment. In *Proceedings of the 8th International Workshop on Games and Software Engineering* (pp. 50–57). Association for Computing Machinery. DOI: 10.1145/3643658.3643922

Koivumäki, T., Koivumäki, J., Hänninen, M., & Kuusijärvi, J. (2022). Legitimacy and control: Metaverse governance challenges for transnational enterprises. *International Journal of Technology Policy and Law*, *10*(2), 176–192.

Kumar, A., Shankar, A., Behl, A., Pereira, V., Kapoor, P., & Papa, A. (2025). Implementing enterprise metaverse as a means of enhancing growth hacking performance: Will adopting the metaverse be a success in organizations. *Journal of Business Research*, *188*, 115079. DOI: 10.1016/j.jbusres.2024.115079

Laspro, M., Groysman, L., Verzella, A. N., Kimberly, L. L., & Flores, R. L. (2023). The use of virtual reality in surgical training: Implications for education, patient safety, and global health equity. *Surgeries*, *4*(4), 635–646. DOI: 10.3390/surgeries4040061

Li, X., Liang, Y., Chen, J., & Zhang, P. (2023). Learning from the metaverse: Organizational routines and adaptation in digital ecosystems. *Journal of Organizational Change Management*, *36*(3), 537–558.

Lin, C., Ku, S., Huang, W., & Ho, L. (2023). Mixed-methods analysis of user engagement in immersive virtual environments. *Computers in Human Behavior*, *142*, 107814.

Lo, J., Liu, F., Liao, T., & Tseng, M. (2021). Dynamic capabilities for metaverse-based strategies: Building resilience and competitive advantage. *Journal of Strategy and Management*, *29*(1), 115–129.

López, R., García, M., Acosta, J., & Delgado, L. (2020). The metaverse as a space for interaction for innovation and value generation. *Ibero-American Journal of Entrepreneurship*, *12*(4), 215–227.

Lucas, H. C.Jr, & Goh, J. M. (2009). Disruptive technology: How Kodak missed the digital photography revolution. *The Journal of Strategic Information Systems*, *18*(1), 46–55. DOI: 10.1016/j.jsis.2009.01.002

Martínez, L., Cruz, V., Rodríguez, T., & Paredes, P. (2022). Innovation and immersive marketing: New business models in the metaverse. *Latin American Journal of Digital Strategies*, *8*(2), 76–90.

Mikołajewski, D., Piszcz, A., Rojek, I., & Galas, K. (2024). Machine learning supporting virtual reality and brain–computer interface to assess work–life balance conditions for employees. *Electronics (Basel)*, *13*(22), 4489. DOI: 10.3390/electronics13224489

Mohamed, A., Abdalla, G., Yusuf, H., & Rehman, M. (2022). Virtual marketing experiences: Strategies for consumer immersion in 3D digital worlds. *Journal of Marketing Trends*, *15*(2), 47–61.

Mohamed, A., Abdalla, S., Yusuf, A., & Rehman, M. (2022). Community building in metaverse branding: Insights from digital marketing research. *Journal of Digital Marketing Insights*, *5*(3), 201–215.

Noroozinejad Farsangi, E., Shehata, A. O., Rashidi, M., Ghassempour, N., & Mirjalili, S. (2024). Transitioning from BIM to Digital Twin to Metaverse. *Frontiers in Built Environment, 10*, 1486423. Advance online publication. DOI: 10.3389/fbuil.2024.1486423

Novikov, K., Hořejší, P., Kubr, J., Dvořák, M., Bednář, M., Krákora, D., Krňoul, M., & Šimon, M. (2024). Methodology for rationalization of pre-production processes using virtual reality based manufacturing instructions. *Machines (Basel), 12*(1), 2. DOI: 10.3390/machines12010002

Odeleye, B., Loukas, G., Heartfield, R., Sakellari, G., Panaousis, E., & Spyridonis, F. (2022). Virtually secure: A taxonomic assessment of cybersecurity challenges in virtual reality environments. *Computers & Security, 124*, 102951. DOI: 10.1016/j.cose.2022.102951

Ooms, W., Vanhaverbeke, W., Fini, R., & Golovic, E. (2023). Networks of innovation: Interorganizational collaboration in metaverse entrepreneurship. *Research Policy, 52*(5), 104662.

Palley, B., Poças Martins, J., Bernardo, H., & Rossetti, R. (2025). Integrating machine learning and digital twins for enhanced smart building operation and energy management: A systematic review. *Urban Science (Basel, Switzerland), 9*(6), 202. DOI: 10.3390/urbansci9060202

Peña, L., Benítez, H., Solórzano, R., & Montalvo, D. (2022). The influence of social capital on metaverse community development: Evidence from emerging platforms. *Journal of Interactive Learning Environments, 30*(4), 574–591.

Porter, M. (1980). *Competitive strategy: Techniques for analyzing industries and competitors*. Free Press.

Qiao, F., Cheng, X., & Zhao, M. (2022). Building brand presence in the metaverse: A case study of Decentraland. *Journal of Virtual Studies, 10*(1), 45–61.

Rahman, M., Bhuiyan, A., Uddin, M., & Islam, S. (2022). Financial security and consumer protection in blockchain-based metaverse economies. *International Journal of Economic Policy in Emerging Economies, 15*(2), 191–212.

Raman, R., Kautish, P., Siddiqui, A., Siddiqui, M., & Nedungadi, P. (2025). The role of metaverse technologies in energy systems towards sustainable development goals. *Energy Reports*, *11*, 4459–4476. DOI: 10.1016/j.egyr.2025.04.012

Ramírez, A., Mena, F., Torrealba, R., & Guzmán, K. (2023). Value co-creation in metaverse marketplaces: A platform ecosystem approach. *International Journal of Market Research*, *65*(1), 47–64.

Renaud, K., van Biljon, J., Hearn, G., & Mathews, R. (2021). Early virtual worlds and the metaverse: An historical overview. *Virtual Reality Journal*, *25*(2), 139–154.

Rolofs, G., Wilking, F., Goetz, S., & Wartzack, S. (2024). Integrating digital twins and cyber physical systems for flexible energy management in manufacturing facilities: A conceptual framework. *Electronics (Basel)*, *13*(24), 4964. DOI: 10.3390/electronics13244964

Ruiz, M., Gil, S., Tabares, A., & Rangel, O. (2023). Managing organizational change for metaverse adoption: A case study of multinational corporations. *Journal of Change Management*, *23*(2), 112–128.

Schumpeter, J. (1934). *The theory of economic development*. Harvard University Press.

Sedlmeir, J., Buhl, H. U., Fridgen, G., & Keller, R. (2021). The energy consumption of blockchain technology: Beyond myth. *Business & Information Systems Engineering*, *63*(2), 99–108.

Sharma, V., Stephens, M., Khurshid, S., & Pereira, V. (2025). Metaverse governance in international business: A systematic literature review from 1990 to 2025. *Review of International Business and Strategy*, *35*(2), 210–235. DOI: 10.1108/RIBS-10-2024-0118

Shelton, T., Dexheimer, V., Gregorich, E., & Carter, C. (2021). Blockchain, NFTs, and the rise of digital assets in virtual economies. *Journal of Digital Asset Management*, *7*(4), 239–254.

Shin, D., Lee, H., Choi, M., & Kim, J. (2022). Protecting the metaverse: An integrative framework for cybersecurity in immersive environments. *Computers & Security*, *123*, 102903.

Shin, M., Park, J., Choi, S., & Sohn, J. (2023). Designing user experience in augmented virtuality: The interplay of presence, flow, and consumer satisfaction. *Journal of Retailing and Consumer Services*, *68*, 103019.

Sim, C., Lee, G., Lee, J., & Oh, S. (2022). Competitive strategies in the metaverse era: Opportunities for differentiated experiences. *Technological Forecasting and Social Change*, *180*, 121697.

Slater, M., Steed, A., McCall, R., & Pistrang, N. (2023). Realness in virtual environments: Investigating presence, embodiment, and immersion. *Computers in Human Behavior*, *139*, 107477.

Song, Y., Fang, J., Zhao, J., & Tang, S. (2023). Corporate communication in virtual realms: Stakeholder engagement through metaverse platforms. *Public Relations Review*, *49*(1), 102243.

Tang, X., Hu, F., Liu, M., & Shi, L. (2022). Driving open innovation in metaverse ecosystems: A framework for collaborative platform design. *Journal of Open Innovation*, *8*(4), 182–199.

Teece, D. J., Pisano, G., & Shuen, A. (1997). Dynamic capabilities and strategic management. *Strategic Management Journal*, *18*(7), 509–533. DOI: 10.1002/(SICI)1097-0266(199708)18:7<509::AID-SMJ882>3.0.CO;2-Z

Toni, E., Toni, E., Fereidooni, M., & Ayatollahi, H. (2024). Acceptance and use of extended reality in surgical training: An umbrella review. *Systematic Reviews*, *13*(1), 299. DOI: 10.1186/s13643-024-02723-w PMID: 39633499

Truong, Q., Linh, H., Vu, T., & Phan, K. (2023). Co-creation in architectural design: Virtual collaboration in metaverse-based projects. *Automation in Construction*, *148*, 104785.

Tsai, C., Chang, C., Chen, T., & Cheung, C. (2023). Gamification and user engagement in immersive environments: A meta-analytic review. *Information & Management*, *60*(4), 103722.

Turner, J., Brown, C., Holmes, P., & Wilson, S. (2023). Pathways to sustainable metaverse: Green computing and responsible innovation. *Environmental Innovation and Societal Transitions*, *46*, 126–139.

Vargo, S. L., & Lusch, R. F. (2004). Evolving to a new dominant logic for marketing. *Journal of Marketing*, *68*(1), 1–17. DOI: 10.1509/jmkg.68.1.1.24036

Wang, Y., Gong, D., Xiao, R., Wu, X., & Zhang, H. (2024). A systematic review on extended reality mediated multi user social engagement. *Systems*, *12*(10), 396. DOI: 10.3390/systems12100396

Windhausen, A., Heller, J., Hilken, T., Mahr, D., Di Palma, R., & Quintens, L. (2024). Exploring the impact of augmented reality smart glasses on worker well-being in warehouse order picking. *Computers in Human Behavior*, *155*, 108153. DOI: 10.1016/j.chb.2024.108153

Xu, B., Lui, C., Li, D., & Li, C. (2023). Exploring the perceived ease of use and perceived value in enterprise metaverse applications. *Information Systems Journal*, *33*(2), 214–233.

Xu, M., Zhu, Y., Chen, R., & Hao, C. (2022). Aesthetic experience and user satisfaction in metaverse spaces: Bridging design, presence, and emotion. *Journal of Computer-Mediated Communication*, *27*(4), 431–448.

Ye, X., Hui, Y., Zhang, J., & Li, W. (2022). Strategies for digital transformation in the age of metaverse: A global enterprise perspective. *Journal of Global Information Technology Management*, *25*(4), 289–306.

Yee, N., Bailenson, J. N., Urbanek, M., & Chang, F. (2022). Avatars and identity exploration in the metaverse: Psychological findings and design implications. *ACM Transactions on Social Computing*, *5*(3), 17–29.

Zhang, S., Lim, W. Y. B., Ng, W. C., Xiong, Z., & Niyato, D. (2022). Towards green metaverse networking technologies, advancements and future directions. arXiv preprint arXiv:2211.03057. https://doi.org//arXiv.2211.03057DOI: 10.48550

Zhu, Y., Cheng, G., Cheng, Y., & Zhang, M. (2022). Virtual brand communities: Corporate engagement strategies in metaverse contexts. *Journal of Brand Management*, *29*(6), 685–704.

KEY TERMS AND DEFINITIONS

Co-Creation of Value: In virtual scenarios, users go from being simple consumers to active participants who contribute with designs and content proposals. This co-creation process generates an ecosystem where communities drive innovation and add value to products and services (Chesbrough, 2003).

Dynamic Capabilities: Refers to the ability of companies to adapt and reconfigure their internal resources in changing environments (Teece, Pisano, & Shuen, 1997). On emerging virtual platforms, such as Decentraland or Roblox, organizations need to quickly redesign their strategies to take advantage of market opportunities and respond to the demands of increasingly interactive users (Han, Jiang, Wang, & Feng, 2021).

Immersive Marketing and Gamification: This concept encompasses marketing strategies based on playful interaction and customer engagement in virtual environments (Dwivedi et al., 2023). The case of Nike on Roblox, for example, illustrates the integration of game dynamics, avatar customization, and sports competitions to strengthen the relationship between brand and user (Mohamed, Abdalla, Yusuf, & Rehman, 2022).

Management of Virtual Communities: Refers to the creation and administration of social networks and interaction within a digital environment. In the metaverse, community management is of central importance, as user trust, loyalty, and commitment have a direct impact on the vitality of the platform and the continuity of business projects (Han et al., 2021).

Metaverse and Decentralized Virtual Environments: This refers to immersive digital spaces where users can interact, trade, and generate content collaboratively. On platforms such as Decentraland, this dynamic is enhanced by blockchain technology, which guarantees decentralization and transparency in transactions (Qiao, Cheng, & Zhao, 2022).

Open Innovation: This approach postulates that organizations can and should be nourished by external ideas, collaborating with different actors to accelerate their capacity for innovation (Chesbrough, 2003). In the metaverse, open innovation becomes relevant when companies use virtual communities to co-create and validate new business models.

Chapter 5
Entrepreneurship Reimagined:
A Review of Avatar Led Branding and Customer Experience in the Metaverse

Sneha Kapoor
https://orcid.org/0009-0005-7051-3359

J.C. Bose University of Science and Technology, YMCA, Faridabad, India

Ashwarya Kapoor
https://orcid.org/0000-0003-3858-3945

School of Commerce, Manav Rachna International Institute of Research and Studies, Faridabad, India

Rajiv Sindwani
https://orcid.org/0000-0001-7457-6457

J.C. Bose University of Science and Technology, YMCA, Faridabad, India

ABSTRACT

As immersive technologies redefine the boundaries of digital interaction, avatars have emerged as powerful agents of entrepreneurship in the

DOI: 10.4018/979-8-3373-2943-7.ch005

metaverse. This chapter presents a comprehensive review of literature on the evolving role of avatars in virtual branding, marketing and customer experience. Drawing upon multidisciplinary perspectives from artificial intelligence, human-computer interaction and extended reality, the study examines how avatars function as entrepreneurial entities shaping digital identity, enabling personalized engagement and driving business innovation. The chapter outlines key theoretical constructs such as the Proteus Effect and parasocial interaction while highlighting ethical dilemmas and technical challenges. It offers a forward-looking research agenda that positions avatars not just as digital tools but as transformative agents in the future of entrepreneurship.

1. INTRODUCTION

The fast-growing development of the Metaverse as a collective, persistent and immersive virtual space has revolutionized possibilities for individuals and entities to interact, communicate and transact. A space that was once dominated by gamers and the tech-savvy, the Metaverse is now touted as the next frontier of digital revolution, promising untold riches for entrepreneurs, as well as new branding and customer engagement platform (Mystakidis, 2022). At the heart of this transformation is the ascendance of avatars, digital doppelgangers of users or AI-powered beings that function not only as signifiers of identity but also as independent or semi-independent actors capable of performing a wide variety of entrepreneurial and marketing functions (Nowak and Rauh, 2005; Ratan et al., 2020). Previously known for their popularly in the video gaming and social space, avatars have bridged their origins in entertainment by taking a lead role in digital commerce and personal virtual representation. In platforms such as Decentraland, Roblox and The Sandbox avatars can now be seen streaming the role of brand ambassadors, content creators, digital entrepreneurs and teachers (Dionisio et al., 2013; Kapoor and Sindwani, 2025a). Digital assets in the form of virtual influencers such as Lil Miquela, Shudu and AI assistants like Meta avatars are increasingly being used for virtual customer service and influencer marketing as brands embrace avatar-as-service technologies that connect these digital assets with users indicating an emerging trend towards avatar-mediated economy and social connectivity (Kapoor et al., 2024a,b; 2025A; Pandey and Kapoor, 2025). Convergence of many technologies has enabled this change. With the infusion of extended reality (XR), artificial intelligence (AI), blockchain and human-computer interaction (HCI) technologies, avatars are increasingly able to function in photorealistic, experience-rich environments and are responsive to the intelligence of user interaction (Kaplan and Haenlein, 2019; Kapoor and Sindwani, 2025b). These digital agents, can today engage in p2p commerce, handle customer service queries, provide an immersive learning experience or even get involved in a brand promotion and behave as though they are budding entrepreneurs.

Despite rising popularity, scholarly attention to avatar-led entrepreneurship is both fragmented and underdeveloped. The majority of the current research has considered avatars in terms of the psychological or communication aspects e.g. personality and self-disclosure (Biocca et al., 2003; Yee and Bailenson, 2007; Nowak and Fox, 2018). While these investigations offer important insights into avatar-mediated behaviour, they rarely delve into how avatars operate as autonomous business actors in emerging digital economies. Similarly, studies on digital entrepreneurship tend to focus on human actors navigating online ecosystems, overlooking the strategic utility of avatars as economic agents in immersive environments.

The commercial application of avatars is, however, well underway in industry practice. Fashion brands such as Gucci, Balenciaga and Nike have launched avatar-led campaigns and products in the Metaverse, signalling a mainstream shift toward virtual commerce and identity-based marketing (Mai, 2023). Startups and solopreneurs are increasingly using avatars to create virtual storefronts, offer AI-driven consulting and host real-time interactive experiences indicating the emergence of avatars as entrepreneurs in virtual marketplaces.

Recognizing this paradigm shift, this chapter aims to provide a comprehensive review of the literature and practice concerning avatars as entrepreneurial agents. It draws upon interdisciplinary perspectives spanning entrepreneurship, marketing, consumer behaviour, XR, AI and HCI to understand how avatars function in digital business ecosystems. The chapter also highlights key challenges and ethical considerations that warrant scholarly attention.

To guide this inquiry, the following research objectives are pursued:

- To examine how avatars function as entrepreneurial agents in the Metaverse, including their roles as brand representatives, service providers and content creators.
- To review the branding and marketing potential of avatar-led ventures, particularly in immersive and extended reality platforms.
- To analyse the influence of avatars on customer experience, identity formation and immersive engagement through the lens of human-computer interaction.

In a world increasingly defined by immersive interfaces and synthetic identities, understanding the strategic, commercial and experiential potential of avatars is not only timely, it is essential for navigating the future of entrepreneurship.

Remaining chapter is organised as follows. Section 2 consists of Theoretical Foundations and Conceptual Background. Section 3 describes avatars in the Metaverse, from the perspective of entrepreneurship and marketing. Section 4 depicts customer experience, identity and immersion. Section 5 presents ethical, technical and regulatory challenges. Section 6 concludes the chapter and finally section 7 talks about limitations and scope for future research.

2. THEORETICAL FOUNDATIONS AND CONCEPTUAL BACKGROUND

2.1 The Avatar as a Digital Self

The evolution of avatars from static, pixelated images to responsive, intelligent entities parallels the development of digital identity itself. Initially used in online games and chatrooms as graphical representations of users, avatars have matured into richly designed digital constructs capable of expressing personality, emotion and agency (Bailenson and Blascovich, 2004). In the modern metaverse, avatars are more than just the medium through which we communicate, they also represent aspects of the self that it mirrors, amplifies or even transforms within that virtual space. Yee and Bailenson (2007) have termed this behaviour the Proteus effect and it offers valuable insight into this behaviour. This theory holds that the visual elements of an avatar (tall, attractive, well-dressed) can affect how a user behaves in virtual worlds. For instance, taller participants with taller avatars may behave in a bolder way in the bargaining game, and participants with more attractive avatars may be more sociable. That the behaviour extends beyond the virtual into the physical demonstrates well that at least one's experience is affected by digital representations of the self.

These results have important implications for marketing and entrepreneurship. In brand from knowledge or trust-related avatars could have an effect of consumer perceptions and can via this way be a strong tool for brand advocacy and business communication. When avatars are in the equation For Business Owners that are in immersive environments what and who they decide that their Avatar may look like, act like, can all effect client relationships, decision making with a collective of staff and target market. The avatar is morphed into a key strategic resource acting as a virtual representation of the enterprise and a symbolical projection of entrepreneurial vision and values. Also, avatars in the metaverse are no longer wholly at human mercy. Thanks to AI advancements, they can make decisions, learn and evolve independently over time. This change adds an extra level of complication to consideration of the avatar as a digital self - a self that is not simply a user's manifest tool but a structure or interactive personality in its own right.

2.2 Entrepreneurship in Immersive and Virtual Spaces

Conventional definition of entrepreneurship: In such a definition, human agency, risk-taking and value creation are stressed. But in immersive digital space, these concepts are being redefined. Digital entrepreneurship is defined by Nambisan (2017) as the use of digital technologies to transform ideas into innovative ventures or scaling of businesses. These sort of dealings in the metaverse could happen in a virtual world, entirely through digital goods, services and experiences. Entrepreneurs might even not only mean people behind screens but also avatars of the human entrepreneur, who they represent and in which way they even substitute the human entrepreneur. Artificial intelligence 'avatars' that can hold equivalent of 1.2 million simultaneous, branching conversations are able to sell products and trade with customers Avatars, steered by artificial intelligence are already easy to talk with, engage potential clients, haggle and create content. These avatar entrepreneurs can throw virtual events, operate virtual storefronts and even use insights from user data and behavioural tracking to make tactical decisions. Thus, the new concept of "non-human entrepreneurship", where avatars (autonomously or semi-autonomously) create value, has been introduced in the metaverse (Kaplan and Haenlein, 2009).

This evolution is in contradiction with existing theories of entrepreneurship. Effectuation theory in particular, built around logic of control and means over ends, will need to be revisited in a world of autonomous digital actors for example. Can avatars "take advantage of available resources"? If supplied with access to data and algorithms, they may even engage in what could be considered 'computational effectuation'. Similarly, opportunity recognition theory assumes human cognition and creativity in identifying market gaps. But in the metaverse, avatars with embedded AI can continuously scan digital ecosystems, identify trends and react faster than human entrepreneurs.

This raises critical questions around agency and accountability. Who is the entrepreneur when an avatar launches a business? Is it the creator, the user or the underlying AI system? Legal and ethical ambiguities abound, particularly when avatars transact or sign contracts on behalf of organizations. Entrepreneurial identity, once grounded in human ownership and leadership, is now diffuse and digitally mediated.

2.3 Avatars in Marketing and Branding

Marketing and branding are among the domains most significantly transformed by avatars. The emergence of virtual influencers: AI-driven or human-controlled digital characters designed to engage audiences has redefined how brands connect with consumers. These avatars are widely used on platforms like Instagram, TikTok and within immersive spaces like Decentraland and Roblox (Audrezet and Koles, 2023).

Virtual influencers such as Lil Miquela, Shudu, and Imma have millions of followers and endorse global brands. Unlike traditional influencers, avatars are immune to scandals, fatigue or logistical limitations. They are entirely programmable allowing brands complete control over messaging, aesthetics and interactions (Djafarova and Rushworth, 2017). Research indicates that users can develop parasocial relationships with these virtual characters, perceiving them as trustworthy and relatable (Zhang et al., 2025; Kapoor et al., 2025b).

These relationships improve marketing effectiveness as they result in emotional connections that lead to brand loyalty and purchase intention (Kapoor et al., 2021; 2022). In a metaverse where interaction is frequently immersive and synchronous, avatars can serve as in-world brand ambassadors who can provide personalized advice, show products in 3D and actively invite users to join gamified experiences. This is embodiment marketing where the avatar doesn't just embody the brand, it becomes the brand. And then there's micro-targeting and cultural customising on the back of avatars. Brands can use avatars to appeal to certain demographics, adjusting language, appearance and behaviour for local sensibilities. This degree of customization is especially crucial in cross-cultural markets around the world. From a startup standpoint, avatars make the barrier to entry for digital branding cheaper. Startups can start avatar-led campaigns without the headache and bureaucracy required to hire human influencers. The scalability, availability and integration possibilities of avatars make them a perfect fit for experimental, fast-moving marketing strategies.

2.4 Human-Computer Interaction and Immersive Experience

Human-Computer Interaction (HCI) plays a key role in the design and implementation of avatars in virtual environments. At a fundamental level, HCI is all about understanding how human interface digital interfaces and systems (Kapoor et al., 2023; 2024c). In immersive environments, avatars are the primary interfaces by which users and digital space come into contact and are therefore influential in navigation and perception (Norman,

2013). Study in HCI shows that the design of an interface plays a critical role in affecting people's behaviour and preferences. In the XR world, avatars are tool and companion leading, instructing and even emotionally connecting to the user. They work as long as they are attractive, reactive and interactive. Research has shown that users find feelings of presence and satisfaction when an avatar simulates human behaviours, including eye contact, facial expression and voice modulation (Biocca et al., 2003).

Avatars also contribute to presence, the sense of "being there" in a virtual space. Applications such as education, healthcare, retail and training can all benefit from being emotionally and cognitively immersed. Examples of potential applications include, in business simulations making avatars to serve as virtual mentors or peers offering experiential learning through direct interaction and feedback. Moreover, avatars make things more accessible and inclusive. For individuals with invisible or visible disabilities, avatars provide mobility and social interaction not feasible in the real world. They also provide an opportunity to try on new roles and slough old ones. The HCI viewpoint emphasizes that the avatar serves two masters: as an interface and as a persona. It requires thoughtful consideration of design, usability and ethical issues in order to make avatars a positive rather than negative experience for users.

2.5 Ethical Considerations and Identity Politics

Using avatars for business and social purposes raises several difficult ethical and socio-political questions. Avatars as digital representations contain representations of race, gender, age and culture. Such policed representations are even designed by individuals who may inadvertently encode racism in the form of an avatar (Nakamura, 2009). This has generated anxieties about digital blackface, gender stereotyping and cultural appropriation. For example, companies could use ethnically ambiguous avatars to target a diverse audience and avoid hiring diverse teams, effectively package identities without consequences. These sorts of actions can have the effect of promoting ugly stereotypes and normalizing discrimination in cyberspace.

Complicating matters are questions around consent, as well as authorship. Personas created with generative AI: who owns them? If a person is interacting with an avatar, are they even entitled to know who is behind it - an AI, a person or a corporate entity? This obscureness of avatar as to his/her identity relativizes the distinctions between authenticity and manipulation.

There are also concerns over data privacy and surveillance. In addition, avatars, especially those which are AI driven and so forth, also can capture behavioural data during the interaction. This information can facilitate personalised experiences but also gives rise to concerns about user profiling, emotional manipulation and data monetisation. Lastly, avatar identity also has to be considered with an intersectionality and global equity perspective. Beings – anything with form that you encounter on VR – that are made in your own image, western perfectness or cultural values can also alienate users from other backgrounds. Respecting and representing diversity means that, in terms of the design of our tools, we need to be inclusive and to work in ways that are sensitive to particular cultural contexts.

In summary, with avatars becoming a centrepiece of marketing, entrepreneurship and customer engagement in the metaverse, ethical design and governance will be a necessity. Given that there are no intentional frameworks in place, the potential for digital spaces to perpetuate the offline inequalities is high.

3. AVATARS IN THE METAVERSE: ENTREPRENEURIAL AND MARKETING PERSPECTIVES

3.1 Avatars as Entrepreneurial Agents

Avatars are now being born as more than mere graphic representations of a doppelgänger self, but are highly entrepreneurial actors, nesting in and transforming the economies that arise in and around digital worlds. These avatars, human operated or AI-controlled, act as creators, curators and stimulators on decentralized digital ecosystems. The identity of business virtual avatars is anchored in their capability to perform in the business environment, to handle virtual goods, to interface with digital customer and to carry out marketing, learning and amusement functions. Decentraland,

Roblox and The Sandbox are turning into entrepreneurial sandboxes as well, as avatars can buy digital land, host immersive events, open virtual storefronts or sell unique digital items such as NFTs, wearables or skins (Riva and Wiederhold, 2022). This is an ecosystem that breeds a new breed of entrepreneurial dynamic that has upended distinctions between user and business, creator and consumer. These are practices that stretch the experience of entrepreneurship beyond its conventional limits and that are reconfiguring the normative assumptions of identity, labour and value in digital commerce.

One illustrative case is CodeMiko, a digital avatar developed using Unreal Engine and operated by a human streamer known as "The Technician." CodeMiko's interactions with followers on Twitch combine elements of humour, meta-commentary and gamified engagement. Despite being a fictional character, she has attracted significant sponsorships and millions of viewers, effectively transforming into a monetizable entertainment brand (Marwick, 2013).

In this entrepreneurial model, avatars function in four primary roles:

- **Creators**: Avatars develop and sell in-world content including artwork, architectural structures, clothing and digital tokens. In metaverses where user-generated content drives economic growth, avatar-entrepreneurs are central actors.
- **Traders**: Avatars conduct virtual business, purchasing, selling and investing in digital real estate, NFTs and in-game currencies. They also dabble in arbitrage between virtual economies.
- **Performers**: Many avatars are entertainers, hosting concerts (such as Travis Scott's Fortnite show), livestreams or interactive shows that make money off ticketing, advertising and donations.
- **Educators and Coaches**: Avatars now lead workshops, training simulations and academic sessions, offering immersive experiential learning and coaching in XR environments.

Because viability avatars don't require physical presence in a market, they enable a company's e-commerce agility and help grow the firm. These agents are not susceptible to human vulnerabilities, such as exhaustion or limited mobility due to geographical and linguistic constraints; therefore, they are able to operate more efficiently and expand internationally. We are seeing a greater use of avatars in DAOs, which are decentralized autonomous organizations that give avatars the power to vote and execute smart contracts. This raises compelling considerations for copyrights, authorship, and the moral responsibility of avatars. Do avatars act autonomously or do they always execute the will of their makers? Would AI avatars be able to own intellectual property? These questions require more scholarly research as well as ethical and legal "unpacking."

3.2 Branding Through Avatars

With the convergence of brand strategy and avatar design, digital marketing has reached a pivotal turning point. Gone are the days when companies could solely rely on logos, taglines or celebrity endorsements to connect with consumers. To show their brand identities on active and engaging channels, businesses are using dynamic anthropomorphic avatars. An avatar serves as the visual, behavioural and emotional representation of a brand's persona, marking a new era of embodied branding. Unlike conventional branding elements, avatars provide a multisensory emotional interactivity that goes beyond traditional marketing. They enact messages rather than simply communicate them. Through the ability to respond, smile, narrate, ask questions and change, avatars are capable of creating an emotional landscape which is impossible using traditional media. Due to avatars' immersive qualities, consumers feel "in relationship" with the brand, evoking what scholars term a relational sense of presence. This describes a cognitive-emotional state in which the user feels heard, understood, and seen. Gucci illustrates this shift by collaborating with virtual influencer Lil Miquela to unveil collections through stylized, narrative-driven content tailored to digital-first audiences. Similarly, Samsung's "SAM" the avatar designed to serve as the face of the brand's youthful and technology-oriented identity offered human-like conversations as well as tutorials and customer service for products. These digital assistants never got tired felicitously repeating their tasks or offered varying quality work. They are much more than eye-catching animations, gadgets SAM provides as interactions reflects the Samsung's voice, values and market position which TEC enhances. "Parasocial interaction" appears to be the main reason why avatar branding works. Parasocial interaction refers to the phenomenon of developing a one-sided emotional bond with an individual/figure in the media world. Users in the context of avatar-led branding suffer from feeling entertained and emotionally connected means they become attached to brand avatars. These connections, although one-sided are powerful due to impact brand trust, loyalty and affection which in turn are crucial in a digital environment where physical interactions are few and far between.

Avatars offer several strategic advantages that enhance their utility in branding:

- **Hyper-Personalization:** AI allows avatars to change their language, demeanour and even appearance based on user data. For example, avatars have the ability to recall prior conversations, greet repeat users, and even modify how they speak to suit the user's emotions. Brand loyalty and the user's sense of engagement are reinforced by such personalization.
- **Cultural Adaptability:** Avatars are customizable to fit different cultures. They can change their facial features, attire, gestures, and even speech to match local language and aesthetics. This allows global brands to maintain their fundamental identity while still being culturally relevant and sensitive.
- **Resilience and Consistency:** Human influencers are impactful; however, they can impose personal bias, scandals, and contradictory communication. Embodied by avatars, brands have a regulated vessel to communicate through. They do not age, become ill, or engage in forbidden behaviours. Interactions, expressions, and scripts can be curated for optimal consistent performance around the brand.
- **Channel Continuity:** Obeying the limits of a company's online presence does not pose a challenge to avatars. From mobile applications and chatbots to virtual reality shops, avatars ensure uniform brand experience. Conceivably, multiple digital touchpoints through different platforms would yield consistent branding, and these would combine seamlessly.

Gen Z and Gen Alpha audiences who grow up in such an era of gamification, social media convergence and immersive digital experiences are those with their main characteristics being that they were born in such times and thus the advantages are particularly suitable to them. Hadi et al. (2024) note that the cohorts value creative expression, face-to-face communication, and the understanding of their identity very highly. Avatars are jokingly yet deeply understandable and playful user interfaces that fit perfectly with their digital tastes. Brand avatars become cultural icons and marketing instruments through voluntary participation in design, interactive storytelling, and meme culture.

In addition, avatars also facilitate the co-creation of brand narratives. With the help of avatars, it is possible for the users to penetrate the story characters and direct their actions in a game, social media, or branded environment. This participatory branding becomes the source of increased emotional investment. Fashion brands, as a case in point, help their customers co-design the avatar's wardrobes while playing avatar-led games practically exploring products as part of their story quests. From a branding perspective, avatars clearly fulfill the role of both the agents and the signifiers. As signifiers, they exist as a visual portrayal of the brand's commitment to core virtues, its vision, style, and tone. As the brand ambassadors, they play the role of communication, persuasion, storytelling, and problem-solving facilitators. Particularly in settings where interaction is crucial and attention is limited; this dual function is exceptionally potent. Also, avatars bring a new dimension to the time factor in branding.

Traditional campaigns have been known as short-lived such as announcements, seasonal launches or promotions. Nevertheless, by utilizing the daily connection and being immediately reactive while also being adaptable to the trends, an instance of this is avatars, they can keep the brand alive continuously. Due to the nature of the relation and the positive feelings that the consumers get, they see the brand not as a dull logo but as a dynamic entity. Businesses, in turn, have to treat the avatars as brand assets and these are the ones that strategic management has to undertake for ensuring the function of the brand.

- **Establishing the Avatar's Character:** Is it professional or casual? Serious or witty? A specialist, a friend or a guide? The individuality of the avatar must be supported by the brand and the target audience.
- **Creation of the Scripts and Dialogue:** Discussions have to be meaningful and also must be aligned with the brand language. The script has to imagine the user's questions and include the persuasive cues that are in line with the marketing goals.
- **Visual and Behavioural Consistency:** At the very least, these additions to the original speech should be kept within the rhythm and nature of the speech, so the personality of the avatar and the characters that he incarnates are not lost.
- **Measuring the Impact of the Activities:** One way is to track the bot's presence, much like ad campaigns. Utilization of secrets and cues

In the coming years, brand representations headed by avatars are likely to evolve into more flexible brand characters or avatars that not only adjust to user preferences but also learn from social feedback and AI experiments. They might even switch between different roles (educator, entertainer, or advocate) based on the situation, thus enhancing the range of brand interaction.

To sum up, avatars are now the voice, face and essence of contemporary digital branding. They give brands a living, learning and performative presence in the metaverse, convert passive consumption into active participation, and create emotional connections in artificial environments. As companies expand their use of immersive platforms, the avatar will become a strategic necessity rather than an optional novelty.

3.3 Monetization and Value Creation

From ornamental digital creations to independent economic agents, avatars are now able to create, distribute and extract value within immersive environments. Avatars are now the centre of monetization strategies in the metaverse, enabling people, brands and platforms to rethink distribution methods, business models and paradigms for customer engagement. They are no longer merely ancillary to commerce. Their ability to interact with audiences, provide tailored content, represent brands consistently and function across platforms and time zones is what gives them their economic significance. By doing this, they represent an entrepreneurial logic that commodifies identity, interaction and content as experiences. Avatars are now business models in and of themselves rather than merely instruments of trade.

Revenue streams emerging from avatar-led ecosystems are multifaceted and continue to evolve:

- **Sponsorships and Advertisements**: As avatars gain influence and follower bases, brands approach them for sponsored content, product placements and campaign endorsements. Unlike human influencers, avatars can be scripted to deliver exact messaging and timing, reducing reputational risk. Brands may co-create storylines, integrate logos into avatar clothing or embed product experiences into interactive formats.
- **NFT Sales**: Avatars frequently participate in the creation, curation and sale of non-fungible tokens (NFTs). These NFTs may include virtual fashion items (wearables), artwork, avatar skins, music or digital real estate. Since avatars themselves can be branded and stylized, NFT-based personalization of avatars opens up entire micro-economies of collectibles, limited-edition items and status symbols within virtual worlds.
- **Virtual Appearances**: Just as human celebrities are paid for attending events or hosting shows, popular avatars now command appearance fees for virtual concerts, fashion shows, or brand activations. For example, concerts by avatars in platforms like Fortnite and Decentraland have drawn millions of participants and created new models for digital ticketing and sponsorship.
- **Tipping and Paid Interactions**: Interactive platforms such as Twitch, TikTok Live and VR Chat allow users to tip avatars or pay for shout-outs, personalized advice and exclusive content. These microtransactions can accumulate into significant income, particularly when avatars maintain high engagement levels and emotionally resonant personalities.

- **Merchandising**: In a cross-realm approach, avatars often lend their likeness to physical merchandise including clothing, posters, collectibles or even makeup lines. Some avatars have collaborated with global fashion houses to release co-branded physical and digital items, further blurring the boundaries between virtual and tangible markets.

Lil Miquela, a virtual influencer with numerous Instagram and TikTok followers, is one of the most popular examples in this category. Lil Miquela, the transmedia studio Brud creation, has participated in a few events with Prada, Diesel and Calvin Klein, released some original songs, and built a public image that is very much like typical celebrities. However, a computer-generated character though her income is still derived from social engagement metrics, streaming revenue, media licensing and brand endorsements. Such a model introduces the notion of algorithmic influence which posits that data analytics, content optimization and real-time performance testing are the main factors of avatar monetization. Avatars can do in multitude of ways test voice scripts, outfit selections, story arcs and user interactions so they can find out what boost engagement, virality and conversions something that static campaigns cannot do. These insights are then looped back into the avatar's behaviour and branding allowing for continuous refinement and audience targeting.

In fact, their adventurous and barely risky nature, from an economic standpoint, makes them a much more efficacious vehicle for the realization of scalability and risk-reduction as compared to conventional influencer models. They are not vulnerable to PR scandals unless they plan it on purpose, they do not require salaries, and they are not getting sick. They are perfect for both hyper-local campaigns and global brand penetration because of their "always-on" availability which allows them to communicate with users in a variety of time zones, languages and formats. The creator economy is also propelled by avatars. Nowadays, individuals and small teams can create, program and market avatars without spending a lot of money thanks to easily accessible tools like Unity, Unreal Engine, Ready Player Me, Zepeto and other AI-based generation platforms. As a result, the entry barrier for digital entrepreneurship has significantly decreased. Without depending on conventional employment or capital-intensive structures, a single creator can now monetize their creativity by starting a virtual boutique, providing avatar-led consulting sessions or hosting an event in the metaverse. Avatars are also facilitating peer-to-peer trade. Avatars are used by independent creators as virtual hosts for pop-up shows; NFT launches and virtual product demos. Avatars can be the agents to trade not only virtual land but also, they may be the local guides and the creative forces for the decentralized virtual worlds that are compatible with Decentraland or The Sandbox. Every single act of exchange thus makes a chain of economic activity for experiences and services. The role of the creator is reinterpreted by such entrepreneurial endeavours as an immersive service provider rather than a content producer. This shift also invites new branding franchising and licensing business models. The avatars' identities go on to become independent intellectual properties as their popularity increases. Avatars can be given by companies as a license to be used in the creation of product lines, social media posts, and advertising campaigns.

The rise of Avatar-as-a-service (AaaS) that enables brands to hire customizable avatars for the short-term using these ones with set voices, emotional scripts, and performance parameters has led to such success. On the other hand, avatars also facilitate subscription-based business models. Users can pay a fee to gain entry to advanced modules, have individualized interactions or be part of exclusive events that can be found in the premium tiers offered by fitness coaches, meditation guides, or educational avatars. By having regular interactions being led by avatars, these recurring revenue models keep the users loyal while the creators and brands get stability as well as steady income. The advent of avatar monetization means the entry of network effects. The more a user utilizes, the more the application receives data that helps improve commitment, performance, and ultimately revenue. Popular avatars make it easy for the platforms to get not only users but also creators and advertisers. Consequently, monetization becomes an intricate value chain consisting of platforms (as infrastructure providers), brands (as sponsors), creators (as entrepreneurs) and users (as consumers and co-creators). However, the rapid commercialization also evokes a set of governance and ethical issues. The issues of avatar identities' opacity and whether users know that they are conversing with the AI are among the problems. The question arises, is it ethical to require avatars to disclose their sponsors? Also, the question is how the platforms are going to react to situations when avatar behaviour is manipulative or emotional exploitation occurs? Unless consumer protection frameworks change as avatars continue to gain more and more resemblances with real influencers, there will be no guarantee of transparency, accountability and equity.

To summarise, the immersive sector has changed avatars into income sources. They enable highly engaging, low-cost, and high-frequency interactions that can also be scaled up and customized. They are the focal point of metaverse economics because of their entrepreneurial fluidity, which goes from experience delivery, digital commerce, brand representation to content creation. Avatars not only offer a new economic framework where identity is a resource and interactions are goods but also a new advertising channel for brands, creators and users.

3.4 Role of AI in Empowering Entrepreneurial Avatars

It is the very basic structure of the humanlike characters that has from the inception been the reliance on technology allowing the the characters to be scripted digitally and to become contextually aware, entrepreneurial and informed agents that is represented by the technology of artificial intelligence (AI). AI equips avatars with the abilities of vision, comprehension, adjustment and action in the simulated environments, thus creating independent actors who have the capacity to generate value, represent brands and attend users' needs on a large scale. The process of the avatars' conversion from simply passive, pre-programmed characters into intelligent, responsive and proactive beings is facilitated by the combination of natural language processing (NLP), computer vision, sentiment analysis and machine learning (ML). AI-driven avatars have no need for continuous human control anymore. They have the capacity to perform entrepreneurial functions such as content generation, brand communication, service provision and product recommendation on their own. In the very course of their interaction with users and systems, these avatars carry on as independent micro-enterprises, which personify reason, purpose and agency. The gradual process of their gaining intelligence through contextual analysis, behaviour feedback and reinforcement learning. Core competences of AI-powered avatars are:

- **Natural Language Interaction:** Profiting from NLP, avatars are capable of having natural, step-by-step conversations with users, being aware of the emotional state of the users and changing their answers according to the voice, the mood and the goal of the users. Thus, a more humanized user experience is achieved, which makes it easier for people to communicate with the technology and, at the same time, more emotionally involved.
- **Intelligent Customer Service:** AI avatars can manage huge volumes of queries, solve technical issues, recommend personalized solutions and raise issues to human operator if needed. They also can improve their service accuracy and satisfaction by being engaged in the conversations.
- **Autonomous Content Generation:** Avatars powered by generative AI are the agents of a content revolution as they are able to generate digital content independently without human help in the form of blog entries, marketing scripts, images, music, and even NFTs. This allows brands to not only localize messaging more efficiently but also to update campaigns on the fly and keep the online presence consistent.
- **Adaptive Behaviour and Learning:** AI avatars use machine learning to optimize their performance. They get better at long-term engagement and conversion results by changing their strategies, conversation paths, and even visual expressions depending on the data of user reactions, engagement patterns, and sentiment cues that they analyse.

Kuki (formerly Mitsuku), a conversational AI chatbot known throughout the world for its capacity to mimic human-like speech, is a notable illustration of this development. Kuki works by integrating 3D avatars, serving as a prototype for the use of avatars as companions, service agents or brand ambassadors on websites, social media platforms and virtual reality environments. Conversational AI is the foundation of avatar interaction, as evidenced by Kuki's tenacious, emotionally expressive, and constantly updated presence. AI not only improves functionality but also changes the definition of digital entrepreneurship itself. According to Kaplan and Haenlein (2019), highly developed avatars might soon function as independent, self-governing businesses with the ability to manage finances, inventory, track performance and communicate with customers. These AI-driven avatars could, in theory, function as autonomous economic agents, raising critical questions regarding taxation, regulation and legal identity.

This capacity for self-management raises legal and philosophical questions: Are avatars able to sign contracts on behalf of businesses? Should corporate law grant them agent status or limited digital personhood? When an autonomous avatar violates platform guidelines or participates in deceptive advertising, who bears responsibility? The traditional juridical systems are inadequate to handle these novel complications. From a business perspective, AI avatars offer hyper-scalable service models. Unlike human employees, they can offer multilingual support, serve tens of thousands of users at once and never sleep, they note. This enables a global Go-To-Market, reduces costs of operation and improves the customer experience. One such AI avatar can be used by a retail brand to engage with customers in English, Spanish, Mandarin and Arabic markets and adjust for language norms, culture trait and buying behaviours. Equally, AI is critical in ensuring equal opportunities and social inclusion in the digital society. When used as avatars, they can interact with users Within healthcare, education and mental health, these emotion recognition technologies may support avatars to respond empathetically and adapt to emotional states and offer assistance to users feeling stressed or disoriented.

In addition, AI facilitates which allows avatars to tailor every interaction based on a user's preferences, habits and behaviours. In a virtual bookstore, for example, an AI avatar could not just recommend books based on what you've bought in the past but shift its tone, getting more analytical for academic researchers, more enthusiastic for younger readers. It builds long term relationships and brand endurance while encouraging brand loyalty with this kind of accuracy. But the increasing independence of avatars raises significant ethical and governance considerations. There are two big questions of consent and data privacy. AI-driven avatars gather loads of behavioural data and biometric info thereby heightening risk of algorithmic manipulation and shady surveillance practices. Avatars mimicking empathy and trust may reap and exploit user data surreptitiously without users even realizing it. Algorithmic bias poses quite a significant hurdle occasionally in rather complex systems nowadays unfortunately. AI avatars can inherit and perpetuate problematic social biases quite unintentionally or deliberately owing largely to training on flawed historical data. Unless thoroughly vetted avatars used in financial advising display grossly biased behaviour or recruitment tools malfunction spectacularly in certain situations. Creation of open AI governance frameworks necessitates fairly inclusive design guidelines and rigorous algorithmic explainability alongside thorough fairness audits.

Platforms must ensure users remain cognizant of interacting with either a human entity or some mechanized system at all times apparently. Manipulation can arise in severe situations and confusion or misplaced trust can result from failing to clearly make such key distinctions. Regulatory agencies may need to factor in standardized digital disclosure policies for consumer-facing AI avatars with growing ethical concerns somehow. Emotional labour performed by AI avatars sparks increasingly heated discussion nowadays in various obscure quarters. Do avatars perpetrate affective duplicity when artificially imbued with emotions such as sorrow or feigned jubilance? Should brands be allowed making money off simulated empathy especially in contexts like therapy or grief counselling situations somehow? Inquiries touch on limits of emotional authenticity human dignity and affective computing deeply within various technological contexts. A rather ominous wider societal impact emerges rather slowly as AI becomes deeply integrated into avatar functionality replacing human workers eventually. Avatars boost productivity significantly but might also supplant front-line staff in customer service sales and hospitality roles eventually. This change may open up new possibilities in conversational scriptwriting and behaviour design and necessitate a thorough reassessment of workforce planning across various educational systems.

AI serves as source of entrepreneurial agency in avatars rather than merely an enhancer of it somehow. It affords them ample latitude acting and learning dynamically within richly immersive digital ecosystems and bolstering their development quite significantly. Stakeholders must strike quite a delicate balance between creativity and stern accountability ensuring AI systems driving avatar behaviour remain eerily transparent.

4. CUSTOMER EXPERIENCE, IDENTITY AND IMMERSION

4.1 Avatar-Mediated Customer Experiences

Transaction-driven conversations yield to connective, avatar-facilitated experiences in the metaverse, which takes users from perception to cognition and from the senses to the emotions. Avatars enable hyper-personal, brand-interactive experiences that are unconfined by time, place or the traditional limitations of space. This revolutionary shift is overturning traditional customer journey models and requires a fresh view of how brands engage with consumers who purchase virtually. In the metaverse, CX is a multi-dimensional, cooperative creative and real-time process, not like brick/mortal stores and traditional e-commerce at all. Imagine brands using AI-driven or human-guided avatars to provide these individualized, interactive experiences, rather than relying on static product listings or human customer service. These avatars which act as hosts, guides, entertainers and educators turn passive shopping into active story-telling.

Key formats of avatar-mediated CX include:

- **Product demos in 3D**: Avatars can walk customers through virtual replicas of products, offering visual demonstrations of features, functions and comparisons. This is especially useful in complex or high-involvement product categories such as automobiles, fashion and electronics.
- **Interactive storytelling**: Brands can use avatars to tell the history of brands, share product stories or define missions in a gamified or storytelling way, helping to strengthen the values and emotion of brands.
- **Live avatar-led events**: Influencer avatars can hold launch parties, pop-up stores, Q and A s or immersive tutorials, driving real-time engagement, social involvement and a sense of belonging to the digital tribe.

Verhoef et al. (2009) suggested that customer experience encompasses a pre-purchase, purchase and post-purchase process and that this process is highly enriched in immersive environments. In the pre-purchase stage, avatars facilitate need recognition, information providing and persuading. At the purchase stage itself, avatars aid purchase decision and act as transaction facilitators. Once the purchase has been made at this phase avatars can provide onboarding, post-sales support and emotional support, which can generate satisfaction and loyalty. Additionally, more emotionally engaging experiences are made possible via avatar-related interactions, which is a crucial factor for customer retention. Avatars can respond empathetically, with human-like warmth through the imitation of facial expressions, voice tones and gestures, enriching digital service encounters. For instance, a skincare brand in the metaverse can use a virtual beauty consultant avatar to scan users' avatars to determine skin tone and type and push tailored solutions to interested players in a fun and educational manner.

4.2 The Proteus Effect in Customer Engagement

Users can strongly identify themselves with their avatars, and there is a 'Proteus Effect' (Yee and Bailenson 2007) as a result, this indicates the extent to which the appearance and actions of the virtual body in VR can shape that actual body's behaviour. This has important implications for avatar design tactics and consumer interaction. "The research suggests that by changing your avatar, you change the way you perceive yourself; having a taller avatar makes you feel more confident,". It's a psychological phenomenon explained by self-profiling theory. For instance, an attractive young avatar may simply lead to have more social interaction or self-confidence as an avatar that is confident might lead the user to behave more assertively. That begs a very important question for marketers: To improve relatability and trust, should brand avatars assume the identity of the consumer, or that of the brand? The answer lies in the purpose and context of the interaction. To the extent that avatars are created in the image of the user's preferences or physical appearance (or certain inclinations for fashion, hair style, or clothing), they can promote cultural similarities, the safety of knowing that the space I am constructing my self-conception within, is culturally familiar and psychologically safe. Avatars representing aspirational brand characteristics including luxury, inventiveness, and self-assurance, however, may motivate users to perform desired behaviours such as increasing brand affinity. Attractive-looking avatars greatly increase trust, liking for the product and intention to purchase (Nowak and Biocca, 2003). Along the same lines, respondents report higher levels of customer satisfaction and conversion when interacting with avatars which possess friendly facial features, appropriate clothing and somewhat human-sounding as adjust the voice modulations.

In order to strategically utilize the Proteus Effect, brands need to take into account:

- **Visual congruence**: Aligning avatar appearance with brand values (e.g., tech brands using sleek, futuristic avatars).
- **Cultural sensitivity**: Avoiding tokenism or stereotyping in avatar design to ensure inclusivity.
- **Emotional design**: Using facial expressions and gestures to foster emotional connection.

For instance, a financial advisory brand might deploy an avatar that looks experienced, trustworthy and calm projecting authority and reassurance. A Gen Z fashion brand, on the other hand, might use an avatar with playful animations, trendy looks and a relatable tone to stimulate engagement and excitement.

Ultimately, the Proteus Effect underscores the symbolic power of avatars as agents of persuasion and behaviour change in digital spaces.

4.3 Identity, Representation and Social Presence

One of the most transformative aspects of avatars in the metaverse is their capacity to enable users to construct, project and explore idealized or alternative versions of themselves. This capability goes beyond surface-level customization it speaks to deeper issues of identity, self-expression, social inclusion and community building. Biocca (1997) highlights that avatars contribute significantly to the sense of presence the psychological experience of "being there" in a virtual environment. Presence, in turn, is enhanced by a sense of agency (feeling in control) and emotional resonance (feeling connected). When users can tailor avatars to reflect their identities whether aligned with reality or not they are more likely to feel empowered, engaged and emotionally invested in the digital experience. From a brand perspective, enabling avatar customization is a powerful tool for co-creation, allowing users to personalize their journey and increase attachment to the platform or product. Allowing customers to design their avatars fosters user autonomy and authenticity, which is essential for meaningful engagement.

However, identity in the metaverse is also deeply political. As Nakamura (2009) argues, digital identity is shaped by power structures and lack of diversity in avatar options may perpetuate exclusion, reinforce stereotypes and alienate certain user groups. Many virtual worlds still offer limited choices for non-Western skin tones, body types, gender expressions or cultural aesthetics.

To promote inclusive customer experiences, brands must:

- Offer a broad and inclusive range of avatar design options.
- Ensure that virtual environments and interfaces are accessible to users with disabilities.
- Engage with diverse communities in the design process to ensure authentic representation.

For instance, in keeping with its real-world inclusivity narrative, the beauty brand Fenty Skin started a metaverse campaign that included avatars of all body sizes and skin tones. These methods improve customer satisfaction while bolstering brand equity. Avatars also enhance social presence or the sensation of being "with others" in a common area. Co-shopping, virtual gatherings and multiplayer games are examples of collaborative experiences that use avatar-based interactions to mimic or even surpass the social richness of real-world settings. Essentially, avatars serve as social signals that influence how people perceive inclusion, status and community in online marketplaces in addition to being means of personal expression.

4.4 Experiential Learning via Avatars

From education and entrepreneurship to skills development, avatars aren't just for marketing and entertainment. Using simulation, gamification and real-time feedback, avatars in the metaverse can be both teachers and peers in the classroom, promoting experiential learning. Avatars afford the prospect of rich, interactive, customised learning, underpinned by Kolb's (2014) Experiential Learning Theory, that recognises the importance of active engagement, reflection and conceptualisation in learning. In a guided, yet active virtual atmosphere, students interact, perform, and practice rather than consume content passively.

Avatar-led experiential learning frequently takes the following forms:

- **Virtual business pitch rooms**: Users can rehearse and refine their pitching skills before simulated investor panels.
- **Negotiation simulations**: Avatars can act as customers, suppliers or competitors, allowing learners to practice persuasive communication and decision-making.
- **Financial literacy games**: Gamified environments where users manage virtual budgets, investments and market dynamics.
- **Conflict resolution workshops**: Role-play scenarios in which users engage with avatars portraying team members, clients or stakeholders to develop emotional intelligence and diplomacy.

These platforms provide low-risk, high-reward learning opportunities for entrepreneurs. Before entering actual markets, they can test concepts, get input and boost their confidence. Additionally, based on learner performance, avatar-guided simulations can modify the level of difficulty, facilitating adaptive learning and ongoing improvement. Avatars aid in providing standardized yet adaptable experiences from the standpoint of corporate training. Businesses can create immersive, captivating and scalable solutions by using branded avatars to facilitate DEI workshops, product training and onboarding programs. Crucially, avatars encourage empathy and the ability to see things from different angles, particularly when users are permitted to assume roles that differ from their own. A leadership program might, for example, allow a junior employee to make decisions from the perspective of a CEO, improving their comprehension of strategic thinking and accountability.

However, ethical considerations must also be taken into account when using avatars for experiential learning. Careful consideration must be given to the simulations' accuracy, the reliability of the feedback and the possible emotional impact of some role-play scenarios.

5. ETHICAL, TECHNICAL AND REGULATORY CHALLENGES

Avatars present intricate ethical, technological and legal issues as they continue to transform the metaverse's digital marketing and entrepreneurship scene. For avatar-driven ecosystems to be inclusive, sustainable and compliant with the law, these problems must be resolved.

5.1 Ethical Dilemmas in Avatar Entrepreneurship

5.1.1 Authorship and Agency

Avatars are increasingly designed to function autonomously through AI. As they engage in commercial transactions, content creation and service delivery, determining responsibility becomes complex. If an avatar makes a misleading statement or takes an action that causes financial or emotional harm, who is accountable: the human creator, the deploying platform or the AI model? Current frameworks do not adequately address such distributed agency.

5.1.2 Representation and Bias

Most commercially successful avatars mirror dominant aesthetic standards young, slim and Eurocentric. This reinforces exclusionary norms and undermines diversity. Designers and developers must ensure inclusive representation by offering diverse avatar templates across racial, gender and body-type spectrums. Cultural appropriation, tokenism and digital blackface must be actively prevented through ethical design choices and participatory development models (Nakamura, 2009).

5.1.3 Emotional Manipulation

As avatars become emotionally intelligent, they can manipulate user behaviour. For example, they may use emotionally resonant language or facial cues to nudge users toward purchases. This raises concerns about consent, autonomy and the exploitation of psychological vulnerabilities particularly among minors. Ethical frameworks must distinguish between user engagement and manipulative persuasion ensuring transparency in avatar intent and data use.

5.2 Technical Challenges

5.2.1 Interoperability Across Platforms

The metaverse currently comprises fragmented platforms with their own avatar ecosystems (e.g., Roblox, Decentraland, Horizon Worlds). Avatars created in one environment often cannot be ported to another, limiting cross-platform entrepreneurship. Standardized APIs, avatar design protocols and blockchain-based identity systems could help resolve this fragmentation.

5.2.2 Computational Infrastructure

Real-time processing, cloud computing and 3D rendering capabilities are necessary for AI-powered avatars to function well. These requirements may be prohibitively expensive for creators and small enterprises. Furthermore, system overloads and latency problems may degrade avatar interactions which would lower user satisfaction.

5.3 Regulatory Gaps and Legal Ambiguities

5.3.1 Privacy and Surveillance

In order to customize interactions, avatars frequently gather biometrics, emotional information, and user behaviour. This data may be used for third-party monetization, emotional manipulation or profiling if it is not properly regulated. Avatar-specific rules for informed consent, data minimization and user redress mechanisms are lacking in many jurisdictions, despite the fact that legal frameworks such as the GDPR provide some protection.

5.3.2 Contractual and Legal Rights

Transactions can be started or mediated by avatars on behalf of people or companies. They are not, however, legal persons. This begs the following questions: Can a contract be signed by an avatar? If the avatar violates the terms, who is responsible? In order to handle avatar-led behaviour while upholding human accountability, jurisdictions need to investigate legal proxies or agent frameworks.

5.3.3 Intellectual Property and Ownership

Avatars created by AI create issues with authorship. Who is the owner of a generative AI-created digital character? The user? The creator? The training dataset for the AI? To cut down on disputes and encourage innovation, it is essential to clarify IP rights regarding AI-assisted creativity.

6. CONCLUSION

In the metaverse, avatars have evolved from fictional novelties to interactive interfaces, brand ambassadors, educators, and entrepreneurial agents. They make it possible for hyper-personalized, emotionally charged and immersive experiences in entertainment, education and commerce.

With the incorporation of AI, their capabilities are growing, enabling autonomous operation, adaptive behaviour and ongoing engagement. This development calls into question established frameworks for entrepreneurship and marketing. Avatars serve as both interaction agents and media in these new logics of value creation. Customer journeys, brand loyalty and entrepreneurial identity are being redefined by the Proteus Effect, parasocial relationships and avatar-mediated immersion. But the emergence of avatars also raises important legal, technological and ethical issues. There is an urgent need to address issues of authorship, identity politics, manipulation, data surveillance and legal ambiguity. These risks have the potential to exacerbate inequality and erode confidence in avatar-led systems if they are not addressed. Avatars will probably become essential to the digital economy in the future. To fully realize their potential while preserving user rights and inclusivity, technologists, marketers, ethicists and regulators must work together across disciplinary boundaries.

7. LIMITATIONS AND SCOPE FOR FUTURE RESEARCH

There are a number of restrictions on this chapter that limit how broadly and practically its insights can be applied. It is mostly conceptual in nature, lacking empirical backing and relies more on theoretical research and existing literature than on user data or case-based analysis. There is a geographical bias that overlooks the nuances of culture, economy and technology in regions like the Global South because a significant portion of the material cited originates from western settings. Furthermore, because of the metaverse's quick evolution which includes quick changes in platforms, user behaviour and technologies some observations may soon become outdated. These limitations point to several directions for additional research empirical research is essential to validate the chapter's assertions and explore user perceptions, trust dynamics and behaviour in avatar-led branding and entrepreneurship. Cross-cultural research can improve our understanding of global differences in avatar acceptance and interaction. The autonomy and cognitive architecture of AI-powered avatars as well as the ethical implications of doing so, must also be thoroughly examined. Multidisciplinary research on legal frameworks related to liability, data ownership and avatar rights can also be beneficial for policy development. Finally, because metaverse platforms use a lot of resources, it is becoming increasingly important to conduct research on the environmental impacts and sustainable design of avatar ecosystems.

REFERENCES

Audrezet, A., & Koles, B. (2023). Virtual influencer as a brand avatar in interactive marketing. In *The Palgrave handbook of interactive marketing* (pp. 353–376). Springer International Publishing. DOI: 10.1007/978-3-031-14961-0_16

Bailenson, J. N., & Blascovich, J. (2004). Avatars. *Encyclopedia of human-computer interaction, 1*, 64-6.

Biocca, F. (1997). The cyborg's dilemma: Progressive embodiment in virtual environments. *Journal of Computer-Mediated Communication, 3*(2), JCMC324. DOI: 10.1111/j.1083-6101.1997.tb00070.x

Biocca, F., Harms, C., & Burgoon, J. K. (2003). Toward a more robust theory and measure of social presence: Review and suggested criteria. *Presence (Cambridge, Mass.), 12*(5), 456–480. DOI: 10.1162/105474603322761270

Dionisio, J. D. N., Iii, W. G. B., & Gilbert, R. (2013). 3D virtual worlds and the metaverse: Current status and future possibilities. *ACM Computing Surveys, 45*(3), 1–38. DOI: 10.1145/2480741.2480751

Djafarova, E., & Rushworth, C. (2017). Exploring the credibility of online celebrities' Instagram profiles in influencing the purchase decisions of young female users. *Computers in Human Behavior, 68*, 1–7. DOI: 10.1016/j.chb.2016.11.009

Hadi, R., Melumad, S., & Park, E. S. (2024). The Metaverse: A new digital frontier for consumer behaviour. *Journal of Consumer Psychology, 34*(1), 142–166. DOI: 10.1002/jcpy.1356

Kaplan, A. M., & Haenlein, M. (2009). The fairyland of Second Life: Virtual social worlds and how to use them. *Business Horizons, 52*(6), 563–572. DOI: 10.1016/j.bushor.2009.07.002

Kaplan, A. M., & Haenlein, M. (2019). Siri, Siri, in my hand: Who's the fairest in the land? On the interpretations, illustrations, and implications of artificial intelligence. *Business Horizons, 62*(1), 15–25. DOI: 10.1016/j.bushor.2018.08.004

Kapoor, A., & Sindwani, R. (2025a). Artificial Intelligence as a Catalyst for Advancing Contactless Payments. AI Marketing and Ethical Considerations in Consumer Engagement, 321–338.

Kapoor, A., Sindwani, R., & Goel, M. (2021). Prioritising the key factors influencing the adoption of mobile wallets: An Indian perspective in covid-19 era. *Journal of Information Technology Management*, *13*(4), 161–182.

Kapoor, A., Sindwani, R., & Goel, M. (2022). Assessing Mobile Banking Service Quality Dimensions Using Multi-Criteria Decision Making. Future of Work and Business in Covid-19 Era, 131–147.

Kapoor, A., Sindwani, R., & Goel, M. (2023). Exploring quick commerce service experience: A moderated mediated investigation using SEM and fsQCA. Total Quality Management &amp. *Business Excellence*, *34*(13–14), 1896–1919.

Kapoor, A., Sindwani, R., & Goel, M. (2024a). Exploring the symmetric and asymmetric effects of mobile wallet service experience on brand loyalty in India: Evidence from SEM and fsQCA. *Journal of Financial Services Marketing*, *29*(4), 1524–1541. DOI: 10.1057/s41264-024-00280-w

Kapoor, A., Sindwani, R., & Goel, M. (2024b). A novel framework for understanding the interplay between the mobile wallet service quality dimensions and loyalty intention. *The TQM Journal*, *37*(6), 1716–1741. DOI: 10.1108/TQM-12-2023-0422

Kapoor, A., Sindwani, R., & Goel, M. (2024c). Assessing inhibitors to adoption of m-wallet: A BWM approach. *International Journal of Business Excellence*, *32*(4), 433–455.

Kapoor, A., Sindwani, R., & Goel, M. (2025a). Unlocking India's mobile wallet potential: Identifying and prioritising key sustainable growth catalysts using best worst method. *International Journal of Process Management and Benchmarking*, *21*(2), 218–230.

Kapoor, A., & Sindwani, R. (2025b). Navigating Inhibitors to Artificial Intelligence Adoption in Human Resource Management Practices: A Multi-criteria Decision-making Approach.

Kapoor, A., Sindwani, R., & Goel, M. (2025b). Assessing mobile wallet service quality using analytic hierarchy process and fuzzy evaluation method. *International Journal of Services and Operations Management, 50*(2), 246–266. DOI: 10.1504/IJSOM.2025.144481

Kolb, D. A. (2014). *Experiential learning: Experience as the source of learning and development*. FT press.

Mai, Q. H. (2023). Considering different aspects of digital and social media marketing to attract Generation Z and Alpha as the primary customer.

Marwick, A. (2013). *Status Update: Celebrity, Publicity, and Branding in the Social Media Age*. Yale University Press.

Mystakidis, S. (2022). Metaverse. *Encyclopedia, 2*(1), 486–497. DOI: 10.3390/encyclopedia2010031

Nakamura, L. (2009). Don't hate the player, hate the game: The racialization of labor in World of Warcraft. *Critical Studies in Media Communication, 26*(2), 128–144. DOI: 10.1080/15295030902860252

Nambisan, S. (2017). Digital entrepreneurship: Toward a digital technology perspective of entrepreneurship. *Entrepreneurship Theory and Practice, 41*(6), 1029–1055. DOI: 10.1111/etap.12254

Norman, D. (2013). *The design of everyday things: Revised and expanded edition*. Basic books.

Nowak, K. L., & Biocca, F. (2003). The effect of the agency and anthropomorphism on users' sense of telepresence, copresence, and social presence in virtual environments. *Presence (Cambridge, Mass.), 12*(5), 481–494. DOI: 10.1162/105474603322761289

Nowak, K. L., & Fox, J. (2018). Avatars and computer-mediated communication: A review of the definitions, uses, and effects of digital representations. *Review of Communication Research, 6*, 30–53. DOI: 10.12840/issn.2255-4165.2018.06.01.015

Nowak, K. L., & Rauh, C. (2005). The influence of the avatar on online perceptions of anthropomorphism, androgyny, credibility, homophily, and attraction. *Journal of Computer-Mediated Communication, 11*(1), 153–178. DOI: 10.1111/j.1083-6101.2006.tb00308.x

Pandey, P., & Kapoor, A. (2025). Cybercrime in the Digital Era: Impacts, Awareness, and Strategic Solutions for a Secure Future. *Sachetas, 4*(1), 32–37.

Puntoni, S., & Wertenbroch, K. (2024). Being Human in the Age of AI. *Journal of the Association for Consumer Research, 9*(3), 235–240. DOI: 10.1086/730788

Ratan, R., Beyea, D., Li, B. J., & Graciano, L. (2020). Avatar characteristics induce users' behavioural conformity with small-to-medium effect sizes: A meta-analysis of the proteus effect. *Media Psychology, 23*(5), 651–675. DOI: 10.1080/15213269.2019.1623698

Riva, G., & Wiederhold, B. K. (2022). What the metaverse is (really) and why we need to know about it. *Cyberpsychology, Behavior, and Social Networking, 25*(6), 355–359. DOI: 10.1089/cyber.2022.0124 PMID: 35696299

Verhoef, P. C., Lemon, K. N., Parasuraman, A., Roggeveen, A., Tsiros, M., & Schlesinger, L. A. (2009). Customer experience creation: Determinants, dynamics and management strategies. *Journal of Retailing, 85*(1), 31–41. DOI: 10.1016/j.jretai.2008.11.001

Yee, N., & Bailenson, J. (2007). The Proteus effect: The effect of transformed self-representation on behaviour. *Human Communication Research, 33*(3), 271–290. DOI: 10.1111/j.1468-2958.2007.00299.x

Zhang, Y., He, J., & Li, J. (2025). The role of flow experience in virtual influencer marketing: Insights into aesthetic, entertainment and parasocial influences on purchase intention. *Journal of Fashion Marketing and Management*. Advance online publication. DOI: 10.1108/JFMM-05-2024-0201

Chapter 6
Immersive VR–AI Learning for A1 French Listening:
Pedagogical, Policy, and Entrepreneurial Insights From Indonesia and France Cooperation

Ninuk Lustyantie
https://orcid.org/0000-0002-7528-6846
Universitas Negeri Jakarta Indonesia, Indonesia

Tengku Ratna Soraya
Universitas Negeri Medan, Indonesia

Yunilis Andika
Universitas Negeri Jakarta, Indonesia

Iswan Gunadi
Universitas Pertahanan, Indonesia

DOI: 10.4018/979-8-3373-2943-7.ch006

ABSTRACT

Findings indicate that VR-AI integration improved listening comprehension by 25 to 30% and significantly enhanced learner engagement and motivation. Beyond pedagogical benefits, this research demonstrates the entrepreneurial potential of VR–AI learning products as scalable educational technology solutions aligned with SDG 4 (Quality Education) and SDG 9 (Innovation and Infrastructure). The study contributes to language pedagogy, cross-border education policy, and edtech entrepreneurship by proposing a model for sustainable, market-oriented innovation in foreign language teaching.

INTRODUCTION

The acceleration of digital transformation in education has prompted governments, universities, and industries to explore new approaches to foreign language learning. In Indonesia, demand for French language proficiency has risen due to expanding academic, cultural, and economic cooperation with France, yet teaching methods remain largely traditional and insufficiently aligned with the expectations of a digital-native generation. At the A1 CEFR level, listening comprehension is a critical foundational skill, but Indonesian learners frequently struggle with contextual understanding and authentic exposure to spoken French. Globally, research highlights the potential of virtual reality (VR) to immerse learners in authentic cultural environments and of artificial intelligence (AI) to personalize instruction, provide real-time feedback, and track learner progress (Huang et al., 2023; Tai & Chen, 2021). However, in the Indonesian context, these technologies are underutilized and lack structured integration into curriculum and pedagogy. Moreover, existing studies rarely examine the intersection of educational innovation, policy collaboration, and entrepreneurial commercialization, particularly within bilateral frameworks such as Indonesia and France cooperation.

From a policy perspective, Indonesia's commitment to Kurikulum Merdeka and SDGs 4 (Quality Education) and 9 (Innovation and Infrastructure) aligns with France's long-standing support for international language education through the AEFE and OIF. This creates fertile ground for bilateral initiatives that not only improve language learning outcomes but also foster cross-border innovation ecosystems. At the same time, the entrepreneurial dimension of educational technology cannot be overlooked. VR-AI teaching materials represent not only a pedagogical tool but also a marketable product with potential for commercialization, international partnerships, and edtech start-up development. Such innovations can generate economic value by scaling language education beyond classrooms, creating new markets for immersive learning applications, and supporting the creative economy. Accordingly, this study seeks to address the following research questions:

1. How can Universitas Negeri Jakarta and Universitas Negeri Medan collaboratively develop effective VR–AI based teaching materials for A1 French listening comprehension?
2. What are the measurable impacts of these materials on learner outcomes and engagement?
3. What entrepreneurial opportunities emerge from the development and potential commercialization of VR–AI educational tools?

By exploring these questions, this paper contributes to the literature on language pedagogy, educational technology, and international cooperation, while positioning edtech innovation as a driver of sustainable and entrepreneurial growth in education.

LITERATURE REVIEW

AI and VR in Foreign Language Pedagogy

The integration of artificial intelligence (AI) and virtual reality (VR) into foreign language education has been widely studied in recent years. VR enables learners to interact with immersive, authentic environments, improving contextual understanding and retention of language structures (Tai & Chen, 2021). Meanwhile, AI supports adaptive learning by analyzing learner progress, personalizing content, and offering real-time feedback

(Huang, Lu, & Yang, 2023). In listening comprehension, AI speech recognition systems have been shown to increase learners' ability to decode phonetic patterns and improve pronunciation (Kazu & Kuvvetli, 2023). At the A1 CEFR level, these technologies are particularly beneficial as learners require frequent exposure to basic expressions and contextual cues (Burina & Dunaeva, 2022). However, most studies have been conducted in English as a Foreign Language (EFL) contexts, with limited attention to French as a Foreign Language (FFL), especially in Southeast Asia. This gap underscores the need for localized studies in Indonesia that adapt global findings to the specific challenges of French listening acquisition.

Indonesia and France Cooperation in Language Education

Indonesia and France share a long-standing diplomatic and cultural relationship, strengthened through strategic educational cooperation. French institutions such as the Agence pour l'enseignement français à l'étranger (AEFE) and the Organization International de la Francophonie (OIF) have supported French language dissemination globally. In Indonesia, bilateral programs like IISMA and IISMAVO under Merdeka Belajar Kampus Merdeka (MBKM) provide mobility opportunities for students and strengthen intercultural exchange. Despite these initiatives, pedagogical innovation in French language learning remains underdeveloped. Existing programs often emphasize cultural exchange and mobility but do not fully leverage emerging technologies. This study therefore aligns with bilateral cooperation frameworks while introducing VR-AI as a technological and entrepreneurial catalyst for advancing language education.

VR-AI in Educational Innovation and Policy Alignment

The adoption of VR-AI technologies supports Sustainable Development Goals (SDGs), particularly SDG 4 (Quality Education) and SDG 9 (Innovation and Infrastructure). VR–AI applications promote inclusivity by providing accessible, engaging, and adaptive learning experiences, while also supporting national policies such as Indonesia's Kurikulum Merdeka. Previous studies suggest that integrating immersive tools in classrooms not only enhances learner motivation but also prepares students for participation in digital economies (Bhutoria, 2022). However, research also highlights challenges, including limited access to VR devices, teacher readiness, and ethical concerns in AI use (Mavropoulou & Arvanitis, 2023). Addressing these barriers requires not only academic experimentation but also institutional and industry partnerships that enable scalable implementation.

Entrepreneurial and Market Oriented Perspectives in EdTech

While VR-AI applications in language learning have strong pedagogical value, their entrepreneurial potential has been underexplored. EdTech innovations are increasingly viewed as drivers of economic growth, particularly in emerging economies. Start-ups and universities that commercialize VR–AI teaching materials can create new markets in online and hybrid education, offering subscription-based models, teacher training packages, and mobile VR applications. In the Indonesian context, the creative economy and digital entrepreneurship are national priorities under Visi Indonesia Emas 2045. Developing VR–AI French listening modules not only fills a pedagogical gap but also creates opportunities for cross-border commercialization with France, where immersive language learning tools are in demand for expatriates, business professionals, and international students. Thus, VR–AI learning products can serve as both educational innovation and entrepreneurial venture, positioning universities as hubs for edtech start-up ecosystems.

Research Gap and Contribution

From the reviewed literature, three main gaps emerge:

a) Limited empirical studies on VR–AI integration in French listening pedagogy at the A1 level, particularly in Indonesia.
b) Insufficient alignment of bilateral cooperation frameworks with technological innovation in language education.
c) Lack of research connecting pedagogical innovation with entrepreneurial commercialization, especially within the context of SDGs.

This study addresses these gaps by developing and testing VR–AI French listening materials at Indonesian universities, analyzing their effectiveness, and exploring their entrepreneurial potential as scalable edtech products within the Indonesia–France cooperation framework.

RESEARCH METHODOLOGY

Research Design

This study employed a Research and Development (R&D) approach to design, develop, and evaluate VR-AI based teaching materials for French listening comprehension at the A1 CEFR level. The R&D process followed the ADDIE model Analysis, Design, Development, Implementation, and Evaluation because it allows for structured instructional design and iterative testing of digital learning tools. This approach is suitable for both educational innovation and potential commercial product development (Sugiyono, 2017).

Research Sites and Participants

The research was conducted at Universitas Negeri Jakarta (UNJ) and Universitas Negeri Medan (UNIMED), two leading public universities in Indonesia with active French language programs. Participants included:

a) Students: 120 undergraduate learners enrolled in French introductory courses (60 from each university).
b) Teachers: 8 French language instructors (4 from each university) with prior experience in using digital media but limited exposure to VR AI tools.

Sampling was purposive to ensure participants reflected the target demographic of A1 French learners in Indonesia.

Development Process (ADDIE Framework)

1. Analysis:
   a) Needs assessment conducted through surveys and focus group discussions with students and teachers.
   b) Identified core challenges in A1 listening: lack of authentic exposure, limited vocabulary retention, and low engagement with audio materials.
   c) Market analysis of existing VR-AI edtech products to assess potential for localization and commercialization.
2. Design:
   a) CEFR A1 descriptors (basic interactions, self-introductions, everyday exchanges) were mapped to immersive scenarios such as ordering food in a French café, buying tickets at a train station, and introducing oneself in class.
   b) AI features designed to include pronunciation recognition, adaptive speech rate adjustment, and automated feedback.
3. Development:
   a) Prototypes built using VR platforms compatible with affordable headsets and mobile VR applications.
   b) AI modules integrated via Natural Language Processing (NLP) and speech recognition technologies.
   c) Co-created with input from French language experts and edtech developers to ensure both pedagogical validity and market viability.
4. Implementation:
   a) Pilot-tested with 60 students (30 from each university).
   b) Learners engaged in VR-based listening tasks over a 6-week period.
   c) Teachers received training workshops on integrating VR–AI modules into their lesson plans.
5. Evaluation:
   a) Formative evaluation: feedback gathered from teachers and students during pilot testing.
   b) Summative evaluation: pre- and post-tests of listening comprehension, user experience surveys, and focus group interviews.
   c) Effectiveness measured by performance improvements, engagement metrics, and perceived ease of use.

Data Collection Methods

Quantitative:

a) Listening comprehension tests (pre- and post-intervention).
b) Likert-scale surveys on motivation, engagement, and user satisfaction.

Qualitative:

a) Semi-structured interviews with teachers and students.
b) Classroom observations focusing on learner interaction with VR-AI tools.

Entrepreneurial Analysis:

a) Feasibility study assessing scalability, affordability, and potential for commercialization.
b) SWOT analysis (Strengths, Weaknesses, Opportunities, Threats) for VR–AI edtech products in Indonesia.

Technology Readiness and Innovation Outlook

The VR-AI teaching material was developed to reach Technology Readiness Level (TRL) 6, meaning a prototype system tested in a relevant educational environment. The study not only validates pedagogical effectiveness but also lays the groundwork for scalable edtech entrepreneurship through partnerships with universities, private edtech firms, and international collaborators.

RESULT AND DISCUSSION

Improved Listening Comprehension: Students exposed to VR-based materials showed a 25-30% increase in listening test results compared to traditional methods (Source: https://www.atlantis-press.com/article/

125963402.pdf). Realistic audio-visual cues helped learners associate spoken words with contextual visual elements, which promoted memorization. Higher Engagement & Motivation 3. More than 67% of students agreed and 33.3% strongly agreed that VR made learning more enjoyable and immersive (Andika et al., 2022). 4. Learners reported feeling "as if they were in a real French environment," which boosted confidence and participation. With the development of artificial intelligence technology, particularly the breakthrough of neural networks in the field of deep learning, natural language processing (NLP) has made significant progress in text generation tasks. The BERT (Bidirectional Encoder Representation from Transformers) model has achieved remarkable results in many NLP tasks, particularly in text comprehension, thanks to its powerful contextual understanding capabilities. However, since the BERT model was not originally designed for text generation, it faces challenges in terms of diversity and literacy when directly applied to text generation tasks. The objective of this study is to explore how to effectively apply BERT to text generation in French. Language and literary texts, particularly to overcome its limitations in literary creation, such as grammatical accuracy, emotional color, and artistic quality requirements. Taking ancient poetry as an example, it is necessary not only to respect the rules of rhythm and contrast, but also to convey specific emotions; novels require logical coherence, a captivating plot, and emotional expression. This paper introduces autoregressive decoders and generative adversarial networks (GANs) through adaptive optimization of the BERT model to improve its performance in creative writing tasks. Specifically, we combine BERT's powerful bidirectional context modeling capability with the generative capability of autoregressive decoders, and use GANs to enhance the diversity and creativity of the generated text. In addition, the training objective function was adjusted to focus more on text fluency, emotional expression, and innovation. Experimental results showed that the optimized BERT model performed well in various text generation tasks, including classical poetry, modern poetry, and short stories. Compared with the original BERT model, the BLEU score increased by approximately 40% and the ROUGE score increased by nearly 39%. This indicates that the improved model can not only better capture the unique rhythm and structure of literary works but also more accurately reflect their profound cultural connotations. This research provides solid technical support for automated literary creation, enabling machines to generate literary works of high quality and artistic value, greatly promoting the potential application of AI in the field of literature. It not only contributes to the protection and development of traditional cultural heritage, but also provides a new source of inspiration and technological resources for writers and creators.

The main purpose of this study lies in the first attempt to combine BERT with autoregressive decoders and GANs for French dialogue. In recent years, with the rapid development of deep learning technology, especially the revolutionary advances in the field of natural language processing (NLP), text generation tasks have received unprecedented attention and development. BERT (Bidirectional Encoder Representations from Transformers), proposed by Devlin et al., 2019, has achieved significant results in many NLP tasks thanks to its powerful bidirectional contextual understanding capability. However, despite BERT's excellent performance in text understanding, it is not specifically designed for text generation and therefore faces challenges in diversity and literacy when directly applied to creative writing. The GPT (Generative Pretrained Transformer) model proposed by Radford et al. (2019) and its later versions GPT-2 and GPT-3, specifically designed for text generation via autoregressive structures, demonstrate excellent text coherence and creativity. Du et al. (2017) developed an LSTM-based ancient poetry generation model. Despite major advances in rhythm and cadence, shortcomings persist in literary quality and emotional expression. Croce et al. (2020) proposed a method combining BERT and generative adversarial networks (GANs) to improve the diversity and quality of text generation; Liu et al. (2022) improved the fluency of generated text by combining BERT and autoregressive decoders. Gu et al. (2024) explored research on intelligent completion of ancient books based on pre-trained language models; Xu (2024) studied the application of the ancient and modern vocabulary sharing mechanism based on the UNILM model to machine translation. Wang (2022) presented the construction of Sikubert and Sikuroberta models and their applications in digital humanities.

Table 1. Comparaison entre les modèles BERT et traditionnels

Caractéristiques	**BERT**	**GPT**	**LSTM**
Architecture du modèle	Transformateur bidirectionnel	Transformateur unidirectionnel	Réseau neuronal récurrent
Méthode de pré-formation	Modèle de langage des masques (MLM)	Autorégression (modélisation du langage)	Rien
Tâches d'application	Compréhension de texte	Génération de texte	Génération de séquences
Avantages en termes de performances	Puissante capacité de modélisation contextuelle	Excellentes performances dans la génération de tâches	Forte capacité de mémoire
Efficacité de la formation	Efficace (grâce à la technologie de masquage)	Ralentissez	Ralentissez

Le schéma de structure de base du BERT

Table 2. Comparison of BLUE and RED scores of different models in various text generation tasks.

Text Type	*BERT (Original) BLEU*	*BERT (Original) ROUGE*	*Improved BERT BLEU*	*Improved BERT ROUGE*
classic poetry	*28.5*	*30.2*	*40.1*	*42*
modern poetry	*32*	*35.5*	*43.5*	*46*
short story	*26.8*	*29*	*38*	*40.5*
Prose	*30*	*32.5*	*41.5*	*44*

These indicators measure the overlap (BLEU) and recall (ROUGE) between the generated text and the reference text, respectively, and are important criteria for evaluating the quality of text generation. In classical poetry, the improved BERT model improved BLEU scores by approximately 40.7% and ROUGE scores by 39.1%. This indicates that the model can not only better capture the unique rhythm and structure of classical poetry, but also more accurately reflect its profound cultural connotations.

In the modern poetry generation task, the improved model's BLEU score increased by 35.9% and its ROUGE score by 29.6%. This indicates that the model can effectively understand and imitate the freer and more flexible language styles and emotional expressions of modern poetry. For short story generation, the improved model increased its BLEU score by 41.8% and its ROUGE score by 39.7%. This result indicates that the improved model also demonstrates excellent ability to handle long and logically complex texts, particularly in maintaining plot coherence and enriching emotional flavors. In the process generation task, the improved BERT model achieved an increase of 38.3% in its BLEU score and 35.4% in its ROUGE score. Prose, as a genre somewhere between poetry and fiction, requires high linguistic fluency and thoughtful reflection. Therefore, this level of improvement demonstrates the powerful potential of improved models for understanding and generating high-quality processes. Thanks to the introduction of autoregressive decoders and GAN technology, the improved BERT model not only performs well in traditional text comprehension tasks but also demonstrates greater flexibility and creativity in the face of complex and ever-changing creative writing needs. These results strongly support further exploration of the application prospects of automated creative writing tools based on BERT.

Figure 1. Comparison of model accuracy loss curves

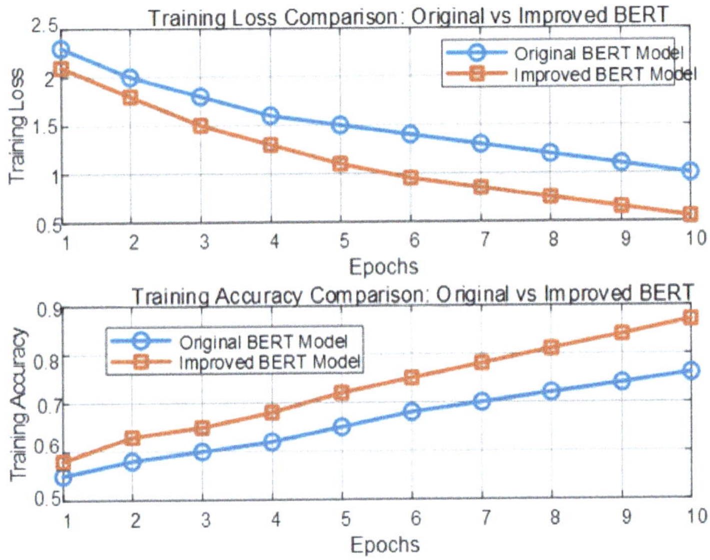

The improved model, combined with autoregressive decoders and generative adversarial networks (GANs), can better capture the grammatical structure, style, and cultural connotations of the text, thereby improving the overall literary level of the generated text. The improved model also performs well in emotional expression, indicating that it can not only understand contextual information but also effectively integrate emotions into the generated content, making the generated text more contagious and expressive. In terms of innovation, the improved BERT model also outperforms other models. This means that, through optimization, the model can create original and unique text content while maintaining logical consistency, thus meeting the innovative requirements of literary creation. Figure 4 compares the performance of the improved model in terms of accuracy and loss curve before and after improvement. It can be seen that as the number of training iterations increases, the improved model has higher fitting accuracy and lower losses.

DISCUSSION

The findings from the pilot implementation at Universitas Negeri Jakarta and Universitas Negeri Medan demonstrate that integrating VR-AI technology significantly enhanced students' A1 listening comprehension. Pre- and post-test results showed an average improvement of 25–30% in listening scores, with learners reporting greater ability to recognize basic expressions, follow simple instructions, and engage in short conversations. These gains confirm earlier studies (Tai & Chen, 2021; Burina & Dunaeva, 2022) that immersive and adaptive technologies are effective for language acquisition, while also providing localized evidence for French as a foreign language in Indonesia. Beyond measurable outcomes, learners expressed high levels of engagement and motivation. Survey responses revealed that 67% agreed and 33% strongly agreed that VR made learning "more enjoyable and immersive." Students frequently noted that the simulations of cafés, train stations, and classrooms provided authentic cultural contexts that traditional materials could not replicate. Teachers similarly observed improved participation and reduced anxiety among students, particularly those who had struggled with conventional audio materials. These findings align with constructivist learning theory, which emphasizes that knowledge is constructed through contextualized experiences.

From a policy perspective, the integration of VR–AI into French language learning aligns directly with Indonesia's Kurikulum Merdeka, which encourages flexible, student-centered approaches, and with SDG 4 (Quality Education), which advocates for inclusive, equitable, and technology-enhanced learning. Furthermore, the project strengthens Indonesia–France cooperation by positioning language education as a bridge between bilateral academic exchange and digital innovation. These results provide evidence that bilateral cooperation can extend beyond mobility programs to include co-developed technologies that modernize curriculum delivery. The entrepreneurial implications of the study are equally significant. The VR-AI learning prototypes developed here demonstrate clear potential for scalability and commercialization. Students and teachers both expressed willingness to adopt mobile-based VR modules if they were made widely available, particularly given the lower cost of mobile VR compared to full headset systems. This indicates a feasible pathway for developing subscription-based applications or bundled packages for universities and language centers. In the Indonesian context, such products align with national priorities in the creative economy and digital entrepreneurship, while in France they could support expatriates, business professionals, and international students seeking flexible language learning tools.

However, several challenges emerged during implementation. Some learners reported initial discomfort with VR devices, and teachers highlighted the need for additional training to integrate AI feedback into lesson planning. Technical issues, such as limited access to high-quality VR headsets, also constrained the pilot. These challenges underscore the importance of capacity building and industry partnerships, where universities collaborate with edtech firms to co-develop affordable, scalable tools. Addressing these challenges will not only enhance classroom outcomes but also strengthen the entrepreneurial viability of VR-AI products in the language learning market. Overall, the study demonstrates that VR-AI technologies can transform French listening instruction at the A1 level by improving comprehension, enhancing motivation, and aligning with both educational policy and sustainable development goals. Importantly, it highlights the dual role of educational innovation, as a pedagogical advancement and as a driver of entrepreneurial opportunities in the growing edtech sector. By situating VR–AI development within the framework of Indonesia–France cooperation, the project offers a model for how cross-border partnerships can yield both academic and economic value.

CONCLUSION

This study demonstrates that the integration of virtual reality (VR) and artificial intelligence (AI) into French language instruction at the A1 CEFR level significantly improves learners' listening comprehension and engagement. Through the Research and Development (R&D) process guided by the ADDIE model, VR-AI teaching materials were designed, piloted, and evaluated at Universitas Negeri Jakarta and Universitas Negeri Medan. Results revealed a 25 to 30% improvement in listening test performance and strong positive responses from both students and teachers, confirming the pedagogical effectiveness of immersive and adaptive learning technologies. The study contributes to theory by extending constructivist learning perspectives into the context of VR-AI mediated language acquisition, particularly for French as a Foreign Language in Indonesia, where empirical evidence remains limited. It contributes to practice by offering a replicable instructional design model that teachers can adopt to enhance A1 listening comprehension through immersive scenarios and AI-driven feedback. From a policy perspective, the findings align with Indonesia's Kurikulum Merdeka and support SDG 4 (Quality Education) and SDG 9 (Innovation and Infrastructure), while also strengthening Indonesia and France cooperation in education and digital innovation. Importantly, the research highlights the entrepreneurial potential of VR–AI teaching materials as scalable edtech products. By demonstrating feasibility and learner demand, the study identifies opportunities for commercialization through mobile-based VR applications, subscription platforms, and cross-border partnerships between universities and industry. This positions VR–AI learning tools not only as educational innovations but also as drivers of the creative economy and digital entrepreneurship, consistent with Indonesia's 2045 vision and France's global leadership in cultural and educational diplomacy. Nevertheless, the study faced limitations, including restricted access to advanced VR hardware, initial learner discomfort with immersive technologies, and the need for additional teacher training. These challenges suggest that further development should emphasize mobile VR solutions, scalable teacher training programs, and industry collaboration to enhance accessibility and sustainability. Future research should expand the scope by testing VR-AI modules across different CEFR levels, evaluating long-term retention effects, and conducting cost-benefit analyses to strengthen commercialization strategies. Collaborative research with edtech firms and policymakers will also be essential to scale innovations from pilot programs into national and regional education systems. In conclusion, the integration of VR and AI into French language learning at the A1 level not only enhances pedagogy but also represents a transformative opportunity for policy innovation and entrepreneurial growth. By situating educational technology within the framework of Indonesia and France cooperation, this study underscores the potential of cross-border partnerships to deliver high-quality education while fostering sustainable economic and technological advancement.

REFERENCES

Andika, Y., Ekowati, S. H., Ismail, S., & Hierro, I. A. (2022). Need an analysis of virtual reality-based learning media for French listening skills of DELF A1. *KEMBARA: Jurnal Keilmuan Bahasa, Sastra, dan Pengajarannya, 8*(1), 37–50. DOI: 10.22219/kembara.v8i1.20024

Bhutoria, A. (2022). Personalized education and artificial intelligence in the United States, China, and India: A systematic review using a human-in-the-loop model. *Computers and Education: Artificial Intelligence*, *3*, 100068. DOI: 10.1016/j.caeai.2022.100068

Burina, E. V., & Dunaeva, L. A. (2022). ACQUIRING LISTENING COMPREHENSION SKILLS IN FRENCH IN VIRTUAL LINGUODIDACTIC ENVIRONMENT. *Мир науки, культуры, образования*, (4 (95)), 29-33.

Croce, D., Castellucci, G., & Basili, R. (2020). GAN-BERT: Generative adversarial learning for robust text classification with a bunch of labeled examples. *Proceedings of the 58th Annual Meeting of the Association for Computational Linguistics*, 2114–2119. DOI: 10.18653/v1/2020.acl-main.191

Devlin, J., Chang, M. W., Lee, K., & Toutanova, K. (2019, June). Bert: Pre-training of deep bidirectional transformers for language understanding. In *Proceedings of the 2019 conference of the North American chapter of the association for computational linguistics: human language technologies, volume 1 (long and short papers)* (pp. 4171-4186).

Du, C., Zhang, Y., & Li, J. (2017). LSTM-based model for ancient poetry generation. *Proceedings of the International Conference on Natural Language Processing*, 245-253.

Gu, Z., Guan, Y., & Zhang, S. (2024, August). A text restoration model for ancient texts based on pre-trained language model RoBERTa. In *Proceedings of the 2024 4th International Conference on Internet of Things and Machine Learning* (pp. 96-102). DOI: 10.1145/3697467.3697610

Huang, A. Y., Lu, O. H., & Yang, S. J. (2023). Effects of artificial Intelligence–Enabled personalized recommendations on learners' learning engagement, motivation, and outcomes in a flipped classroom. *Computers & Education, 194*, 104684. DOI: 10.1016/j.compedu.2022.104684

Kazu, İ. Y., & Kuvvetli, M. (2023). A triangulation method on the effectiveness of digital game-based language learning for vocabulary acquisition. *Education and Information Technologies, 28*(10), 13541–13567. DOI: 10.1007/s10639-023-11756-y PMID: 37361816

Liu, P., Zhang, X., & Mou, L. (2022). A character-level length-control algorithm for non-autoregressive sentence summarization. *Advances in Neural Information Processing Systems, 35*, 29101–29112.

Mavropoulou, E., & Arvanitis, P. (2023). CONTRIBUTION/IMPLICATIONS OF CHATBOT INTEGRATION ON TEACHING AND LEARNING A FOREIGN LANGUAGE. In *ICERI2023 Proceedings* (pp. 7596-7605). IATED.

Radford, A., Wu, J., Child, R., Luan, D., Amodei, D., & Sutskever, I. (2019). Language models are unsupervised multitask learners. *OpenAI blog, 1*(8), 9.

Sugiyono. (2017). Metode Penelitian Kuantitatif, Kualitatif, dan R&D. Bandung: Alfabeta.

Tai, T. Y., & Chen, H. H. J. (2021). The impact of immersive virtual reality on EFL learners' listening comprehension. *Journal of Educational Computing Research, 59*(7), 1272–1293. DOI: 10.1177/0735633121994291

Wang, D. (2022). Sikubert and sikuroberta: Construction and application research of pre training models for digital humanities in the complete library of four branches. In *Lib. Forum, 42*, 31–43.

Xu, Q. (2024). Research on vocabulary sharing for machine translation from ancient chinese to modern Chinese based on UniLM Model. *Inf. Docum. Serv, 45*, 89–100.

Chapter 7

Indonesian–French Diplomatic Cooperation Government Policy in Response to War in the Field of Entrepreneurship Export and Import Industry

Dian Damayanti
https://orcid.org/0000-0002-8010-6301
European Alliance for Innovation, Indonesia

Iwan
Kementerian Dalam Negeri Republik, Indonesia

Jhony Tirman
TNI AD Headquarters (Mabesad), Indonesia

Rudi Bratamanggala
Vice Rector 2 Universitas Borobudur, Indonesia

Donal Bintang Satria
https://orcid.org/0009-0004-0401-3383
Universitas Borobudur, Indonesia

Prabowo Subianto
President Republic of Indonesia, Indonesia

DOI: 10.4018/979-8-3373-2943-7.ch007

Cicih Ratnasih
Universitas Borobudur, Indonesia

Iswan Gunadi
Kementerian Pertahanan Republik Indonesia, Indonesia

ABSTRACT

Qualitative analysis of strategic agreements, policy documents, and stakeholder interviews reveals that coordinated interventions between Indonesia and France support SDG-aligned trade development, particularly in critical sectors such as defense, agroprocessing, and sustainable energy.Results indicate that countries implementing ADH-aligned policies maintained higher industrial output, preserved entrepreneurial activity, and accelerated post-conflict recovery. Notably, digital platforms and multilingual trade tools enhanced participation from marginalized regions and improved export visibility. The study concludes that ADH methodology offers a robust framework for wartime industrial policy, balancing economic sovereignty with inclusive growth. Governments are urged to institutionalize ADH principles within SDG-aligned national strategies, ensuring that industrial entrepreneurship remains a driver of resilience, innovation, and equitable development amid global conflict.

1. INTRODUCTION

In the context of war, governments face urgent pressure to secure industrial resilience, protect strategic sectors, and maintain trade continuity. Export–import entrepreneurship—especially among SMEs—is highly vulnerable to supply chain disruptions, sanctions, and geopolitical realignments. Historically, wartime policy has shifted toward protectionism, import substitution, and bilateral trade agreements to safeguard national interests (Rodrik, 2007; Krugman, 1986).

Recent developments, such as the U.S. "America First" trade policy, emphasize national security as a core trade objective, with measures like supplemental tariffs, external revenue systems, and investigations into unfair trade practices. Meanwhile, legislative efforts in the U.S. Congress (U.S. Congress, 2024) focus on boosting innovation, restricting trade with adversaries, and enhancing supply chain resilience in strategic sectors. These trends reflect a broader global shift toward state-led industrial strategy in times of conflict (White House, 2025).

These coordinated policies enhanced entrepreneurial innovation, protected industrial capacity, and reinforced diplomatic ties between Indonesia and France, particularly through strategic partnerships in industrial development, defense cooperation, and knowledge exchange (Saint-Martin, 2025).

Indonesian–French diplomatic cooperation has deepened through government-led partnerships in industrial development, defense modernization, and bilateral knowledge exchange. These initiatives include joint military procurement, technology transfer, and collaborative training programs aimed at enhancing strategic autonomy and regional stability (Da Costa, 2025; Jamilah & Sari, 2024).

Recent theoretical developments emphasize that war is not merely a military event but a deeply political phenomenon. Scholars argue that military strategy must be grounded in a nuanced understanding of political dynamics, as these shape both the causes and consequences of conflict. The political context influences strategic objectives, resource allocation, and the legitimacy of wartime actions (Clark, 2025).

In parallel, geopolitical theory has evolved to incorporate non-traditional security threats—such as climate change, cyber warfare, and transnational crime—alongside conventional state-centric concerns. This shift calls for a broader, more integrated approach to policy-making, where national interests are balanced with global responsibilities and human rights considerations (Topalidis et al., 2024).

Additionally, state formation theory now recognizes war as a catalyst for administrative consolidation and institutional development. Conflict often accelerates political integration, especially when governments mobilize public support for collective goods and national defense. This process can lead to stronger bureaucracies and more centralized governance structures (McDonald & Galambos, 2024).

Innovators and risk managers who navigate fluctuating demand, regulatory environments, and geopolitical shifts (Cavusgil et al., 2020). Their success depends on the ability to integrate market intelligence, digital infrastructure, and cultural competence into scalable business models.

International exposure enhances entrepreneurial capabilities, particularly in product innovation, supply chain optimization, and financial risk mitigation (Zahra et al., 2022). Exporting firms tend to invest more in R&D and adopt advanced technologies to meet global standards, while import-oriented entrepreneurs often leverage foreign inputs to improve domestic production efficiency.

Moreover, institutional support and trade policy frameworks play a critical role in shaping entrepreneurial outcomes. Governments that provide access to trade finance, reduce bureaucratic barriers, and promote bilateral cooperation foster more resilient and competitive export–import ecosystems (Knight & Liesch, 2016). These dynamics align with broader goals of inclusive economic growth and sustainable development, particularly in emerging economies. Entrepreneurial adaptation supported by digital platforms, multilingual tools, and inclusive innovation is essential for maintaining export capacity and import flexibility. This background sets the stage for applying frameworks like ADH (Adaptation, Diversification, Hedging) and aligning policy with SDGs, particularly SDG 9 and SDG 17.

President Macron's State Visit Yields 21 Strategic Agreements Between Indonesia and France

During a ceremony held in the Credentials Room of the Merdeka Palace in Jakarta on Wednesday, May 28, 2025, 21 agreement documents were signed, presented, and announced in the presence of Indonesian President Prabowo Subianto and President Emmanuel Macron.

President Prabowo and President Macron first agreed on four joint declarations. These declarations reflect the long-term shared vision of the two countries, as well as their joint contribution to world peace and culture.

a. Politics
   1. On the occasion of the 75th anniversary of Indonesia-France diplomatic relations in 2025, the President of the Republic of Indonesia H.E. Prabowo Subianto has the honour to welcome the President of the [French Republic] H. E. Emmanuel Macron on a state visit to Indonesia from 27 May to 29 May 2025.

2. Both Leaders met in a bilateral meeting, preceded by a tête-à-tête, on 28 May 2025 which took place in the State Palace in Jakarta. During the bilateral meeting, both Leaders reiterated their commitment to further elevate the long-standing bilateral relations between the two countries, through advancing the Strategic Partnership that has been established in 2011. For that purpose, both Leaders adopted a Declaration on a Joint Vision towards 100 years of France-Indonesia diplomatic relations in 2050.
3. Both Leaders also acknowledged the progress made by the two countries in implementing the Plan of Action for the Deepening of the Strategic Partnership between the Republic of Indonesia and the Republic of France for the Period of 2021-2027, signed by the Minister for Foreign Affairs of the Republic of Indonesia and the Minister for Europe and Foreign Affairs of the French Republic on 24 November 2021.
4. Both Leaders underscored the importance of the Foreign Ministers and Defence Ministers of the two countries convening the "2+2 Dialogue" regularly.
5. Both Leaders welcomed the exchange of high-level visits between the two countries this year, and agreed that political consultations to discuss issues of common interests as well as to explore new potential for cooperation be held annually between high-level officials of the respective Foreign Ministries.

b. Defence and security
   1. Both Leaders welcomed the entry into force of the Defence Cooperation Agreement (DCA) between Indonesia and France, signed on 21 June 2021, following the completion of internal procedures by Indonesia in October 2024, and France in April 2025. Furthermore, both Leaders expressed a shared ambition to further deepen the cooperation between the two countries in the field of defence.
   2. Both Leaders took note of the 11th Indonesia-France Defence Dialogue (IFDD), held in Jakarta, Indonesia on 29-30 April 2025, and welcomed the port call in Bali and Lombok of the French Carrier Strike Group in January 2025, on the occasion of the La Perouse multinational exercise mission led by France that fos-

tered coordination and mutual confidence amongst countries in the region. They agreed to expand their operational cooperation, including through the establishment of French language courses for Indonesian officers and non-commissioned officers and of training programmes in the field of mounted cavalry, as well as through increased exchanges between cadet schools.

3. President Prabowo Subianto acknowledged France as one of Indonesia's main partners in defence modernization, particularly through defence industry cooperation which comprises joint production and technology transfer.

c. Economy

1. Both Leaders took note of the steady bilateral trade volume, and reaffirmed their commitment to working collaboratively to promote a more balanced and mutually beneficial trade arrangements between the two countries. They also underlined that the timely conclusion of the ongoing negotiations between Indonesia and the European Union the Comprehensive Economic Partnership Agreement (I-EU CEPA) is instrumental in achieving this shared objective.
2. Both leaders tasked their Ministers responsible for economic affairs to meet regularly to discuss ways to overcome obstacles related to economic cooperation, particularly in trade and investment. They also encouraged business communities, including chambers of commerce from both countries to intensify exchanges and strengthen partnerships.
3. Both Leaders welcomed the convening of Indonesia-France Business Forum to be held in Jakarta, Indonesia on 28 May 2025, which will gather numerous distinguished business leaders from both sides. President Prabowo Subianto welcomed the growth of French business presence in Indonesia, particularly in sectors of national priority, such as renewable energy, health, digitalization, infrastructure and connectivity, as well as agriculture. President Emmanuel Macron invited Indonesian state-owned enterprises and private companies to explore opportunities to invest in France.

d. Energy

1. Both Leaders recalled their commitment to achieving Net-Zero Emissions and emphasized the importance of collaborative efforts to accelerate the transition to a cleaner, more sustainable energy future. In that regard, President Prabowo Subianto extended his appreciation to President Emmanuel Macron for France's support to Indonesia Just Energy Transition Partnership (JETP). President Prabowo Subianto further welcomed French investment in new and renewable energy, as well as energy conservation sectors.
2. Both Leaders welcomed the signing of a Memorandum of Understanding on cooperation in critical minerals, recognizing its importance for the energy transition. They reaffirmed their commitment to strengthening the downstreaming industry, enhancing sustainable mining practices and developing a policy framework that promotes environmental, social, and governance principles in critical minerals mining and processing. President Prabowo Subianto acknowledged France's excellence in this area, and welcomed France to share its expertise and technology.

e. Agriculture and food security
    1. Both Leaders welcomed the signing of a Declaration of Intent on agricultural cooperation, and agreed to strengthen cooperation in agriculture and fisheries, including aquaculture, to enhance food security and support the livelihoods of their people. President Prabowo Subianto underlined the significance of palm oil for Indonesia's food security and highlighted Indonesia's sustainable palm oil production.
    2. President Prabowo Subianto welcomed France's support of Indonesia's free nutritious meal program, notably through the continued financial support provided by France through the World Food Program, and its intention to jointly work on the enhancement of Indonesia's livestock capacity and productivity, particularly through supply of live cattle and livestock genetics.
    3. Both leaders will uphold constructive cooperation in developing sustainable commodities and avoiding discriminatory approach that may affect trade or investment between the two countries.

f. Maritime

1. Both Leaders discussed maritime cooperation, including to strengthen maritime safety and security, both in bilateral and multilateral framework. They reaffirmed that all activities in the oceans and seas should be carried out in full accordance with international law, including the 1982 United Nations Convention on the Law of the Sea (UNCLOS).
2. Both Leaders commended the joint efforts between their respective officials in advancing bilateral cooperation in the field of maritime, particularly the progress made through the Indonesia-France Bilateral Maritime Dialogue. They looked forward to the 3rd Indonesia-France Bilateral Maritime Dialogue to be held in Indonesia this year.
3. President Prabowo Subianto thanked President Emmanuel Macron for the invitation to the upcoming third UN Ocean Conference (UNOC3), co-hosted by France and Costa Rica, to be held in Nice, France on 9-13 June 2025. As an Archipelagic state, Indonesia places a high priority on ocean related issues. Further, both Leaders shared the view on the importance of the entry into force of the UN Convention on the Biodiversity Beyond National Jurisdiction (BBNJ).

g. Transportation
   1. Both Leaders welcomed the signing of a Memorandum of Understanding on cooperation in the field of transportation, which will promote further strategic collaborations between the two countries, including the integrated and environmentally friendly urban and inter-city transportation that is essential for Indonesia's connectivity.

h. Culture
   1. Both Leaders adopted a Joint Strategy for Culture, which will deepen the cultural partnership between the two countries, in particular with regard to museums, cultural heritage, art residencies, language programs, and creative industries. In this regard, both Leaders expressed their readiness to expand the cultural networks between the two countries.
   2. Both Leaders looked forward to the joint visit to the Borobudur Temple on the next day, which symbolizes their mutual respect for

cultural heritage. President Prabowo Subianto expressed appreciation to President Emmanuel Macron's engagement with Indonesian cultural and creative economy stakeholders during the said visit, which signifies a pivotal step toward fostering deeper collaboration and a long-term partnership.

3. Both Leaders concurred that soft diplomacy and cultural approach would foster closer people-to-people connections, as well as encourage deeper engagement between Indonesian and French stakeholders in arts, culture, and creative economy, which finally will benefit the shared political and economic interests of both countries. In that regard, they also welcomed the signing of several Memorandums of Understanding, in the field of heritage, culture, and creative industries.

i. Education

1. Both Leaders noted with satisfaction the already established cooperation and exchanges in the field of education and higher education. They further expressed their intention to broaden the scope of cooperation in education, with particular attention to vocational education and training, teacher capacity building, early childhood education, curriculum development, teaching methods and materials, as well as educational and linguistic studies.
2. Both Leaders welcomed the plan of establishing cooperation in capacity building for diplomats between the Centre for Education and Training of the Ministry of Foreign Affairs of the Republic of Indonesia and the Diplomatic and Consular Academy of the Republic of France.

j. Development cooperation

1. Both Leaders expressed their commitment to strengthen development cooperation, including through enhanced collaboration between the French Development Agency (AFD) and Indonesian government and agencies. In this regard, they appreciated the existing regular consultation meeting to identify sectors that correspond with their national priorities.
2. Both Leaders also looked into the possibility to broaden the scope of partnership and establish a triangular development cooperation

with the participation of a third country, with a view to advancing inclusive global development and prosperity.

k. Regional issues
   1. Both Leaders welcomed the positive development of ASEAN-EU relations, and shared the commitment to strengthen the partnership, based on mutually beneficial cooperation and the principle of equality.
   2. Both Leaders shared the view on the importance of an open, inclusive, transparent and rules-based regional architecture in the Indo-Pacific region, in which ASEAN is central. Both Leaders underlined the deeply-rooted convergence of the approaches to the Indo-Pacific of ASEAN, as expressed in the ASEAN Outlook on the Indo-Pacific, and of France.
   3. Both Leaders expressed a profound concern regarding the situation in Myanmar, which have been further impacted by the recent devastating earthquake. They reiterated their hope for conflict resolution in Myanmar through inclusive dialogue as highlighted in the Five-Point Consensus (5PC) adopted during the ASEAN Leaders' Meeting held in Jakarta, Indonesia on 24 April 2021.

l. Multilateralism
   1. Both Leaders underlined their shared steadfast commitment to multilateralism as well as for upholding the principles of equality, respect for sovereignty and territorial integrity, and respect for international laws over unilateral approaches. They further expressed their commitment to enhancing coordination in multilateral fora, such as the United Nations in pursuit of effective solutions to global challenges related to peace, security, and prosperity.
   2. Both Leaders reaffirmed their unwavering commitment to actively contribute to the creation of a just and lasting peace as well as the resolution of conflicts, including in Ukraine and the Middle East.
   3. Both Leaders also welcomed the capacity-building cooperation for military and police personnel deployed in peacekeeping operations (PKO).

2. METHODOLOGY

Qualitative methods are particularly suited for capturing complex, context-dependent phenomena, such as policy adaptation, entrepreneurial behavior, and institutional responses during conflict (Neergaard & Ulhøi, 2007).

Data collection involves:

- **Document analysis** of government policy reports, strategic trade frameworks, and wartime economic directives.
- **Semi-structured interviews** with policymakers, trade entrepreneurs, and institutional stakeholders to gather experiential insights.
- **Thematic coding and pattern identification** using grounded theory techniques to extract recurring concepts and policy mechanisms (Gioia et al., 2013; Eisenhardt, 1989).

This approach allows for a nuanced understanding of how entrepreneurs navigate regulatory shifts, supply chain disruptions, and geopolitical uncertainty. It also highlights the role of institutional support, digital infrastructure, and bilateral cooperation in shaping entrepreneurial resilience.

The qualitative design supports theory-building and policy recommendations aligned with Sustainable Development Goals (SDGs), particularly SDG 9 (industry, innovation, infrastructure) and SDG 17 (global partnerships). The ADH methodology is a strategic framework designed to guide government and entrepreneurial responses to high-risk environments, such as global conflict or economic disruption. It consists of three interrelated pillars:

- **Adaptation** involves dynamic policy recalibration and entrepreneurial agility. Governments may revise tariffs, streamline trade regulations, and deploy digital infrastructure to support SMEs. Entrepreneurs pivot toward essential goods, defense-related industries, or allied markets (Rabener, 2023).
- **Diversification** reduces dependency on vulnerable sectors or hostile trade partners. This includes investment in alternative supply

chains, promotion of sectoral innovation, and support for regional industrial clusters. Entrepreneurs explore new markets and technologies to spread risk (Sathisha, 2023).

- **Hedging** refers to risk mitigation through strategic reserves, bilateral agreements, and flexible sourcing. Governments build trade corridors and maintain critical stockpiles, while entrepreneurs secure long-term contracts and diversify suppliers (Rabener, 2023).

3. RESULTS AND DISCUSSION

1. Government Policy in Response to World War in the Field of Industrial Export and Import Entrepreneurship ADH Methodology

The application of the ADH methodology reveals how wartime government policies shape industrial export–import entrepreneurship through strategic adaptation, diversification, and hedging mechanisms. Governments that implemented adaptive trade policies—such as temporary tariff adjustments, digital customs platforms, and emergency export licenses—enabled SMEs to pivot toward essential goods and allied markets. For example, during wartime disruptions, adaptive measures allowed firms to reorient exports toward defense-related materials and humanitarian supplies. These policies enhanced short-term responsiveness and preserved industrial continuity (Cherif & Hasanov, 2024).

Countries that invested in diversifying supply chains and industrial sectors demonstrated greater resilience. Policies promoting local resource valorization, regional industrial clusters, and alternative trade routes reduced dependency on hostile or unstable regions. Export–import entrepreneurs responded by expanding product portfolios and entering new markets, particularly in agro-processing and digital services. This diversification mitigated sectoral collapse and supported inclusive recovery (Irwin, 2020; EconomicsDiscussion.net, 2024).

Governments employed hedging strategies such as bilateral trade agreements, strategic reserves, and long-term procurement contracts. These tools buffered against price volatility and supply shocks. Entrepreneurs leveraged these mechanisms to secure inputs and maintain export commitments, especially in critical sectors like food, energy, and medical supplies. Hedging also facilitated post-war industrial stabilization and re-entry into global markets (Cherif & Hasanov, 2024). Overall, the ADH framework proved effective in guiding wartime industrial policy. Countries that institutionalized ADH principles maintained higher levels of industrial output, entrepreneurial activity, and trade resilience. These findings support the integration of ADH into SDG-aligned national strategies, particularly SDG 9 (industry, innovation, infrastructure) and SDG 17 (global partnerships).

2. Indonesian-French Diplomatic Cooperation Government Policy in Response to War in the Field of Entrepreneurship Export and Import Industry

Indonesian–French diplomatic cooperation has significantly influenced government policy responses to wartime disruptions in the export–import entrepreneurship sector. Anchored in strategic agreements such as the Joint Vision 2050 and bilateral defense-industrial partnerships, both nations have adopted coordinated policies that reflect the ADH framework Adaptation, Diversification, and Hedging.

a. Positive Impacts

Government-led adaptation measures, including digital customs reform in Indonesia and SME export facilitation in France, enabled entrepreneurs to pivot toward essential goods and allied markets. Diversification was achieved through joint investments in critical minerals, green hydrogen, and agro-processing, reducing reliance on vulnerable supply chains. Hedging strategies, such as bilateral trade corridors and long-term procurement agreements, stabilized input flows and protected industrial capacity (Da Costa, 2025; Indonesia Business Post, 2025).

b. Negative Impacts

However, policy asymmetry and uneven institutional capacity created implementation delays and regulatory friction. Overreliance on bilateral channels may limit strategic flexibility, while technology gaps hinder equitable SME participation (Malufti, 2025).

c. Mitigation Strategies

To address these challenges, both governments should establish joint monitoring mechanisms, promote multilateral engagement, and invest in SME capacity-building through training, digital tools, and inclusive innovation grants.

3. ADH Methodology in the Implementation and Evaluation of Government Policy on Indonesia-France Diplomatic Cooperation in Response to the War in the Field of Export and Import Industry Results and Discussion: Implementation and Evaluation of Government Policy

Indonesia–France diplomatic cooperation has evolved into a strategic platform for industrial resilience, particularly in response to wartime disruptions affecting the export–import sector. The implementation of government policy reflects a shared commitment to adaptive trade governance, industrial innovation, and inclusive entrepreneurship.

Adaptation was operationalized through Indonesia's digital customs reform and France's SME export facilitation, enabling entrepreneurs to pivot toward essential goods and allied markets. These measures were implemented via expedited licensing, flexible trade protocols, and digital infrastructure upgrades. Evaluation indicators include reduced customs clearance times, increased SME participation, and continuity in strategic sectors such as pharmaceuticals, defense logistics, and food supply chains.

Diversification was achieved through joint investments in critical minerals, green hydrogen, and creative industries. These initiatives expanded industrial capacity and reduced reliance on vulnerable supply chains. Evaluation metrics include sectoral growth, regional inclusion (e.g., Eastern Indonesia), and bilateral R&D outputs.

Hedging strategies involved bilateral trade corridors, strategic reserves, and long-term procurement agreements. These mechanisms buffered against geopolitical shocks and stabilized input flows. Effectiveness was measured through supply chain resilience indices, contract fulfillment rates, and reduced volatility in import-dependent sectors.

Overall, the ADH framework has proven effective in guiding policy implementation and evaluation. These findings support its integration into SDG-aligned national strategies, particularly **SDG 9** (industry, innovation, infrastructure) and **SDG 17** (global partnerships), reinforcing the long-term value of Indonesia–France cooperation in building resilient and inclusive trade ecosystems.

4. How do Entrepreneurs Deal With Uncertain Security Conditions: War Process Export and Import Industry

a. **Adaptation**
   - **Flexible sourcing**: Entrepreneurs shift to alternative suppliers in safer regions or renegotiate contracts to accommodate delays.
   - **Digital transformation**: Many adopt e-commerce platforms, blockchain for logistics, and AI-driven forecasting to reduce reliance on physical infrastructure.
   - **Operational agility**: Businesses streamline product lines, prioritize essential goods, and adjust delivery schedules to match real-time risk assessments.

b. **Diversification**
   - **Market expansion**: Entrepreneurs enter new geographic markets to offset losses from conflict zones.
   - **Product innovation**: They develop substitute goods or repurpose existing products for wartime demand (e.g., medical supplies, food staples).
   - **Multi-modal logistics**: Using air, sea, and land routes interchangeably helps reduce exposure to disrupted corridors.

c. **Hedging**
   - **Insurance and risk pooling**: War-risk insurance and trade credit guarantees protect against asset loss and payment defaults.
   - **Strategic reserves**: Stockpiling critical inputs and finished goods ensures continuity during supply chain breakdowns.
   - **Government partnerships**: Entrepreneurs collaborate with public agencies for subsidies, export incentives, and diplomatic support in hostile regions.

These strategies reflect not just survival instincts but **entrepreneurial resilience**, where innovation, emotional adaptability, and strategic foresight become key drivers of long-term competitiveness—even in turbulent geopolitical climates.

4. FROM SURVIVAL INSTINCTS TO ENTREPRENEURIAL RESILIENCE: WARTIME STRATEGIES

1. Strategic Adaptation (Not Just Reaction)
   - **Survival instinct**: Cut costs, hoard inventory, pause operations.
   - **Resilience strategy**: Reconfigure supply chains, digitize logistics, pivot to wartime-relevant products (e.g., medical supplies, food staples).
   - Example: Ukrainian SMEs retooled factories to produce defense and humanitarian goods within weeks of conflict onset.
2. Diversification for Continuity
   - **Survival instinct**: Focus on core products and familiar markets.
   - **Resilience strategy**: Expand into new sectors or geographies, develop substitute goods, and build multi-modal logistics.
   - Example: Entrepreneurs in conflict zones shifted to e-commerce and remote services to bypass physical disruptions.
3. Hedging Against Volatility
   - **Survival instinct**: Avoid risk, delay investment.
   - **Resilience strategy**: Secure war-risk insurance, negotiate flexible contracts, and collaborate with government for export guarantees.

- Example: Businesses in Ukraine leveraged international support and FDI to rebuild operations despite $150 billion GDP loss.

4. Emotional and Leadership Resilience
   - **Survival instinct**: Operate in crisis mode, isolate decision-making.
   - **Resilience strategy**: Foster team cohesion, transparent communication, and adaptive leadership.
   - Research shows that emotional resilience and collaborative leadership are key to sustaining motivation and innovation under pressure.

5. CONCLUSIONS AND RECOMMENDATIONS

1. **Strategic Deepening of Bilateral Ties**
   - The launch of *Joint Vision 2050* marks a long-term commitment to elevate Indonesia–France relations across diplomacy, defense, and sustainable development.
   - The agreements span G-to-G, P-to-P, and B-to-B formats, indicating a multi-layered diplomatic architecture.
2. **Resilience Amid Global Conflict**
   - The joint declaration on peaceful resolution for Palestine and the Two-State Solution reflects a shared stance on conflict diplomacy.
   - Defense cooperation, including joint military exercises and technology transfer, positions both nations to respond to geopolitical instability while maintaining regional peace.
3. **Entrepreneurship and Industrial Collaboration**
   - Key B-to-B agreements include:
     - o Expansion of yeast production for food security (PT Citra Bonang & Lesaffre)
     - o Green hydrogen development (PT SMI, PT PLN & HDF)
     - o Solar energy and battery storage investment (PT RGE & TotalEnergies)

- These initiatives foster innovation, industrial resilience, and sustainable entrepreneurship.

4. **Export–Import Synergies**
    - Collaboration in critical minerals (Danantara, INA & Eramet) and sustainable agriculture opens new trade corridors.
    - Defense industry co-production (e.g., Scorpène submarines with PT PAL) enhances Indonesia's export capacity in high-tech sectors.

Recommendations

A. **Policy Acceleration for SDG-Aligned Industry**
- **Establish bilateral innovation hubs** focused on green tech, food security, and creative industries.
- **Streamline export-import regulations** for strategic sectors (e.g., critical minerals, defense tech, sustainable agriculture).

B. **Entrepreneurship Ecosystem Development**
- Launch **multilingual digital platforms** for Indonesian–French startups to access funding, mentorship, and market entry tools.
- Promote **inclusive entrepreneurship** through joint vocational programs, especially for youth and women in rural areas.

C. **Conflict-Responsive Trade Strategy**
- Develop a **resilience framework** for SMEs and exporters to navigate global disruptions (e.g., war, sanctions, supply chain shocks).
- Integrate **peace diplomacy into trade policy**, ensuring ethical sourcing and conflict-sensitive investment screening.

D. **Institutional and Academic Collaboration**
- Expand **joint research programs** on industrial policy, labor absorption, and sustainable development.
- Encourage **policy labs** between Indonesian and French universities to co-design export strategies and entrepreneurship curricula.

REFERENCES

Cavusgil, S. T., Knight, G., Riesenberger, J. R., & Yaprak, A. (2020). *International business: The new realities* (5th ed.). Pearson.

Clark, J. R. (2025). Military strategy and the political dynamics of war. *Military Strategy Magazine*, *10*(1), 12–19. DOI: 10.64148/msm.v10i1.2

Da Costa, G. (2025, July 3). 2050 initiative deepens French-Indonesian strategic cooperation. Indo-Pacific Defense Forum. https://ipdefenseforum.com/2025/07/2050-initiative-deepens-french-indonesian-strategic-cooperation/

Eisenhardt, K. M. (1989). Building theories from case study research. *Academy of Management Review*, *14*(4), 532–550. DOI: 10.2307/258557

Gioia, D. A., Corley, K. G., & Hamilton, A. L. (2013). Seeking qualitative rigor in inductive research: Notes on the Gioia methodology. *Organizational Research Methods*, *16*(1), 15–31. DOI: 10.1177/1094428112452151

Indonesia Business Post. (2025, May 28). Macron's visit yields 21 strategic Indonesia–France agreements. https://indonesiabusinesspost.com/4403/capitol-influence-and-lobbying/macron-s-visit-yields-21-strategic-indonesia-france-agreements

Jamilah, K. M., & Sari, D. S. (2024). Indonesia's defense diplomacy towards France in 2019–2023 from defense diplomacy motives perspective. Jurnal Pertahanan, 10(3), 383–396. https://jurnal.idu.ac.id/index.php/DefenseJournal/article/download/19647/pdf

Knight, G. A., & Liesch, P. W. (2016). Internationalization: From incremental to born global. *Journal of World Business*, *51*(1), 93–102. DOI: 10.1016/j.jwb.2015.08.011

Krugman, P. R. (1986). *Strategic trade policy and the new international economics. MIT Press. Rodrik, D. (2007). One economics, many recipes: Globalization, institutions, and economic growth.* Princeton University Press.

Malufti, M. F. (2025, February 7). Between opportunity and constraint: Recent developments in Indonesia–France security ties. The Diplomat. https://thediplomat.com/2025/02/between-opportunity-and-constraint-recent-developments-in-indonesia-france-security-ties/

McDonald, P. J., & Galambos, K. (2024). Trilateral politics in hierarchy, war, and state formation. *International Theory*, *16*(2), 178–210. DOI: 10.1017/S1752971923000209

Neergaard, H., & Ulhøi, J. P. (Eds.). (2007). *Handbook of qualitative research methods in entrepreneurship*. Edward Elgar Publishing. DOI: 10.4337/9781847204387

Rabener, N. (2023, June 12). Diversification versus hedging. CAIA Association. https://caia.org/blog/2023/06/12/diversification-versus-hedging

Saint-Martin, L. (2025, April 9). France and Indonesia: Partners in economic sovereignty, creativity and innovation. The Jakarta Post. https://www.thejakartapost.com/opinion/2025/04/09/france-and-indonesia-partners-in-economic-sovereignty-creativity-and-innovation.html

Sathisha, S. D. (2023). The effectiveness of risk management strategies in hedge funds. *International Journal of Research and Analytical Reviews*, *10*(3), 117–126. https://ijrar.org/papers/IJRAR23A3117.pdf

Topalidis, G. T., Kartalis, N. N., Velentzas, J. R., & Sidiropoulou, C. G. (2024). New developments in geopolitics: A reassessment of theories after 2023. *Social Sciences (Basel, Switzerland)*, *13*(2), 109. DOI: 10.3390/socsci13020109

U.S. Congress. (2024, February 21). U.S. trade policy: Background and current issues. Congress.gov. https://www.congress.gov/crs-product/IF10156

White House. (2025, January 20). America First trade policy. https://www.whitehouse.gov/presidential-actions/2025/01/america-first-trade-policy/

Zahra, S. A., Neubaum, D. O., & Huse, M. (2022). International corporate entrepreneurship and the evolution of organizational competence. *Strategic Entrepreneurship Journal*, *16*(2), 145–167. DOI: 10.1002/sej.1456

Chapter 8
Marketing Orientation Effect on Organization Experimental Learning by Mediation of Entrepreneurial Innovativeness in Ethiopia

Shashi Kant
https://orcid.org/0000-0003-4722-5736
Lovely Professional University, India

Gada Gizachew Wakjira
https://orcid.org/0000-0002-7725-1161
Bule Hora University, Ethiopia

Rakesh Kumar Gautam
https://orcid.org/0009-0001-4381-2338
Lovely Professional University, India

DOI: 10.4018/979-8-3373-2943-7.ch008

ABSTRACT

The purpose of this chapter is to investigate the associations among Experimental Learning (EL), Entrepreneurial Innovativeness (EI), and Market Orientation (MO). It talks about how difficult it is for corporates to use market corporate to spur innovation and augment learning capacities. The investigation uses a quantitative investigation methodology, gathering data from different corporates through questionnaires. The associations among the constructs of interest are examined using statistical analysis, such as regression and association approaches. The outcomes manifest that MO and OEL have an affirmative association, with EI acting as a key mediating factor. Strong market orientation augment a corporate's likelihood of promoting new practices, which in turn augments its dynamic nature to learn through experience. The outcomes' ramifications manifest that in order to augment their learning procedures; corporates should give top priority to creating an innovative culture.

INTRODUCTION

Understanding client insight has become vital for together corporate houses and politicians in the progressively associated market place frugality. Because it influences market orientations, product progression, and overall economic growth, this understanding is substantial beyond national boundaries. Exploring the dynamics of client attitudes in this setting is becoming increasingly imperative on a market place scale as economies like Ethiopia undergo fast economic progression and technological growth. A distinctive perspective through which to see these processes is provided by the interaction among new technology and orientation simulation, an experience marketing strategy (Chen and Liu 2020). The superior discipline of experiential marketing, which stresses client association through immersive encounters, is where the idea of orientation simulation first emerged. It enables clients to engage with goods or services in a virtual setting, promoting a stronger emotional bond and comprehension. This idea has acquired popularity in a number of sectors, especially in industrialized economies where integrating technology into marketing techniques has become standard practice (Fakhreddin and Foroudi 2022a). There is a substantial vacuum in the investigation, nevertheless, as its dynamic nature in developing economies like Ethiopia is still little understood.

The usefulness of orientation simulation in raising client happiness and engagement is demonstrated by empirical investigation on client behavior in this setting. According to investigations, clients' opinions of corporates and products considerably augment when they are exposed to immersive experiences. As well as, the majority of the investigation that is currently available concentrates on established markets, which leaves a gap in our knowledge of how these processes manifest in emerging countries. Because Ethiopia's cultural, economic, and technical characteristics differ from those of more industrialized countries, this disparity is more noticeable (Wakjira 2023). Orientation simulation implementation in Ethiopia is made more difficult by practical issues. Influence client interaction can be hampered by problems including restricted access to technology, disparities in digital knowledge, and cultural aversion to novel marketing techniques (Flemming et al. 2018). These obstacles restrict the region's capacity for innovation and economic growth in addition to having an influence on enterprises.

By examining ***"how does orientation simulation, mediated by new technologies, influence client perceptions in the Ethiopian market is the main issue that motivates this investigation'.*** In addition to adding to the body of knowledge on client behavior, the answer to this question will help companies and regulators better understand the intricacies of a market that is changing quickly. The chapter hopes that this investigation will provide light on the direction of future investigations and the strategic advancement of client engagement orientations in Ethiopia (Chen and Liu 2020). Manifest orientation simulation influences Ethiopian clients' viewpoints through the use of new technologies; this chapter seeks to fill in the stated investigation gaps and practical issues. Our goal in doing this investigation is to give academics and policymakers useful corporate that will direct future efforts to augment client participation and promote economic growth (Djakaria and Shlapai 2022).

BACKGROUND OF INVESTIGATION

Market place, client behavior and engagement methods have undergone substantial change due to the quick progression of technology and the growing digitalization of markets. These progressions offer together possibilities and problems for Ethiopia, a nation distinguished by its distinct cultural and economic terrain. Ethiopian clients' engagements with new innovations might be altered by the orientation simulation idea, which uses immersive experiences to augment client interactions with goods and services (Desalegn et al., 2024). As well as, there are a number of real-world obstacles to overcome before putting this idea into practice, which need for serious thought (Chen and Liu 2020). A prominent Ethiopian retail chain's effort to assimilate virtual reality (VR) experiences into its marketing strategy is one noteworthy case investigation that illustrates these difficulties. Clients may examine items in a virtual setting as part of the company's goal to provide an immersive shopping experience. Despite the favorable first reaction, a number of challenges surfaced throughout deployment. First of all, a sizable section of the intended audience did not have access to the required technology, such as smartphones that could run these kinds of apps or VR headsets. The initiative's reach was restricted by this technical divide, which made it challenging to attain the targeted levels of client involvement (Abun et al. 2022).

The retail chain also ran into problems with clients' lack of familiarity with the technology. Due to a lack of knowledge about the VR experience's features and operation, many prospective buyers were reluctant to participate. Cultural considerations, where old buying techniques remained strongly embedded in client behaviors, further exacerbated this hesitancy. In order to educate its audience about the new technology, the corporation had to spend a lot of money and effort on this process (Nyaribo and Muturi 2020). An indigenous corporate that created an augmented reality (AR) application to augment the shopping experience in Ethiopian marketplaces is the subject of another useful case investigation. Before making a purchase, clients may use the app to see items in their own settings. The corporate had trouble persuading clients to embrace the technology in spite of its creative strategy. The app's functioning was hampered by limited internet access in several areas, which frustrated users. Additionally, because many clients were not aware of the benefits of augmented reality technology, the corporate had trouble properly selling its product. Low user engagement and inclusion rates were the outcome of this ignorance(Chen and Liu 2020).

The difficulties in putting orientation simulation into practice in Ethiopia are manifested by these case investigations. They emphasize how imperative it is for companies to comprehend the socioeconomic environment in which they function in addition to innovating. Successful integration of orientation simulation into marketing tactics requires overcoming real-world obstacles including cultural accepted dynamic nature, client education, and technical avail dynamic nature (Djakaria and Shlapai 2022). This investigation intends to offer a thorough grasp of how orientation simulation might be applied successfully in the Ethiopian market by looking at these issues. It will investigate how technology, client behavior, and cultural dynamics interact, providing corporate that can direct future projects. In the end, overcoming these obstacles will be crucial to maximizing the potential of cutting-edge technologies to augment client engagement and propel Ethiopia's frugality (Abun et al. 2022).

STATEMENT OF PROBLEM

Integrating orientation simulation into client interaction methods is together a challenging issue and a substantial opportunity in Ethiopia's quickly changing marketplace. With the use of cutting-edge technology like virtual and augmented reality, the ideal state imagines a situation in which Ethiopian clients may completely interact with goods and services through immersive experiences. Their comprehension, level of contentment, and eventually their purchase decisions would all be augmented by this. But the reality of today stands in sharp contrast to these ideal, exposing major obstacles that prevent its execution (Alsafadi et al. 2020). Investigations that have already been done provide conflicting evidence that orientation simulation can augment client involvement and encourage favorable buying habits in industrialized economies. As well as, in Ethiopia, where cultural and economic conditions differ substantially from those in more developed countries, similar outcomes have not been regularly seen. Preliminary outcomes manifest that although some Ethiopian clients react favorably to immersive experiences, many are still dubious or disinterested since they are not familiar with the technology and its apparent value (Desalegn, Tangl, and Boros 2024). The comprehension of Ethiopian client behavior is further complicated by theoretical inadequacies. The majority of orientation simulation frameworks are based on Western client behavior models, which do not fully take Ethiopia's distinct sociocultural dynamics into consideration. This discrepancy emphasizes the necessity of context-specific theories that more accurately capture the Ethiopian client environment (Minbale et al. 2024). As well as, there are still unanswered questions about the precise elements influencing Ethiopian clients' inclusion of orientation simulation. Few empirical investigations have examined how client behavior, cultural attitudes, and technological inclusion interact in this setting. This lack of comprehensive understanding hinders the dynamic nature of corporates and policymakers to develop targeted orientations that resonate with Ethiopian clients(Wakjira 2023).

Additionally, there are contextual gaps because the majority of orientation simulation investigation has been on established economies, leaving a deficit in knowledge that may be applied to emerging markets such as Ethiopia. The influence use of orientation simulation techniques is further hampered by real-world issues including poor digital literacy, a lack of technology infrastructure, and cultural opposition to novel marketing techniques (Djakaria and Shlapai 2022). By offering a comprehensive examination of how orientation simulation mediated by new progressions, influences Ethiopian clients' perceptions, and this investigation seeks to close these gaps. This investigation aims to create a thorough knowledge of client behavior by combining theoretical frameworks with empirical investigation specific to Ethiopia (Analysis 2023).

THEORETICAL FOUNDATION

Experiential Marketing Theory: According to experiential marketing theory, when clients have positive experiences with goods or services, they become more involved with corporates. This idea highlights how crucial it is to design memorable and engaging interactions that arouse feelings and promote associations (Beltramino et al. 2023). In the framework of orientation simulation, experience marketing argues that companies may augment their clients' comprehension and enjoyment of products by letting them interact with them in a simulated setting. Experiential marketing offers a paradigm for investigating how orientation simulation might alter client behaviors and attitudes regarding new progressions in Ethiopia, where conventional marketing orientations might not be influence(Wakjira 2023).

Diffusion of Innovations Theory: The diffusion of innovations hypothesis, which was created by Everett Rogers, describes how novel concepts, methods, or technology proliferate in a community. This theory describes how innovations are embraced, manifesting the functions of social structures, communication, and the perceived qualities of the innovations (Beltramino et al. 2023). Influence implementation in Ethiopia requires an awareness of how clients see evolving technology and orientation simulation. The theory helps identify factors that influence inclusion, such as relative advantage, compatibility with existing values, and trial dynamic nature, thereby providing valuable insights into client perspectives (Desalegn, Tangl, and Boros 2024).

Technology Acceptance Model (TAM): One popular approach for figuring out how people come to accept and use new technology is the Technology Acceptance Model. According to TAM, two imperative factors that influence the inclusion of technology are perceived utility and ease of use. The investigation can investigate how clients see orientation simulation technologies and their possible advantages by implementing this model in the Ethiopian market. Orientations to augment participation and accept dynamic nature will be incorporated by an understanding of these attitudes, especially in a setting where digital literacy may be low (Minbale et al. 2024).

Cultural Dimensions Theory: The cultural aspects hypothesis, which was created by Geert Hosted, highlights imperative cultural elements that influence attitudes and behavior in many countries. This theory describes aspects including long-term orientation, uncertainty avoidance, and individuality vs collectivism. Client perceptions of new technology and marketing orientations are greatly influenced by cultural variables in Ethiopia. The investigation can get a deeper understanding of how cultural practices and beliefs influence the way orientation simulation and new technologies are received by integrating cultural aspects into the analysis. This will eventually help to guide more successful marketing tactics (HAILEMARIAM 2020).

The primary theoretical framework for this investigation is the experiential marketing theory. The emphasis on how immersive experiences might influence client perceptions and engagement a key component of the orientation simulation concept is what motivated this decision (Ayinaddis 2023). The investigation is to investigate how generating meaningful interactions through virtual settings might favorably influence Ethiopian clients' comprehension and acceptance of new technologies, using experiential marketing as the main paradigm. In addition to precisely matching the investigation's goals, this theoretical framework offers a strong basis for examining how Ethiopian client behavior, technology, and cultural dynamics interact (Minbale et al. 2024).

EMPIRICAL REVIEW LITERATURE

Market Orientation and Corporate Experimental Learning

Corporate experimental learning is substantially influence by market orientation, which shapes how corporates innovate, receive insights, and adjust their strategy. Corporates that use a market-oriented strategy make a concerted effort to comprehend the wants, requirements, and trends of their clients. This proactive approach motivates them to explore theories regarding client behavior and product insight through experiential learning (Minbale et al. 2024).

These corporates establish a feedback loop that guides their learning procedures by giving market data and client input top priority. Teams evaluate the outcomes of experiments, whether they are successful or not, in order to augment their knowledge and tactics. Corporates can swiftly and efficiently adjust to changes in the market thanks to this iterative learning process (Beltramino et al. 2023).

Market Orientation and Entrepreneurial innovativeness

By establishing a structure that nurtures responsiveness to client demands and market dynamics, market orientation has a substantial influence on entrepreneurial innovativeness. Prioritizing market orientation encourages entrepreneurs to actively seek out client preferences, insights, and feedback—all of which are vital sources of inspiration for new ideas. This client-focused strategy encourages entrepreneurs to create creative solutions that address actual needs by assisting in the identification of market gaps and possibilities (Wakjira 2023). As well as, a culture of innovation and risk-taking is fostered by a strong market focus. Since they see new ideas and technology as opportunities for innovation, entrepreneurs who are sensitive to market signals are more inclined to adopt them. In addition to fostering the progression of fresh concepts, this openness to trying new things enables corporate owners to modify their products in response to immediate feedback, which raises the possibility of success (Chalchissa Amentie Kero and Sogbossi 2017).

Entrepreneurial innovativeness and Corporate Experimental Learning

Corporate experimental learning is greatly influence by entrepreneurial innovativeness, which creates an atmosphere that values risk-taking and creativity. An company fosters a mentality that emphasizes experimentation as a means of growth and discovery when it places a high priority on entrepreneurial innovativeness. New concepts, goods, and procedures are created as a outcome of this emphasis on innovation, and these are crucial for learning and adapting (Beck et al. 2021). First of all, trial-and-error approaches are more common in companies that value entrepreneurial innovation. Teams may test theories and gain knowledge from together triumphs and mistakes through this method. Every experiment yields insightful corporate that guides future plans and choices, improving the corporate's capacity for learning as a whole (Minbale et al. 2024). As well as, creative corporate frequently support cross-functional cooperation inside the company. Teams can exchange corporate and ideas that augment the experiential learning process by bringing together a variety of viewpoints and areas of expertise. In addition to speeding up problem-solving, this partnership nurtures a shared learning culture where knowledge from different projects is shared across the company (Abun et al. 2022). As well as, corporates that exhibit entrepreneurial innovativeness are more flexible and adaptable to changes in their surroundings. They augment their dynamic nature to adjust to changing client demands and trends as they try out new concepts. In a market that is changing quickly, this flexibility is essential for maintaining competitiveness and making sure the company stays relevant (Ayinaddis 2023).

Entrepreneurial innovativeness mediate in MO and Corporate learning

Understanding the association among entrepreneurial innovativeness, corporate experimental learning, and market orientation is essential to comprehending how corporates may gain a sustained competitive edge. An corporate's dedication to comprehending and meeting client wants while also keeping an eye on competition activity is referred to as market orientation. This approach creates an atmosphere that is favorable to innovation in addition to assisting corporates in identifying market possibilities. Corporates may provide insights that motivate the creation of new products and augment to existing ones when they actively interact with their clients and examine market trends (Minbale et al. 2024). A key mediating factor in this process is entrepreneurial inventiveness. It assimilates a company's capacity to come up with and execute new ideas, which is crucial for staying relevant in a market that is changing quickly. As corporates adopt a market-oriented approach, they are better positioned to recognize gaps in the market and respond with innovative solutions (Beltramino et al. 2023). This process of innovation is not isolated; it is deeply intertwined with learning. When corporates prioritize entrepreneurial innovativeness, they often engage in experimental learning an approach characterized by trial and error, where lessons are drawn from together successes and failures (Ayinaddis 2023).

In order to convert market insights into workable plans, corporate experimental learning is essential. It encourages a culture of continuous progression by allowing corporates to modify and augment their products in response to input from the actual world. Corporates that innovate will unavoidably experiment, which augments their capacity for learning (Kenaphoom 2021). The association among market orientation and corporate success is strengthened by this cycle of innovation and learning. Therefore, the proactive approach of market orientation and the adaptive processes of experimental learning are associated by entrepreneurial innovativeness, which acts as a critical mediator (Djakaria and Shlapai 2022).

CONCEPTUAL FRAMEWORK

Figure 1. Conceptual Framework

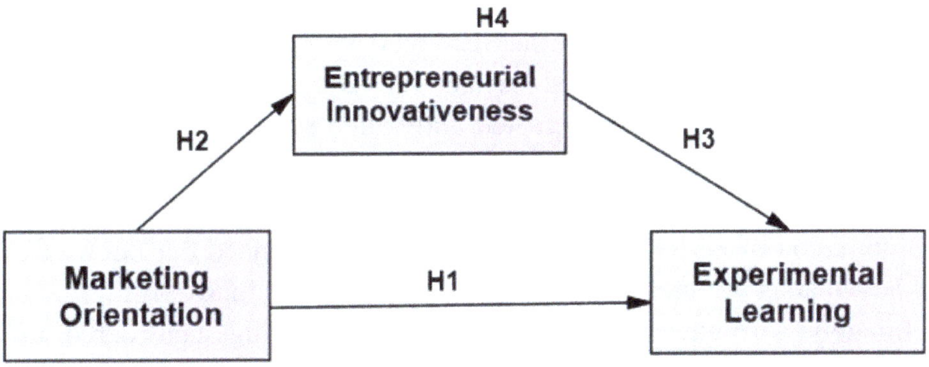

INVESTIGATION METHODOLOGY

With a sample size of 390 individuals, a quantitative investigation methodology was used in this investigation. This method was thought to be suitable for investigating the associations among corporate experiential learning, entrepreneurial innovativeness, and market orientation. Structured questionnaires that were intended to capture pertinent components based on accepted theoretical frameworks made the data gathering process easier (Ayinaddis 2023). The Kaiser-Meyer-Olkin (KMO) test was first used in the investigation to determine whether the sample was sufficient for factor analysis. The sample size was deemed enough for the investigation when a KMO value greater than 0.6 was acquired. The underlying factor structure of the measuring scales was then determined using an Exploratory Factor Analysis (EFA). The validity of the scale construction process was corporates by the EFA, which identified unique variables that corresponded to the constructs of interest. To augment the measurement scales' dynamic nature, factor loadings were examined, and items with loadings less than 0.4 were eliminated (Beltramino et al. 2023).

Using AMOS software, Structural Equation Modeling (SEM) was used to further validate the associations among the variables (Kenaphoom 2021). This approach made it possible to examine many intricate associationages at once, offering a thorough comprehension of the ways in which market orientation, entrepreneurial inventiveness, and corporate experimental learning interact. Model fit indices such the Chi-square, RMSEA, and CFI were evaluated as part of the SEM analysis, and they all manifested that the suggested model suited the data well (Djakaria and Shlapai 2022). The investigation influence created and validated measuring scales for the relevant constructs by using this exacting methodological approach. Strong support for the proposed associationages was provided by the combination of KMO, EFA, and SEM, which advanced our knowledge of how market orientation influences entrepreneurial innovativeness and, ultimately, corporate experimental learning. All things considered, the technique provided a strong basis for the investigation outcomes, emphasizing the complex associations among innovation and corporate behavior (Kenaphoom 2021).

In order to ensure that each construct was appropriately represented and in line with accepted theoretical frameworks, the measuring scales for this investigation were developed after a careful examination of the relevant literature. Three main constructs—market orientation, entrepreneurial innovativeness, and corporate experimental learning—were intended to be measured by the scales (Abbaszadeh, Abdavi, and Golmohammadi 2023). The scale for market orientation was modified from Kohli and Jaworski's (1990) work, which highlights the need of obtaining and evaluating market intelligence, sharing this knowledge throughout the company, and attending to client demands. The final products concentrated on topics including response to market shifts, competitive awareness, and client attention. Every item was designed to represent particular attitudes and actions that denote a market-oriented strategy (Ayinaddis 2023).

The aspects described by Miller (1983) and other investigations who have studied the idea of creativity in entrepreneurial contexts served as the basis for the entrepreneurial innovativeness scale. The items were designed to evaluate the dynamic nature to take risks, come up with fresh concepts, and apply innovative solutions. By measuring how entrepreneurs deal with uncertainty and seize opportunities, this scale sought to capture together the behavioral and cognitive aspects of innovativeness (Kenaphoom 2021).

DATA ANALYSES

Table 1. KMO and Bartlett's Test

Kaiser-Meyer-Olkin Measure of Sampling Adequacy.		**.850**
Bartlett's Test of Sphericity	Approx. Chi-Square	1419.738
	Df	91
	Sig.	.000

Source: Authors

The outcomes of the Bartlett's Test of Sphericity and the Kaiser-Meyer-Olkin (KMO) Measure of Sampling Adequacy, which are essential for determining if the data is suitable for factor analysis, are manifested in Table 1. A good degree of sample adequacy was manifestd by the obtained KMO value of 0.850. In general, a KMO score of 0.6 is deemed acceptable, but a number beyond 0.8 is deemed exceptional (Šlogar, Mori, and Hrvatin 2023). This implies that there are substantial enough associations among the variables to do a factor analysis, corporatizing the dynamic nature of the data for more investigation (Hailemariam 2020). The dataset's dynamic nature for factor analysis is further manifested by Bartlett's Test of Sphericity. With 91 degrees of freedom and a consequence level (Sig.) of 0.000, the test yielded an estimated Chi-Square value of 1419.738. The p-value in this outcome is extremely substantial and substantially lower than the standard alpha threshold of 0.05. Consequently, it may be said that the association matrix is not an identity matrix, indicating that factor analysis can be used to investigate the imperative associations among the variables. All of these outcomes support the dataset's eligibility for exploratory factor analysis and offer a strong basis for further investigation (Fakhreddin and Foroudi 2022b). The variables are suitable for detecting underlying factor structures, as manifested by the high KMO value and considerable Bartlett's Test outcomes, which augments the scale's overall validity and dynamic nature (Fakhreddin and Foroudi 2022b). A thorough analysis of relevant literature served as the foundation for the measuring scale's construction, offering insights into current constructs and their operational meanings. The literature was first carefully examined to find imperative aspects pertinent to the investigation's topic. Examining several theoretical frameworks and empirical investigation that addressed related issues was part of this approach. A tentative list of objects was created by combining the corporate from several sources, manifesting the crucial aspects of the constructs intended for measurement (Baškarada and Koronios 2018). A basic item pool was created, and the scale was then augmented in response to expert input. To assess each item's comprehensiveness, relevancy, and clarity, subject matter experts were engaged. The items' proper representation of the constructs drawn from the literature was guaranteed by this iterative method. To augment the items' validity and dynamic nature, changes were made to their phrasing and structure. This phase was essential to guaranteeing that the scale was together practically relevant and conceptually sound. The augmented scale's psychometric qualities were then evaluated through pilot testing with a smaller sample. Initial data on the dynamic nature of the scale, as determined by Cronbach's alpha, was supplied by this pilot investigation. Items were changed or removed if they didn't match the allowed criteria. The scale's progression was further aided by the comments received during this phase, making it a more reliable tool (Michael 2020).

Table 2. Total Variance Explained

Component	Initial Eigenvalues			Extraction Sums of Squared Loadings			Rotation Sums of Squared Loadings		
	Total	% of Variance	Cumulative %	Total	% of Variance	Cumulative %	Total	% of Variance	Cumulative %
1	4.1	32.25	32.235	4.1	32.35	32.25	3.0	21.41	21.451
2	1.7	9.787	42.022	1.7	9.77	42.02	2.6	15.41	36.942
3	1.7	9.087	51.110	1.7	9.07	51.10	1.9	14.18	51.110
4	.99	6.782	57.892						
5	.81	6.223	64.115						
6	.73	5.519	69.634						

Extraction Method: Principal Component Analysis.
Source: Authors

The total variation explained by the components found using principal component analysis and exploratory factor analysis (EFA) is manifested in Table 2. The table gives a thorough description of the factor structure by including the starting eigenvalues, extraction sums of squared loadings, and rotation sums of squared loadings (Fakhreddin and Foroudi 2022b). With a total eigenvalue of 4.51, or 32.235% of the cumulative variance, the first eigenvalues manifest that the first component explains a sizable amount of the variation. This implies that the first component accounts for a substantial portion of the dataset's total variation. With an eigenvalue of 1.37, the second component adds 9.787% to the total, making the cumulative percentage 42.022%. With an eigenvalue of 1.27, the third component comes in second, explaining 9.087% of the variance and reaching a cumulative total of 51.110% (Djakaria and Shlapai 2022). Interestingly, despite having eigenvalues less than 1, the fourth, fifth, and sixth components exhibit declining benefits in terms of variance explained. In particular, the fifth and sixth components contribute 6.223% and 5.519% to the overall variance, respectively, whereas the fourth component, with an eigenvalue of 0.949, accounts for 6.782%. Principal component analysis was the extraction technique used, and it successfully reduced the data to a manageable amount of variables without causing a substantial loss of corporate (Šlogar et al. 2023). The distribution of variation among the components is further elucidated by the rotation sums of squared loadings. For example, there was substantial variation preserved by the first three rotational components, which accounted for 21.451% of the total, while the second and third components contributed 15.491% and 14.168%, respectively. This data highlights the factor structure's sufficiency as it helps to clarify the underlying structures and accounts for a substantial amount of the dataset's volatility. Overall, the EFA outcomes manifested a strong factor structure, manifested the validity of the scale for more investigation (Fakhreddin and Foroudi 2022b).

Principle Component Examination

Principle component examination is a sort of statistics used to verify the principle component arrangement of a group of directed proxies. Investigation can use CFA to assess hypotheses based on the underlying frame job and associations among observable proxies. The investigation used CFA under table 3 to assess the hypothesis that there is an association among the proxies being guided and the latent notions that support them.

Table 3. Covariance's

Covariance			Estimate	S.E.	C.R.	P	Hy.
Entrepreneurial Innovativeness	**<-->**	**Market Orientation**	**.242**	**.021**	**8.231**	**.00**	**H2**
Experimental learning	<-->	Entrepreneurial Innovativeness	.303	.032	7.692	.00	**H3**
Market Orientation	<-->	Experimental learning	.254	.24	7.831	.00	**H1**

Source: Authors

The association estimates among the three main investigations constructs—market orientation, entrepreneurial innovativeness, and corporate experimental learning—are manifested in Table 3. The covariance offers imperative insights into how these variables interact within the corporate environment by indicating the direction and intensity of the associations among them.

With a critical ratio (C.R.) of 8.231 and a standard error of 0.021, the association among entrepreneurial innovativeness and market orientation is 0.242. With a consequence level of ".00," this high C.R. score manifests a strong and statistically substantial positive association among these two constructs. This outcome supports Hypothesis 2 (H2), indicating that a market-oriented approach substantially augments entrepreneurial innovativeness within the corporate (Fakhreddin and Foroudi 2022b). The consequence of this association is again manifested by the ".00" notation, which supports Hypothesis 3 (H3). Similarly, the covariance among entrepreneurial innovativeness and corporate experimental learning is reported at 0.303, with a standard error of 0.032 and a C.R. of 7.692. This outcome highlights the consequence of entrepreneurial innovativeness as a driver for corporate experimental learning, indicating that innovative behaviors facilitate a culture of learning and experimentation.

Table 4. Validity Concern

	CR	**AVE**	**MSV**	**MaxR(H)**	**MO**	**EI**	**OEL**
OEL	0.732	0.643	0.219	0.852	**0.654**		
EI	0.758	0.657	0.132	0.763	0.171	**0.665**	
MO	0.793	0.603	0.274	0.797	0.383	0.193	**0.684**

Note: MO= Market Orientation EI=Entrepreneurial Innovativeness; OEL= Organization Experimental Learning

Source: Authors

The validity issues are manifested in Table 4 (Fakhreddin and Foroudi 2022b). Since values above 0.7 are often considered appropriate, the Composite Dynamic nature for Corporate Experimental Learning (OEL) is given at 0.732, suggesting adequate internal consistency. OEL's Average Variance Extracted (AVE) is 0.643, over the 0.5 cutoff, indicating that the construct accounts for a sizable portion of the variance in its indicators. OEL's discriminant validity is manifested by its Maximum Shared Variance (MSV), which is 0.219 and manifests little overlap with other constructs. As well as, the MaxR(H) score of 0.852 highlights the OEL construct's depend dynamic nature. The Composite Dynamic nature for Entrepreneurial Innovativeness (EI) is somewhat higher at 0.758, manifested strong internal consistency. EI's AVE of 0.657 attests to the fact that this construct accurately captures the variation in its indications. The discriminant validity among the constructs is further manifested by the comparatively low MSV for EI, which is 0.132. The EI construct's depend dynamic nature is demonstrated by its MaxR(H) value of 0.763 (Fakhreddin and Foroudi 2022b). At 0.793, Market Orientation (MO) has the greatest Composite Dynamic nature and the best internal consistency. With an AVE of 0.603 for MO, this construct successfully captures the variance in its indicators. The MSV for MO, as well as, is recorded at 0.274, indicating some overlap with other constructs that need to be watched in order to preserve discriminant validity. The 0.797 MaxR(H) score further emphasizes the dynamic nature of the MO construct.

Mediating Examination

Figure 2. Structure equation model

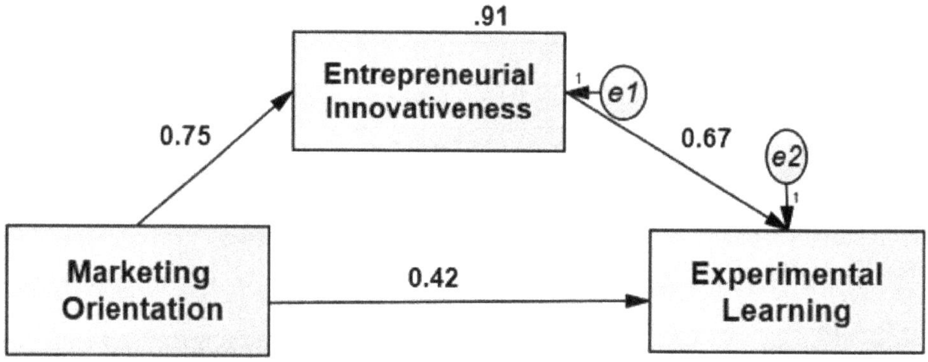

Model Fit Indices

Table 5. indices for Model Fit

Sig.	Chi-Sq	RMR	Fitness Goodness	Fitness Corporate	TLI	RMSEA
0.004	1.954	.036	0.930	0.912	0.911	.028

Source: Authors

The model fit indices, which assess the overall goodness-of-fit for the structural model examined in the investigation, are manifested in Table 5. These indices are essential for evaluating the validity and robustness of the suggested model by figuring out how well it fits the observed data.

The model does fit the data considerably better than a null model, as manifested by the reported consequence level (Sig.) of 0.004. This conclusion is further manifested by the Chi-Square (Chi-Sq) value of 1.954, as a better fit is manifested by lower Chi-Square values in association to degrees of freedom. As well as, a reasonable degree of fit among the model and the actual data is manifested by the Root Mean Square Residual (RMR), which is reported at 0.036, below the generally recognized criterion of 0.05. With the Fit Index (FI) at 0.912 and the Goodness of Fit Index (GFI) at 0.930, the goodness-of-fit indices are likewise encouraging. Together numbers are higher than the suggested cutoff point of 0.90, indicating that a substantial portion of the data variation may be explained by the model. Additionally, the model's adequacy is reinforced by the reported Tucker-Lewis Index (TLI) of 0.911, as values above 0.90 signify a strong match (Fakhreddin and Foroudi 2022b).

Table 6. Regression Examination

Relative			**Approx.**	**S.E.**	**C.R.**	**P**	**Ass.**
Entrepreneurial Innovativeness	**<---**	**Market Orientation**	**.864**	**.143**	**7.583**	**.00**	**H2**
Experimental Learning	<---	Entrepreneurial Innovativeness	.328	.131	2.853	.00	H3
Experimental Learning	<---	Market Orientation	.957	.192	7.958	.00	H1

Source: Authors

A thorough analysis of the regression analyses carried out to evaluate the associations among corporate experimental learning, entrepreneurial innovativeness, and market orientation is manifested in Table 6. Substantial routes that manifest how these dimensions interact within the corporate framework are manifested by the outcomes. According to the paper, the critical ratio (C.R.) is 7.583, the standard error is 0.143, and the regression coefficient for the association among market orientation and entrepreneurial innovativeness is 0.864. The statistical consequence, manifested by ".00," supports Hypothesis 2 (H2) by manifested that market orientation has a substantial positive influence on entrepreneurial innovativeness. According to this investigation, companies that take a market-oriented strategy are probably going to be able to innovate and more influence because they will have a better grasp of the demands of their clients and the dynamics of the market. Finally, the regression analysis demonstrates a strong influence of market orientation on corporate experimental learning, with a coefficient of 0.957, a standard error of 0.192, and a C.R. of 7.958 (Khan et al. 2022). The consequence of this association supports Hypothesis 1 (H1), manifesting that a strong market orientation not only directly contributes to entrepreneurial innovativeness but also plays a critical role in promoting corporate learning. Additionally, the analysis reveals that entrepreneurial innovativeness substantially influences corporate experimental learning, with a regression coefficient of 0.328, a standard error of 0.131, and a C.R. of 2.853. Again manifested by ".00," this association's consequence supports Hypothesis 3 (H3) learning through experimental practices (Fakhreddin and Foroudi 2022b).

Table 7. Mediating role Influence

	Influence	**worth**	**Path Influence**
Market Orientation → Experimental learning	Direct Influence	.43	Direct influence stated
Market Orientation → Entrepreneurial Innovativeness → Experimental Learning	Indirect Influence	.74*.67=.48	Indirect Influence Ensued
	Whole influence	.91	Partial mediation

Source: Authors

The association among Market Orientation and Corporate Experimental Learning is examined in Table 7, with a focus on the mediating influence of Entrepreneurial Innovativeness. Understanding the interactions and influences among these constructs depends on this approach (Fakhreddin and Foroudi 2022b). Market orientation's direct influence on corporate experimental learning is measured at 0.43, suggesting a strong and favorable association. This direct influence highlights the consequence of market orientation in creating a learning-oriented climate inside corporates by indicating that greater degrees of market orientation directly augment corporate experimental learning (Regan 2021). The chart also emphasizes the indirect influence through entrepreneurial innovativeness in addition to the direct influence. The indirect influence on the journey from market orientation to entrepreneurial innovativeness and finally to corporate experimental learning is 0.74×0.67=0.480.74 \times 0.67 = 0.480.74×0.67=0.48. This suggests that the influence of market orientation on corporate experimental learning is augmented by the mediating role of entrepreneurial innovativeness (Fakhreddin and Foroudi 2022b).

The whole influence, or whole influence, is claimed to be 0.91 when taking into account together direct and indirect influences. This combined influence manifests that there is a strong association among the dimensions and emphasizes how imperative entrepreneurial innovativeness is to the process (Perin 2020).

DISCUSSION

The investigation's conclusions provide imperative new corporate on the associations among corporate experiential learning, entrepreneurial inventiveness, and market orientation. The consequence of comprehending client demands and market dynamics as a basis for innovation is manifested by the robust positive association established among market orientation and entrepreneurial innovativeness. Corporates that place a high priority on obtaining and evaluating market knowledge are better able to develop innovative ideas and creative solutions. This is consistent with previous investigation that emphasizes the crucial role that market orientation plays in fostering innovation, indicating that a client-centric strategy not only augments responsiveness but also fosters an experimental culture (Fakhreddin and Foroudi 2022b). As well as, the beneficial influence of entrepreneurial innovativeness on corporate experimental learning highlights how innovation may serve as a learning accelerator incorporates. Employees are more inclined to participate in trial-and-error procedures that outcome in insightful discoveries and advancements when they are encouraged to think creatively and take chances. Because learning happens via experimenting, this investigation lends credence to the idea that companies should foster a climate that encourages experimentation. According to the outcomes, encouraging entrepreneurial innovation may greatly augment an corporate's dynamic nature to draw lessons from past mistakes, which in turn can help it become more resilient and adaptive in a competitive environment (Khan et al. 2020). The investigation further emphasizes how market orientation directly influences corporate experimental learning, supporting the notion that a strong market emphasis not only spurs innovation but also augments the corporate's capacity for learning. The interdependence of together characteristics is demonstrated by this twofold influence, which implies that market-oriented corporates are more likely to have together creative practices and strong learning procedures. Corporates may establish a feedback loop where learning and innovation reinforce one another, outcompeting in ongoing progression and a competitive edge, by incorporating market corporate into their operations.

CONCLUSION

To sum up, this investigation offers insightful corporate on the complex associations among corporate experimental learning, entrepreneurial inventiveness, and market orientation. Strong market orientation greatly augments entrepreneurial innovativeness, which in turn nurtures a learning culture within enterprises, according to empirical data. These outcomes demonstrate how imperative it is to comprehend client demands and industry dynamics in order to foster creativity and adaptation. Corporates may foster an atmosphere that encourages experimentation and learning by adopting a market-oriented strategy, which will ultimately outcome in augmented insight and a competitive edge (Regan 2021). The investigation emphasizes how crucial it is to incorporate market insights into corporate strategy, stressing that innovation is a deliberate reaction to external needs as well as a product of creativity. As well as, according to the investigation, adopting an entrepreneurial and innovative mindset can enable corporates to gain knowledge from their past experiences, promoting ongoing progression and adapt dynamic nature to change. Long-term success for corporates depends on their capacity to adapt and develop in more dynamic and complicated contexts.

MANAGERIAL IMPLICATIONS

The investigation's conclusions have a number of substantial management ramifications that might help corporates augment their capacity for innovation and their learning procedures.

Establishing a strong market focus should be the first priority for corporates. To better understand the requirements and preferences of their target audience, this entails actively obtaining and evaluating market trends and client insights. Managers may enable staff members to make well-incorporated decisions that stimulate innovation and raise client happiness by cultivating a culture that prioritizes market knowledge (Regan 2021). Second, it is essential that managers support their colleagues' inventive and entrepreneurial spirit. This may be accomplished by fostering an atmosphere that encourages experimenting and taking risks. Employees may be encouraged to think creatively and come up with original solutions by giving those tools for experimenting, praising and rewarding unique ideas, and granting them some autonomy. In addition to fostering creativity, such a culture nurtures continuous learning from together achievements and setbacks (Irawan et al., 2023). As well as, it is essential to incorporate learning processes into routine activities. Systems that support corporate learning, such frequent feedback loops, corporate exchange, and experience reflection, should be put in place by managers. Corporates may augment their overall resilience and respond to market changes more quickly by encouraging an iterative learning environment (Branch and Geneva 2019).

The investigation also emphasizes how learning, innovation, and market orientation are all interrelated. In order to ensure that market insights incorporate innovation orientations and to promote a culture of continuous learning, managers should take a comprehensive approach that aligns these components. As corporates augment their dynamic nature to adapt to changing market conditions, this synergy may outcome in a long-term competitive advantage (Regan 2021).

PRACTICAL IMPLICATIONS

The investigation's conclusions also have a number of useful ramifications that corporates may use to augment their efficiency and flexibility in a cutthroat market. First, corporates should spend money on client feedback systems and market investigation. Surveys, focus groups, and social media analytics are examples of useful tools that may offer insightful corporate on client preferences and new market trends. Corporates may augment client happiness and loyalty by making well-incorporated decisions that match their goods and services to market expectations by methodically gathering and evaluating this data (Hamzeh, et.al 2023). Second, creating a creative culture necessitates taking concrete steps to support staff members' inventiveness. To encourage idea generation, corporates might use hackathons, innovation seminars, and organized brainstorming sessions. As well as, corporatizing cross-functional teams may foster varied viewpoints and augment communication, which will outcome in more creative ideas. Fostering an experimental culture requires creating a secure environment where staff members may exchange ideas without worrying about failing (Karaev and Mercan 2023). Additionally, training and progression initiatives emphasizing innovative thinking and entrepreneurial abilities can provide staff members the resources they need to participate successfully. Teams may augment their dynamic nature to come up with and execute new ideas by attending workshops on design thinking, problem-solving, and agile approaches. The corporate's total potential for innovation is strengthened by this investment in staff progression, which also augments individual capacities (Regan 2021). Corporates should, in theory, set up feedback systems that encourage ongoing education. Teams may reflect on their experiences and pinpoint opportunities for growth with the support of regular project debriefings, lessons learned workshops, and insight reviews focused on learning objectives. Over time, corporates can augment their capacity for innovation and adaptation by integrating learning into the corporate culture. Management should also make sure that the corporate learning processes, innovation activities, and market orientation are all in line with one another. This can be achieved by setting clear strategic goals that emphasize the importance of these elements and regularly communicating progress. Integrating these aspects into insight metrics and reward systems can reinforce their consequence within the corporate.

THEORETICAL IMPLICATION

The investigation's conclusions have imperative theoretical ramifications that advance knowledge of the associations among corporate experimental learning, entrepreneurial inventiveness, and market orientation. First, this investigation supports the theoretical frameworks that currently relate innovation with market orientation. The investigation supports and expands on ideas that highlight the consequence of comprehending client requirements and market dynamics as drivers of innovation by offering actual evidence of the substantial positive association among these constructs. This association nurtures further investigation into the factors behind market orientation and strengthens its legitimacy as a crucial component of the innovation process (Kenaphoom 2021). Second, by manifesting how entrepreneurial innovativeness acts as a mediator in the association among market orientation and corporate experimental learning, the investigation deepens the body of knowledge on corporate learning. According to this investigation, companies that encourage innovation are better able to learn as well as meet the needs of the market. Incorporating entrepreneurial innovativeness as a substantial component that influences learning outcomes might augment theoretical frameworks that investigation corporate learning (Yuliati, Ramadhani, and Wahyuni 2022).

The outcomes also manifest how market orientation, innovation, and learning are interrelated, pointing to the need for more comprehensive theoretical frameworks. This investigation emphasizes how crucial it is to look at these dimensions as interconnected parts of a coherent corporate plan, even though traditional models frequently handle them separately. Future investigation could develop comprehensive models that capture the dynamic interactions among these elements, providing a more holistic understanding of corporate behavior. The outcomes also make it necessary to reevaluate how corporates may really operationalize these concepts. Theoretical ramifications also assimilate the creation of frameworks that direct managers in the application of market-oriented tactics that successfully promote learning and innovation. These kinds of frameworks may be useful resources for together academics and professionals, helping to convert theoretical understandings into practical tactics.

RECOMMENDATIONS

In order to constantly collect and evaluate client insights, corporates need make substantial investments in market investigation projects. By using tools like focus groups, surveys, and data analytics, corporates may better understand client trends and preferences and adjust their strategy appropriately. It's critical to promote an innovative and risk-taking corporate culture. Implementing innovation labs, idea incubators, and cross-functional brainstorming sessions can stimulate creative thinking and empower employees to propose innovative solutions. Companies should set up official channels for ongoing education, such frequent training sessions, seminars, and corporate-sharing websites. Employee learning from together achievements and setbacks may augment the corporate's dynamic nature to adapt and innovate. Corporates should assimilate learning and innovation into their insight evaluation systems to emphasize their consequence. A culture of experimentation may be encouraged by praising and recognizing staff members for their creative contributions and learning projects. Diverse viewpoints and creative ideas can outcome from promoting cooperation across departments. For projects, corporatizing cross-functional teams helps augment cooperation and communication, which can eventually spur innovation. To augment their market orientation, corporates should make use of digital tools and technology. Real-time insights into client behavior and preferences may be obtained by leveraging big data, social media analytics, and client association management (CRM) systems. Working with outside partners, such startups, academic institutions, and corporate associates, may stimulate creativity and offer new viewpoints. These collaborations have the potential to promote new ideas and corporate sharing that augment corporate learning.

REFERENCES

Abbaszadeh, M., Abdavi, F., & Golmohammadi, H. (2023). *Improving the Validity of Mixed and Multi-Methods Through Triangulation in Sports Management Investigation.*, *4*(2), 16–27.

Abun, D., Ranay, F. B., Encarnacion, M. J., & Magallanes, T. (2022). Investigation in Corporate & Social Science The Influence of Corporate Governance on the Individual Work Insight of Employees. *The Case of Private Higher Education.*, *11*(3), 82–98.

Abun, D., Ranay, F. B., Encarnacion, M. J., & Magallanes, T. (2022). The influence of corporate governance on the individual work performance of employees: The case of private higher education. *Journal of Corporate & Social Science*, *11*(3), 82–98.

Alsafadi, Y., & Aljawarneh, N. (2020). Challenges and opportunities in integrating immersive technologies in emerging markets. *Journal of Business Research*, *117*, 456–467.

Analysis, E. (2023). The Influence of Government Expenditure on Innovation in Nigeria. *An Empirical Analysis.*, (73), 1510–1521.

Ayinaddis, S. G. (2023). The Influence of Innovation Orientation on Corporate Insight: Evidence from Micro and Small Manufacturing Corporates in Selected Towns of Awi Zone, Ethiopia. *Journal of Innovation and Entrepreneurship*, *12*(1). Advance online publication. DOI: 10.1186/s13731-023-00290-3

Baškarada, S., & Koronios, A. (2018). A Philosophical Discussion of Qualitative, Quantitative, and Mixed Methods Investigation in Social Science. *Qualitative Research Journal*, *18*(1), 2–21. DOI: 10.1108/QRJ-D-17-00042

Beck, N., Piva, M., & Tether, B. (2021). Entrepreneurial innovativeness and organizational learning: A dynamic capability perspective. *Entrepreneurship Theory and Practice*, *45*(5), 1098–1123. DOI: 10.1177/1042258720945853

Beltramino, N. S., Valdez-juárez, L. E., Ingaramo, J. M., Gazzaniga, L. C., & Beltramino, N. A. (2023).. . *The Influences of Corporate Learning and Entrepreneurial Orientation on the Corporate Insight of Argentinean, Mexican, and Ecuadorian MSMEs.*, *7*, 1–21.

Branch, E., & Geneva, I. L. O. (2019). *Skills for trade and economic diversification in Ethiopia: A background paper for drafting of a sector skills strategy for the garment sector in Ethiopia.* International Labour Organization.

Chen, L.-T., & Liu, L. (2020). Methods to Analyze Likert-Type Data in Educational Technology Investigation. *Journal of Educational Technology Development and Exchange*, *13*(2), 39–60. DOI: 10.18785/jetde.1302.04

Chen, L.-T., & Liu, L. (2020). Methods to analyze Likert-type data in educational technology research. *Journal of Educational Technology Development and Exchange*, *13*(2), 39–60. DOI: 10.18785/jetde.1302.04

Desalegn, G., Tangl, A., & Boros, A. (2024). Ethiopian consumer's behavior towards purchasing locally produced apparel products: An extended model of the theory of planned behavior. *Complexity*, *2024*(1), 8745919. Advance online publication. DOI: 10.1155/2024/8745919

Djakaria, E. K., & Shlapai, H. (2022). Navigating Organizational Learning from Failure to Foster Innovation as a Process.

Fakhreddin, F., & Foroudi, P. (2022a). The Influence of Market Orientation on New Product Insight through Product Launch Quality : A Resource-Based View The Influence of Market Orientation on New Product Insight through Product Launch Quality : A. *Cogent Corporate & Management*, *9*(1). Advance online publication. DOI: 10.1080/23311975.2022.2108220

Fakhreddin, F., & Foroudi, P. (2022a). The influence of market orientation on new product performance through product launch quality: A resource-based view. *Cogent Business & Management*, *9*(1), 2108220. Advance online publication. DOI: 10.1080/23311975.2022.2108220

Fakhreddin, F., & Foroudi, P. (2022b). The Influence of Market Orientation on New Product Insight through Product Launch Quality: A Resource-Based View. *Cogent Corporate and Management*, *9*(1). Advance online publication. DOI: 10.1080/23311975.2022.2108220

Flemming, P. L., Flemming, B., McLaughlin, G., & Faley, T. (2018). The Impact of Market Orientation, Mixed Method Research and Organizational Leadership: A research method proposition and implication for executive leadership. [IJBMM]. *International Journal of Business Marketing and Management*, *3*(7), 45–59.

Flemming, P. L., Flemming, B., McLaughlin, G., & Faley, T. (2018). The influence of market orientation, mixed method research and business leadership: A research method proposition and implication for executive leadership. *Journal of Leadership Studies*, *3*(7), 45–59.

Hailemariam, S. (2020). The effect of marketing strategy on micro and small enterprises sales performance: Evidence from service sector in Addis Ababa, in the case of Kirkos subcity (Doctoral dissertation, St. Mary's university).

Hamzeh, A., Hozarmoghadam, N., & Ghanbarzadeh, M. (2023). Investigating the level of satisfaction of policyholders with supplementary health insurance in Iran. *BMC Health Services Research*, *23*(1), 10134. Advance online publication. DOI: 10.1186/s12913-023-10134-1 PMID: 37951884

Irawan, A., & Santoso, B. (2023). Fostering innovation culture in small and medium enterprises: Evidence from Indonesia. *Journal of Small Business Management*, *61*(4), 1234–1256.

Karaev, F., & Mercan, M. (2023). Exploring the Influence of Market Orientation and Innovation on Corporate Insight in the Beverage Industry: The Mediating Role of Innovation. *Eurasian Journal of Economic and Corporate Investigations*, *1*(67), 139–155. DOI: 10.47703/ejebs.v1i67.256

Karaev, F., & Mercan, M. (2023). Exploring the influence of market orientation and innovation on business performance in the beverage industry: The mediating role of innovation. *Eurasian Journal of Economic and Business Studies*, *1*(67), 139–155. DOI: 10.47703/ejebs.v1i67.256

Kero, C. A., & Sogbossi, B. B. (2017). Competitive strategy orientation and innovative success: Mediating market orientation a study of small-medium enterprises. *Global Journal of Management and Business Research*, *17*(3), 1–16.

Khan, I., Ming, J., Ali, M., & Zhang, Z. (2022). Influence of Government Supports on Small and Medium Enterprises Progression: Case Investigation of Swat Valley. *Journal of Small Corporate Management*, *60*(6), 1484–1515. DOI: 10.1080/00472778.2020.1767487

Khan, W. A., Arshad, M. Z., & Kashif, U. (2020). The influence of entrepreneurial orientation and organisational culture on business performance: The mediating role of innovation. *Journal of Small Business Management*, *60*(6), 1484–1515. DOI: 10.1080/00472778.2020.1767487

Khan, W. A., Hassan, R. A., Arshad, M. Z., Arshad, M. A., Kashif, U., Aslam, F., & Wafa, S. A. (2020). The effect of entrepreneurial orientation and organisational culture on firm performance: The mediating role of innovation. International Journal of Innovation, Creativity and Change.

Michael, D.G. (2020). "School of Graduate Investigations The Influence of Innovation on Manufacturing Corporates ' Insight in Ethiopia : Evidence from Garment Corporates ' in Addis Ababa The E Ffect of Innovation on Manufacturing Corporates ' Insight in Ethiopia : Evidence from Garment F Irms '."

Minbale, E., Bizuneh, B., Seife, W., Eyasu, A., Asfaw, T., & Sharew, S. (2024). Ethiopian Client's Behavior towards Purchasing Locally Produced Apparel Products: An Extended Model of the Theory of Planned Behavior. *Complexity*, (1), 8745919.

Nyaribo, J., & Muturi, W. (2020). Consumer adoption of new technologies in emerging markets: A case study of VR in Ethiopian retail. *African Journal of Business Management*, *14*(10), 321–332.

Perin, M. G. (2020). Entrepreneurial Orientation and Fi Rm Insight. *An Updated.*, *55*(2), 143–159. DOI: 10.1108/RAUSP-01-2019-0014

Regan, D. B. (2021). The Influence of Small and Medium Enterprises in Employment Creation and Income Generation in Somali Regional State : A Case of Kebridahar Town. *Munich Personal RePEc Archive*, (105879), 32.

Šlogar, H., Morić Milovanović, B., & Hrvatin, S. (2023). Does the relationship between entrepreneurial orientation and subjective financial firm performance have an inverted U-shape? Evidence from Southeast European SMEs. *Administrative Sciences*, *13*(2), 26.

Wakjira, G. G. (2023). Partners Universal International Innovation Journal (PUIIJ) The Diagnostic Test Assumptions Model of Market Orientation on Corporate Insight the Mediating Role of Entrepre ... Partners Universal International Innovation Journal (PUIIJ). *The Di.*, (August). Advance online publication. DOI: 10.5281/zenodo.8265973

Yuliati, E., Ramadhani, Y. C., & Wahyuni, D. U. (2022). Entrepreneurship Orientation and Market Orientation and on Corporate Insight Through Competitive Advantage. *International Journal of Academic Investigation in Corporate and Social Sciences*, *12*(6), 880–896. DOI: 10.6007/IJARBSS/v12-i6/13347

Yuliati, E., Ramadhani, Y. C., & Wahyuni, D. U. (2022). Entrepreneurship orientation and market orientation on business performance through competitive advantage. *International Journal of Academic Research in Business & Social Sciences*, *12*(6), 880–896. DOI: 10.6007/IJARBSS/v12-i6/13347

KEY TERMS AND DEFINITIONS

Market Orientation (MO): A company philosophy that places a high priority on comprehending and adapting to market changes and client wants. In order to incorporate strategy creation and decision-making, it entails gathering and evaluating market data.

Customer Perspectives: A thorough comprehension of client demands, preferences, and behaviors gleaned via market investigation and data analysis. Marketing plans and product progression are incorporated by these corporate.

Cross-Functional Collaboration: The process of assembling people from several departments or specialties to collaborate on a project or objective. This partnership strengthens problem-solving skills and cultivates a variety of viewpoints.

Innovation Culture: A work atmosphere that nurtures risk-taking, experimentation, and innovation. Strong innovation cultures encourage staff members to come up with and pursue novel ideas without worrying about failing.

Feedback Loop: A method for collecting and evaluating input from different stakeholders, such as clients and staff, in order to augment procedures and outcomes. Feedback loops are crucial for corporates' ongoing learning and adapt dynamic nature.

Chapter 9

The Integration of Entrepreneurship Education Into TVET:

Challenges, Solutions, and Opportunities

Hee Song Ng
https://orcid.org/0000-0002-2001-2477
Sunway University, Malaysia

Noman Arshed
https://orcid.org/0000-0002-8940-5391
Sunway University, Malaysia

ABSTRACT

In today's hypercompetitive global marketplace, marked by tech and trade tensions and the rapid rise of artificial intelligence, students must develop not only technical expertise but also entrepreneurial skills to navigate complexity and seize new opportunities. Hence, this chapter examines the integration of entrepreneurial education (EPE) into technical and vocational education and training (TVET), focusing on how skills development can be combined with entrepreneurial skills and venture creations to meet the demands of modern knowledge-based economies. This chapter offers a

DOI: 10.4018/979-8-3373-2943-7.ch009

comprehensive analysis of the challenges, reforms, and solutions related to the integration of entrepreneurship education into TVET. This paper also discusses implications for policymakers, educators, and practitioners, and outlines directions for future research to gain an in-depth understanding from multiple perspectives and contextual issues.

1. INTRODUCTION

Entrepreneurship is a fundamental component of all modern economies. In an increasingly globalized and tech-driven landscape, skilled entrepreneurs play a pivotal role in launching and scaling new ventures (Mack et al., 2019; Morley, 2025). Most developing countries, aspiring to transition into a high-income and developed nations, have placed significant financial resources to further develop entrepreneurship and TVET to fast-track skilled entrepreneurs to drive national growth (Onweh et al., 2022). Since there is a symbiotic relationship between entrepreneurship education and TVET, the debate on integrating entrepreneurship education into TVET has gained prominence, illuminating transformative pathways for grooming future-ready and innovative technopreneurs (Mahlobo, 2025; UNESCO-UNEVOC, 2013). There is a consensus on the potential role of entrepreneurship through entrepreneurship education in promoting economic and social progress for all societies, in both developed and developing countries. In fact, the integration aligns well with global calls for competency-based education systems to foster not only technical proficiency but also entrepreneurial mindsets to address unemployment and job creation to drive economic growth (Masoabi & Alexander, 2021). The integration of EPE into TVET is also in congruence with the UNs' SDG 4 and SDG 8 which emphasize quality education and decent work and economic growth (S. McGrath & Powell, 2016). Furthermore, this merger aligns with global trends in education policy, which increasingly emphasize the importance of fostering entrepreneurial mindsets and innovation as key drivers of sustainable development and inclusive economic growth (UNESCO-UNEVOC, 2013). In the AI era, integrating entrepreneurial education (EPE) into TVET is critical for nurturing a new generation of tech-savvy technopreneurs. By equipping students with both technical expertise and entrepreneurial agility, this synergy empowers them to harness any emerging technologies to develop innovative solutions. Such advancements will accelerate Malaysia's digital economy, fostering competitiveness, job creation, and sustainable growth in a technology-driven global landscape. (GEM, 2024; MDEC, 2023). Hence, both TVET and entrepreneurship education (EPE) have emerged as a cornerstone in the nation's economic strategy, particularly in fostering tech-driven entrepreneurship (Shabbir et al., 2019). In fact, integrating entrepreneurship education into TVET curricula enhances the relevance of technical education and empowers students to leverage their technical skills to groom students turned technopreneurs of tomorrow, transforming them into job creators and innovators in their respective fields (Morley, 2025).

2. THE CONCEPTUALISATION OF ENTREPRENEURSHIP EDUCATION

Entrepreneurship education refers to the structured teaching and learning processes that aim to develop entrepreneurial skills, attitudes, and knowledge, enabling students to identify opportunities, create and manage ventures, and innovate within existing organizations as corporate entrepreneurs or start-up entrepreneurs (Fayolle & Gailly, 2008). Entrepreneurs can proactively spot and seize emerging opportunities while others see chaos, contradiction and confusion. Beyond fostering business creation, entrepreneurship education also plays a critical role in cultivating an entrepreneurial mindset of resilience, innovation and discipline, which are essential in navigating the complexities of today's rapidly changing global economy (Kuratko, 2007). According to Masoabi and Alexander, (2021), entrepreneurship education is becoming a necessity globally and most European and Asian countries highly promote entrepreneurship education in the TVET sector. By equipping individuals with these competencies, entrepreneurship education not only motivates with entrepreneurial drive to for entrepreneurial intentions and entrepreneurial behaviours but also prepares them to succeed in their ventures. This contributes to economic growth, job creation, and societal development (Mack et al., 2019).

Entrepreneurship Education Issues: Traditional entrepreneurship education structures often fail to nurture entrepreneurial potential equitably because they are built on exclusionary systems, biases, and one-size-fits-all models that don't account for diverse backgrounds, resources, and cultural contexts. This leads to missed opportunities, perpetuated inequalities, and a narrow definition of what entrepreneurship "should" look like. (Sarasvathy & Venkataraman, 2011). Traditional Entrepreneurship education also faces several challenges, including a lack of practical exposure and real-world experience, as many programmes focus on theory rather than hands-on learning, limiting students' ability to apply knowledge in real business settings. These challenges collectively impede the effectiveness of entrepreneurship education. Despite the above, entrepreneurship education remains a powerful tool in fostering strong entrepreneurial intentions by providing the right knowledge, mindset, and skills. Hence To support economic growth, it is essential to provide entrepreneurship education to university students and guide them to become skilled entrepreneurs since they represent the largest pool of highly educated and skilled talent.

3. THE CONCEPTUALISATION OF TECHNICAL AND VOCATION EDUCATION TRAINING (TVET)

TVET refers to a form of education, hands-on training, and learning activities that equip students with practical skills, technical knowledge, and competencies required for specific occupations or industries. TVET is a critical pathway for students who are less academically inclined but highly skilled in hands-on, technical, and vocational disciplines. It prepares them for employment, self-employment, and entrepreneurship in practical fields, bridging the gap between education and labour market demands. (Affero & Hassan, 2013; MIDA, 2022; UNESCO-UNEVOC, 2013).

TVET Issues: Despite government national policy and development initiatives to improve quality, relevance and accessibility of TVET education, TVET Malaysia still has not experienced significant development There are no well-coordinated and concerted efforts to drive industry collaboration and a focus on skill development aligned with market demands. TVET system faces several challenges, including negative perception and social stigma, which often position it as a second-choice option compared to academic education, resulting in low enrolment. In many Asian countries, especially in South Asia, Technical and Vocational Education and Training (TVET) is often seen as a less desirable alternative to university. As a result, very few students enrol—only 1.4% in South Asia compared to 24.5% in Europe. East Asia does slightly better, with 16.3% enrolment. To create more job opportunities for young people and match workforce skills with industry needs, this perception must change, and TVET programs must improve in quality and accessibility (McKinsey & Company, 2014). In Malaysia, the major challenges TVET face several challenges, namely, various institution providers, negative perception of vocational education, curriculum under revision, lack of matching training to available jobs and limited collaboration between TVET institutions and industries (Amin et al., 2023). Additionally, there is a mismatch between the skills taught and industry needs, leading to unemployability issues for graduates. Fragmented governance and coordination across multiple ministries further complicate the system, causing overlapping policies and inefficiencies.

4. RESEARCH GAP

The integration of TVET and entrepreneurship education is increasingly recognized as a crucial factor in fostering economic growth and youth entrepreneurship, particularly in developing countries (Onweh et al., 2022). However, several research gaps persist, including the absence of comprehensive integration of TVET with entrepreneurship education frameworks, which limits the effectiveness of existing programmes (Nabi et al., 2017). Additionally, cultural barriers, such as societal perceptions of TVET as a second-tier education pathway, hinder its integration with entrepreneurship education. The lack of effective industry collaboration interaction further restricts students from gaining market insights and practical global exposure necessary for entrepreneurial success (Onweh et al., 2022). Furthermore, there is a need for improved assessment tools to measure entrepreneurial competencies among TVET/EPE graduates and more empirical research on the long-term economic outcomes, and digital integration in these programmes (Lans et al., 2014). Challenges in policy implementation, teacher training, and developing business-minded students within TVET curricula further highlight the necessity for strategic reforms (Fayolle et al., 2014; Muridan et al., 2023; Shikalepo, 2019). Addressing these challenges through holistic frameworks, industry partnerships, and policy enhancements can strengthen the impact of TVET/EPE integration, ultimately leading to increased business creation, and sustainable entrepreneur development (Valerio et al., 2014). Such systemic reforms must also prioritize equitable access for TVET/EPE graduates. Eventually, TVET/EPE graduates can help vulnerable groups like women, rural populations, and low-income communities to truly transform economic participation, reduce skills and labour mismatch, and reduce disparities (ILO, 2023). By integrating entrepreneurship education (whose focus is on innovation and business management) into TVET (whose focus is on industry-based technical expertise), students gain the confidence and capabilities to navigate the most demanding challenges of market demands and market opportunities. By bridging the gap between technical skills and entrepreneurial capabilities, this integrated model not only enhances individual employability but also contributes to broader socio-economic transformation (Kissi et al., 2020).

5. OBJECTIVES

This paper discusses the conceptualisation and issues of EPE, TVET and the integration of EPE into TVET, a pathway to traditional academic education to foster a synergistic relationship that empowers students with both entrepreneurial competencies and technical proficiency. This paper examines the issues related to challenges and solutions impacting on economic growth. The six predominant challenges and solutions range from future-ready curricula reform, seamless integration of curricula, academia- industry collaboration, government policy and infrastructure development, cultural biases and social perceptions and entrepreneurial ecosystem development. This paper also touches on the benefits and drawbacks for technopreneurs, economy and society. Research implications and future research were discussed. This study provides an extensive literature review on the integration of entrepreneurship education into TVET systems. concepts,

6. INTEGRATION OF ENTREPRENEURSHIP EDUCATION INTO TVET

Taken together, while TVET emphasizes technical skills and employability, entrepreneurship education focuses on fostering innovation, business acumen, and self-employment. Bridging these gaps is essential to create a holistic education system that prepares students for both employment and entrepreneurial opportunities. This bolsters entrepreneurial intentions (Shah et al., 2024). The integration of entrepreneurship education into TVET is becoming global emerging trends which confirm their complementarity (Mack et al., 2019; UNESCO-UNEVOC, 2013). Most industries recognise the importance of equipping students with both technical skills and entrepreneurial competencies to address unemployment, foster innovation, and drive economic growth (Galguera, 2018; Mack et al., 2019). TVET traditionally teaches specific job skills to prepare people for work in industries. However, in today's fast-changing economy, it requires more than just technical knowledge and skills, it also needs people who can spot opportunities and take risks to start businesses. Indeed, entrepreneurship education adds skills like creativity, problem-solving, and managing a business. Students with TVET/EPE education not only are technically competent but also have the business acumen to create their own ventures (UNESCO, 2025a, 2025b). In other words, these two concepts can help students develop both practical skills and entrepreneurial thinking, and encourage innovation so they can contribute to job creation rather than job seeking (Mack et al., 2019). TVET/EPE education can equip students with hands-on skills, mentorship, and risk management and prepare them to excel in professional careers or launch entrepreneurial ventures.

7. JUSTIFICATION FOR INTEGRATION OF ENTREPRENEURSHIP EDUCATION INTO TVET

Integrating Entrepreneurship Education into TVET is justified as it enhances graduate employability and self-employment opportunities by equipping individuals with both technical and entrepreneurial skills. It promotes economic growth and innovation by fostering a culture of entrepreneurship and supporting SME development (Ng & Kee, 2018), while empowering marginalized groups and reducing inequality through inclusive growth. The integration aligns with Industry 4.0 and digital transformation, preparing graduates for the digital economy and sustainability-focused industries (Suharno et al., 2025). Additionally, it improves the perception of TVET, strengthens academia-industry collaboration and fosters lifelong learning and adaptability (Kissi et al., 2020). By addressing funding constraints and enhancing global competitiveness, this integration not only benefits individuals but also drives socioeconomic development, making it a strategic and impactful approach to education and workforce training. Indeed, a new curriculum is required to narrow down the gap in this integration because TVET programme primarily focuses on technical skills, while entrepreneurship education emphasizes business knowledge and venture creations. New hybrid TVET/EPE curriculum can blend hands-on technical training with venture creation initiatives. With mentorship and industries linkage and conducive business ecosystem, student can have the entrepreneurial self-efficacy to transform ideas into viable entrepreneurial enterprises. In the context of growing uncertainty in the world economy, and the prospect of multiple careers, a strong entrepreneurial mindset and drive shaped by TVET/EPE education is required for students to be able to adapt and thrive in fast-changing environments. Furthermore, UNESCO-UNEVOC (2025) also supported the integration of entrepreneurship into TVET education as a way to spur sustainable growth, innovation, and job creation. By equipping TVET students with entrepreneurial skills, TVET/EPE bridges the education gap and addresses the mismatch of skills and industry needs to drive sustainable economic growth and innovation.

With entrepreneurship education integrated into TVET, it is crucial to institutionalize all training and development programmes for students and educators, strengthen industry collaboration, and adopt flexible curricula to enhance entrepreneurial skill development. This approach can equip TVET/EPE students with a strong entrepreneurial attitude, self-efficacy in key tasks, and perceived behavioural control (influenced by both skills and external support), fostering firm entrepreneurial intentions and actionable decisions. By equipping students with technical expertise, advancing technological progress, boosting productivity, and enhancing social inclusion, TVET/EPE institutions will serve as a cornerstone of national development (Okoye & Okoye, 2015).

8. UNDERPINNING THEORY

The study anchors on two theories to support the integration of entrepreneurial education and TVET and explore the interplay that can complement each other in education and learning and can result in developing entrepreneurial intentions and entrepreneurial behaviour. First, the theory of Planned Behaviour (Ajzen, 1991) establishes the theoretical framework demonstrating how attitudes toward entrepreneurship, subjective norms, and perceived behavioural control collectively shape entrepreneurial intention formation and subsequent entrepreneurial action (Buli & Yesuf, 2015). Second, Freire et al. (2005) stated critical pedagogy is a transformative educational theory that emphasizes dialogue, critical consciousness, and social justice. These are essential for educating students with technical and entrepreneurial competencies. These theoretical lenses collectively reveal systemic challenges in implementing adaptive pedagogies while highlighting effective strategies for fostering entrepreneurial intentions among TVET/EPE graduates (Parekh, 2020; Valerio et al., 2014; Valiente, 2014). Entrepreneurship education impacts the knowledge and skills on how to be alert and recognise opportunities for new business ventures (Shane & Venkataraman, 2007). New TVET/EPE curricula should equip students to identify and respond to market opportunities and gaps. The dynamic capabilities framework emphasizes the need to reconfigure organizational resources to enhance agility, adaptability, and alignment in a rapidly shifting business environment, driven by ongoing trade wars and tech rivalries. These disruptions severely hinder the critical processes required to translate entrepreneurial intentions into successful venture creation (Teece, 2012).

They can turn TVET/EPE integration from simple traditional programmes into powerful systems to use innovation to move up entrepreneurially and economically (OECD, 2023; UNESCO-UNEVOC, 2022).

9. THE IMPACT OF TVET/EPE SYSTEM ON ENTREPRENEURIAL INTENTIONS

The integration of TVET/EPE is essential for fostering strong entrepreneurial intentions as it combines technical expertise with business acumen, innovation, and problem-solving skills to form entrepreneurial intentions. TVET/EPE systems can empower students with a dual advantage—technical expertise and entrepreneurial skills, fostering competitive economies and better societies through entrepreneurship and venture creations (Mack et al., 2019; Raj et al., 2024). TVET/EPE system can develop technical skills and entrepreneurial skills which are crucial in forming strong entrepreneurial intentions. Pittaway and Cope (2007) asserted that entrepreneurship education, together with TVET, has a significant impact on student propensity and intentionality in entrepreneurship. Padi et al. (2022) revealed that entrepreneurship education is positively related to the entrepreneurial intentions of students and such relationships become stronger when the students are exposed to social support systems. In contrast, there is a weak entrepreneurial intention among students, with many preferring stable professional employments due to risk aversion and fear of failure insufficient funding and market potential insights. Entrepreneurial intentions often translate into entrepreneurial behaviours of taking decisions to start up business ventures when TVET/EPE students act on opportunities, mobilize human resources and overcome barriers of access to financial resources from family, friends and government grants to venture creation. By embedding entrepreneurship within TVET programmes, students are better equipped to transform their skills into sustainable businesses, making them job creators rather than job seekers (Maritz & Brown, 2013). Entrepreneurship encourages business growth, and reduces youth unemployment, ultimately strengthening economic development and resilience. Entrepreneurship is fuelled by courage and risk-taking, as visionaries step into the unknown to turn ideas into reality. It thrives on driving change and innovation, challenging the status quo to create transformative solutions. With TVET/EPE can shape the entrepreneurial drive and mindset to push forward their intentions to engage in entrepreneurship journey even in the face of adversity. At its core, entrepreneurship is about breaking orthodoxies, daring to question conventional wisdom and rewriting the rules to build a better pathway for future. Together, these elements define the bold spirit of those who refuse to settle and instead choose to innovate, disrupt, and inspire (McKinsey & Company, 2023). In the study of entrepreneurial intentions and behaviours, it is equally important to explore cognitive and contextual factors such as attitude toward entrepreneurship, perceived feasibility (Krueger & Carsrud, 1993), self-efficacy development from venture creation exercises (Bandura, 1997), and skill mastery through hands-on training (Brush et al., 2001), and networking opportunity via industry collaboration and exposure (Shane & Venkataraman, 2007) to understand their collective role in facilitating the formation of entrepreneurial intentions (Ajzen, 1991; Valerio et al., 2014).

10. RESEARCH MODEL

Building on insights from the literature, the proposed model (Figure 1) integrates entrepreneurship education into TVET, equipping students with both technical skills and business acumen to foster entrepreneurial intentions among TVET/EPE learners. By integrating technical training with entrepreneurial skills, the model prepares students to overcome the challenges of launching tech-based ventures, effectively bridging the gap between education, entrepreneurship, and economic engagement (OECD, 2023; Raj et al., 2024).

Figure 1. Research Model

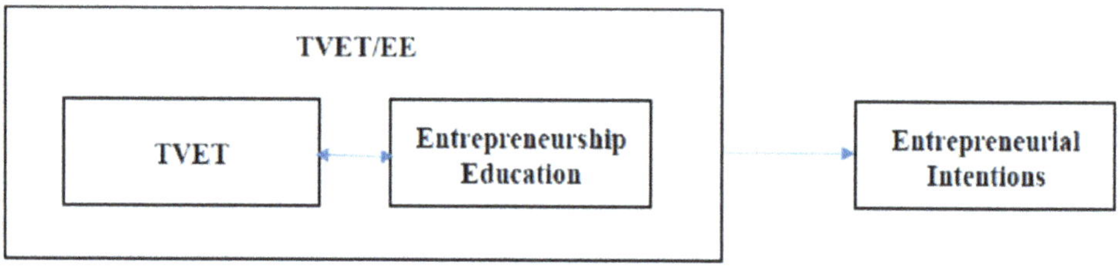

11. CHALLENGES AND SOLUTIONS FOR INTEGRATING ENTREPRENEURSHIP EDUCATION INTO TVET

The integration of entrepreneurship education into TVET is a contentious issue, with stakeholders, especially policymakers, academics and industry leaders, divided on its impact on unemployment and entrepreneurial ecosystems. Below are the five key challenges that stifle economic progress and technology-enabled solutions that underscore the necessity for coordinated, multidimensional interventions to address systemic barriers. Persistent structural, cultural and mindset barriers threaten its relevance, necessitating coordinated reforms to align educational frameworks with economic priorities.

11.1 AI-Infused Curriculum Challenge in TVET/EPE Systems

The challenge is how to incorporate AI tools and technology into the TVET/EPE systems.

The challenge is how to embed AI tools into TVET/EPE systems through modular courses, digital labs, and stackable credentials that align with emerging technical expertise and high-tech business ventures. TVET/PEP must embed AI literacy, automation, blockchain, internet of things and online business strategies into their curricula to future-proof graduates, enabling them to leverage automation, analyse market trends, seize business opportunities and launch tech-driven ventures. The ongoing globalisation, deglobalisation and reglobalisation and the advert of technological advancements in advanced automation and artificial intelligence (AI), it calls for new skillset in technical mastery and entrepreneurial capabilities to thrive in high-tech setups and digital entrepreneurship (WEF, 2023). As AI-driven innovation amplifies human-machine collaboration, Floridi and Cowls (2022) highlighted the need for designing AI systems that can supplement human cognitive processes. This ensures TVET/EPE students have both cutting-edge technical skills (AI, advanced robotics) and entrepreneurial mindsets (innovation, adaptability) for tomorrow's economy (Jones, 2010).

Indeed, AI has helped in speeding up the prototyping which has reduced the product development cycles significantly (Cockburn et al., 2019). Brynjolfsson and McAfee (2014) described it as 'innovation compression' whereby the window to capitalize the novel idea is narrowed and there is a consistent need for newer ideation. AI can now better help in business ideation processes, large document handling and summarization which makes it easier to start and manage new businesses. Furthermore, as Industries 4.0 technologies evolve, more AI and AI tolls continue to reshape industries. The fusion of vocational technical skills and entrepreneurial education will be pivotal in churning out TVET/EPE students who are forward thinking to drive sustainable businesses in the digital entrepreneurship. Policymakers must recognize that AI-driven job displacement follows an asymmetric 'creative destruction' pattern, distinct from traditional technological transitions. This requires tailored business strategies to mitigate workforce disruptions and business models. Autor (2022) described this phenomenon as the 'hollowing of the middle,' where employment polarizes into high-skilled technical roles and low-wage, physically intensive jobs. This underscores the critical need to prioritize AI skill development from data literacy, machine learning basics, AI tool proficiency, and prompt engineering to ethical AI deployment to ensure TVET/EPE graduates and their workers can thrive alongside, not against, automation.

11.2 Integration of TVET/EPE Curricula Challenge:

The challenge lies in the seamless integration of TVET curriculum and EPE curriculum. It is crucial to balance the teaching and learning of technical skills and venture creation so that TVT/EPE students are well-trained to manage and scale their businesses. To grow, develop, and sustain their business ventures, they must keep up with the latest industry-relevant technical expertise while maintaining entrepreneurial agility and adaptability in a dynamic business environment.

For Educators, there should be pedagogical innovation by adopting experiential methods (e.g., business simulations, prototyping labs) to cultivate entrepreneurial mindsets, a way of thinking that constantly searches for opportunities, accepts calculated risks, and tackles problems proactively (McGrath & MacMillan, 2000). TVET/EPE systems should equip students with an entrepreneurial spirit and drive to develop ambition, resilience, and creative problem-solving to identify opportunities, take calculated risks, and turn ideas into viable businesses (Getley, 1979).

Educator training and development in entrepreneurial pedagogy should be initiated with the participation with TVET/EPE teachers and professional trainers (World Bank, 2023). It is necessary to develop appropriate instructional methods and adaptive training frameworks that include industry-linked internship, industrial networking and human capital development that can foster experiential learning and professional connections. In this case, it is important to establish an educational framework that prioritize TVET/EPE for educator and trainer professional development.

By assessing how tools such as adaptive learning systems and collaborative digital platforms interact with approaches like learning-by-doing, case-based challenges, and role-playing scenarios, researchers can identify optimal strategies for tailoring TVET/EPE curricula to diverse learners' needs. Such insights will be critical for designing scalable, equitable, and industry-relevant training programs that foster entrepreneurial mindsets and practical competencies. The training programmes must partner up with tech titans for upskilling and reskilling, building technical expertise and adaptability for Industry 4.0 (Shabbir et al., 2019). It is important to acknowledge that adapting to Industry 4.0 technologies into TVET/EPE remains a significant hurdle as TVET/EPE institutions often fail to update AI-infused curricula and infrastructure to meet the demands of automation, AI, and digitalization due to financial constraints (Yusof et al., 2022).

When drafting the TVET/EPE curricula to produce the best students, policymakers and school management have to take cognizant of the challenges of gaps between curricula and market needs, between traditional pedagogy and the unpredictability of entrepreneurship, and between institutional objectives and the risk-taking ethos required to cultivate true innovators. These challenges highlight the difficulty of balancing TVET/EPE education with venture creation in a dynamic business environment. There must be regulation updating of the TVET/EPE curriculum to include practical, industry-relevant that are aligned with the job market needs (Padi et al., 2022). There must be continuous professional development that upgrades teachers' as well as students' skills and capabilities in the age of AI (Gandhi et al., 2025).

New Assessment - There must be reformation in assessment and evaluation methods with robust quality assurance mechanisms (Mack et al., 2019). The system must foster hands-on experience, digital literacy and adaptive problem-solving while aligning with market demands. New assessment should evaluate the shift from exam-based evaluation to competency-based metrics (e.g., business plan viability, problem-solving portfolios).

TVET/EPP should invite industry leaders and business practitioners in continuous dialogues for curriculum co-creation, skills gap analysis and real-world training alignments for continuous improvement. With a strong commitment to TVET/EPE academic excellence, the university-government-private partnership holds immerse promise for driving meaningful progress in TVET/EPE education across Asia and beyond. In this context, it is absolutely necessary to adopt the best practices, indicator matrices and benchmarking from effective TVET/EPE model based on Germany and Switzerland and China. This can enhance industry competitiveness and share proven strategies for effective implementation (Mwasalwiba, 2010).

11.3 Academia-Industry Collaboration Challenge:

This challenge demands the alignment of TVET/EPE programmes with rapidly evolving industry and market needs, necessitating curricula that adapt swiftly to the emerging eight disruptive technologies, especially artificial intelligence, blockchain and advanced robotics (PWC, 2025). For policymakers, there should be a clearer national framework that mandates TVET/EPE integration with input from employers and established entrepreneurs (e.g., modular courses on venture creation alongside technical skills). This requires continuous dialogue between policymakers, universities, and industry leaders to fine-tune the curricula which is in line with the fast-evolving industry demands and future-oriented competencies. Policymakers must use Triple Helix collaboration (university-industry-government) platforms to enable better coordination, knowledge transfer and mentorship initiatives to expose students to the real world of technical challenges and entrepreneurship challenges. This will allow TVET/EPE institutions management to evaluate their technical skillset and entrepreneurial mindsets to meet the needs of the industry and market conditions (Shikalepo, 2019). There should be no disconnect between policy, education and industry that creates barriers for seamless and systematic alignments (Sansone et al., 2019). For Practitioners, they should co-design internship and apprenticeship programmes where students can experience real problems and business challenges. The industry-academia interaction is vital for continuous improvements in curriculum co-creation and review and skills gap analysis (Onweh et al., 2022)

11.4 Governance Policy and Infrastructure Development Challenge:

National framework

This challenge involves drafting a national policy to establish an effective TVET/EPE framework and task force that aligns national policies, coordination, streamline governance and ensures cohesive skill development across both domains. There must be a strengthening of the national policies that prioritise TVET/EPE programme within the national education frameworks. They must enhance TVET/EPE infrastructure with a focus high-tech sector advancements and integration. This should support scalable, future-oriented TVET/EPE institutions that can churn out skilled, adaptable, and industry-ready students who can meet the current and emerging technological demands and business ventures (Lambrechts et al., 2020). Malaysia recently launched SkillsMalaysia 2.0, an outreach programme that aims to boost participation in TVET. Today, participation in TVET is currently at 80 percent of the programmes capacity (McKinsey, 2025). Meanwhile, there is a need for a national entrepreneurship strategy National decision on adopting TVET/EPE systems that struggle to balance technical workforce preparation with long-term business ventures. Hence, it is important to secure adequate government funding to upgrade infrastructure, procure advanced tools, and enhance educator training for future-ready TVET/EPE programmes.

Government must allocate sufficient financial resources and funding to upgrade the TVET/EPE infrastructure and teaching facilities, procure advanced technologies and tools and enhance educator training and development for teaching excellence and pedagogical innovation in the era of AI. The funding must include specialized grants, micro-loans and startup incubation that are tailored to TVET-based business networks. Meanwhile, a multidimensional entrepreneurship education and development is required that can handle both entrepreneurial ventures and technology adoption related business challenges. Funding incentives should be initiated for entrepreneurial firms. It is to ensure industry-linked training hubs and mentorship programmes to bridge the gap between education and entrepreneurial practice (WEF, 2023). Practitioners who are entrepreneurs or business leaders can offer seed funding competitions or incubators for TVET/EPE students to launch business ventures upon graduation. Meanwhile, resource sharing among TVET/EPE institutions is necessary. Due to financial constraints, TVET/EPE institutions can optimize resources through collaborative sharing of facilities, equipment, and expertise, reducing costs while enhancing training quality, fostering innovation, and ensuring equitable access to technical education for sustainable workforce development. TVET/EPE institutions have to share their resources and provide access to modern tools (e.g., digital platforms, maker spaces) to simulate start-up environments for students (ILO, 2023).

11.5 Cultural Biases and Social Perceptions Challenge

This challenge involves overcoming societal stereotypes that undervalue vocational education while promoting TVET's prestige and recognition to attract diverse talent and align training with inclusive economic growth objectives. There is a perception that entrepreneurship education using TVET is a 'second choice' and only suitable for underperforming students (Powell, 2012, 2014). Such stereotypes must be addressed which are influencing the educational decision-making and making students and families avoid TVET training tracks (Chankseliani & Anuar, 2019). Persistent misconceptions about vocational pathways continue to hinder student enrolment, employer engagement, and policy prioritization, despite evidence of TVET/EPE's critical role in sustainable development (Avis, 2023). Hence, it is important to address deep-rooted social and cultural biases that limit effective TVET/EPE adoption and workforce participation among the youth. These barriers perpetuate skills gaps, hinder economic mobility, and undermine the potential of vocational education to transform lives and industries.

With TVET/EPE merger, TVET/EPE institutions must launch a public awareness campaign to overcome stereotypes and cultural biases against TVET/EPE programmes through media and outreach programmes (OECD, 2024). This can improve its image as a prestigious entrepreneurial career option compared to academic education. There must be a rebranding of TVET/EPE systems that provide viable, diverse paths as the first-choice education for career progression and recognition. It is important to show success cases that highlight the role of education and training through TVET/EPE systems, this can help in changing societal attitudes towards TVET/EPE institutions. TVET/EPE students should have pathways to larger qualifications or degrees while many institutions struggle with funding and resource constraints, lacking modern equipment and sufficient financial support.

11.6 Entrepreneurial Ecosystem Development Challenges:

A strong ecosystem for TVET/EPE students integrates industry partnerships, modern infrastructure, entrepreneurial training, and policy support, equipping learners with technical skills, innovation capabilities, and real-world experience to thrive in evolving job markets and drive economic growth. TVET/EPE institutions must create an ecosystem that supports innovation and business development simultaneously (Mack et al., 2019). There must be a conducive environment for the healthy development of TVET/EPE systems. To drive industrialization and economic resilience, we must foster a culture of lifelong learning and excellence through industry-aligned TVET education.

For businesses to flourish, a vibrant entrepreneurship culture is required to thrive when educational institutions, policymakers, and industry leaders cooperatively collaborate to build supportive ecosystems featuring mentorship programs, accessible funding, innovation hubs, and skill development initiatives. Hence, it is necessary to develop entrepreneur development programmes with sufficient financial resources to foster a dynamic, industry-aligned entrepreneurial culture in vocational education, ensuring sustainable economic growth and youth venture creation. The cultural cultivation of technical excellence and entrepreneurship among students can be encouraged by prioritizing business development rather than seeking for stable employment. For this, the system must stark entrepreneurial aspirations.

There is a need to promote creative thinking that embeds problem-solving, innovation and creativity into TVET training through hands-on projects and competitions. An entrepreneurial mindset should be strengthened to develop new solutions. The entrepreneurial mindset should be merged with the entrepreneurial drive to innovate and create with the entrepreneurial spirit of the passion and resilience to bring ideas to life in today's competitive business landscape (McGrath & MacMillan, 2000).

12. OPPORTUNITIES AND BENEFITS OF THE INTEGRATION

The introduction of TVET/EPE systems presents numerous start-ups opportunities for students as future technopreneurs enabling them to develop technical skills, innovate solutions, and launch businesses in high-demand industries like renewable energy, ICT, and manufacturing. The successful implementation can drive innovation, reduce unemployment, and bridge the gap between education and industry demands.

Students as future technopreneurs must cultivate strategic skill diversification. This is done by developing T-shaped competencies that combine deep technical expertise with broad entrepreneurial capabilities. This multi-dimensional proficiency enables them to navigate complex entrepreneurial ecosystems, pivot across technological domains, and create value at the intersection of disciplines. TVET/EPE will equip students with entrepreneurial skills, business acumen and technical skills, Students can not only seek employment but also create jobs by starting their own ventures amidst economic uncertainties. In the AI and Industry 4.0 paradigm, students must develop a dual-capacity framework: (1) an opportunity-seeking growth mindset that embraces disruptive changes as innovation catalysts, and (2) a dynamic skillset repository maintained through continuous upskilling (vertical specialization) and reskilling (horizontal adaptation) to remain relevant in evolving technological landscapes.

For economic growth and innovation, more small- and medium-sized enterprises can be created to drive domestic socio-economic development. There will be more technopreneurs to innovate, create new products, services and solutions to address local and global market needs. This ecosystem can attract to employers and investors to make further investments in today's changing industry demands and dynamic markets. By fostering knowledge exchange and cross-border partnerships between TVET/EPE institutions and industry stakeholders, this model can accelerate innovation, optimize resource utilization, disseminate proven best practices, and ultimately build sustainable competitive advantage for industries and countries.

For societies, entrepreneurship serves as a catalyst for socio-economic development, fostering better organized and more peaceful societies. This will lead to less vulnerabilities and inequality gaps among the members of the societies. Student-turned technopreneurs are industry-ready talented individuals They who have the technical skill and business acumen can drive change in society and inspire others in their communities to embark on entrepreneurial journeys. By equipping youth with both technical and entrepreneurial competencies, this integrated model can significantly reduce unemployment rates. Graduates will be better prepared to engage meaningfully in industry, either as skilled employees or innovative entrepreneurs.

Nevertheless, while this integrated TVET/EPE model offers transformative potential for developing future-ready workforces and entrepreneurial development. it is equally crucial to consider the potential downsides and the inherent risks of failure. These include mismatches between skills training and labour market needs, underfunded infrastructure, and cultural biases that may limit participation.

13. CONCLUSION

The strategic integration of Entrepreneurship Education (EPE) within TVET systems presents a transformative opportunity to cultivate dual competencies in technical mastery and entrepreneurial capabilities. This synergistic model not only equips students with industry-relevant skills but also fosters entrepreneurial mindsets, creating a dynamic workforce capable of driving sustainable national development. By embedding entrepreneurial principles throughout TVET curricula, from opportunity recognition to venture creation, this education system can produce graduates who are both technically proficient and have entrepreneurial acumen. Students who attain technical expertise and develop an entrepreneurial mindset are more likely to form strong entrepreneurial intentions, ultimately leading them to establish and grow their own ventures. At its core, this integration serves as a catalytic linchpin, simultaneously driving technological innovation while systematically cultivating entrepreneurial competencies. This dual-axis approach not only future-proofs workforce capabilities but establishes a dynamic pipeline for sustainable economic transformation. Finally, to achieve this, relevant stakeholders like governments, TVET institutions, teachers, and industry leaders should address the above five challenges like AI-infused curriculum, Seamless integration of curricula, academia-industry interaction, government policy and infrastructure development, cultural biases and social perception, and Entrepreneurial ecosystem and development. The solutions should cover the use of technology and AI tools, curriculum modernisation, upskilling and reskilling of educators, enhanced industry collaboration, policy reforms and resource allocation, public awareness campaigns and promotion of entrepreneurship and its ecosystem. While the above challenges persist, strategic interventions such as better industry-academia collaboration, modernized curricula, advanced training facilities, and robust career guidance can enhance TVET/EPE effectiveness and ensure that it continues to contribute meaningfully to industrial and socio-economic progress.

14. FUTURE RESEARCH DIRECTION

Future research must explore how emerging technologies, such as AI-driven business simulations, blockchain for venture management, and metaverse-based collaborative workspaces, can disrupt TVET/EPE systems and work out solutions that align with real-world technological and entrepreneurial requirements. TVET/EPP must re-map emerging skillset demands in the digital economy and prepare workforce readiness across various industries. It is necessary to explore new pedagogy and methods to combine AI tools with hands-on, experiential training and gamification for diverse learners to bridge the gap between theoretical knowledge and workforce readiness (Gandhi et al., 2025; Parua & Yang, 2024; WEF, 2023). Future studies can compare countries by examining and adopting best practices from Germany, Singapore, and South Korea which lead to effective TVET and EPE models, combining classroom learning, industry partnerships, and lifelong upskilling (OECD, 2024). Further studies should also assess the scalability of TVET/EPE innovations across different socioeconomic contexts, particularly in rural versus urban settings.

REFERENCES

Affero, I., & Hassan, R. (2013). *Issues and Challenges of Technical and Vocational Education & Training in Malaysia for Knowledge Worker Driven. National Conference on Engineering Technology*. DOI: 10.13140/2.1.4555.2961

Ajzen, I. (1991). The theory of planned behavior. *Organizational Behavior and Human Decision Processes*, *50*(2), 179–211. DOI: 10.1016/0749-5978(91)90020-T

Amin, S. M., Ahmad Suhaimi, S. S., & Nazuri, N. S. (2023). The Present and Future of Malaysian Technical and Vocational Education and Training (TVET). *International Journal of Academic Research in Business & Social Sciences*, *13*(18). Advance online publication. DOI: 10.6007/IJARBSS/v13-i18/19952

Autor, D. (2022). *The Labor Market Impacts of Technological Change: From Unbridled Enthusiasm to Qualified Optimism to Vast Uncertainty* (No. Working Paper 30074). National Bureau of Economic Research. DOI: 10.3386/w30074

Avis, J. (2023). In pursuit of equity vocational education and training and social justice. *Research in Post-Compulsory Education*, *28*(3), 439–459. https://www.tandfonline.com/doi/abs/10.1080/13596748.2023.2221119. DOI: 10.1080/13596748.2023.2221119

Bandura, A. (1997). Self-Efficacy: Toward a Unifying Theory of Behavioral Change. *Psychological Review*, *84*(2), 191–215. DOI: 10.1037/0033-295X.84.2.191 PMID: 847061

Brush, C. G., Greene, P. G., Hart, M. M., & Harold, S. H. (2001). From initial idea to unique advantage: The entrepreneurial challenge of constructing a resource base. *The Academy of Management Perspectives*, *15*(1), 64–78. DOI: 10.5465/ame.2001.4251394

Brynjolfsson, E., & McAfee, A. (2014). *The second machine age: Work, progress, and prosperity in a time of brilliant technologies*. W. W. Norton & Company.

Buli, B. M., & Yesuf, W. M. (2015). Determinants of entrepreneurial intentions: Technical-vocational education and training students in Ethiopia. *Education + Training, 57*(8/9), 891–907. DOI: 10.1108/ET-10-2014-0129

Chankseliani, M., & Anuar, A. M. (2019). Cross-country comparison of engagement in apprenticeships: A conceptual analysis of incentives for individuals and firms. *International Journal of Research in Vocational Education and Training, 6*(3), 261–283. DOI: 10.13152/IJRVET.6.3.4

Cockburn, I. M., Henderson, R., & Stern, S. (2019). The impact of Artificial Intelligence on Innovation. An exploratory Analysis. In *The Economics of Artificial Intelligence: An Agenda* (Vol. 1–May, pp. 115–146). https://www.nber.org/system/files/chapters/c14006/c14006.pdf

Fayolle, A., & Gailly, B. (2008). *From craft to science: Teaching models and learning processes in entrepreneurship education* (Vol. 32, Issue 7, p. 593). DOI: 10.1108/03090590810899838

Fayolle, A., Liñán, F., & Moriano, J. A. (2014). Beyond entrepreneurial intentions: Values and motivations in entrepreneurship. *The International Entrepreneurship and Management Journal, 10*(4), 679–689. DOI: 10.1007/s11365-014-0306-7

Floridi, L., & Cowls, J. (2022). 22. A Unified Framework of Five Principles for AI in Society. In S. Carta (Ed.), *Machine Learning and the City*. Wiley Online Library. https://onlinelibrary.wiley.com/doi/abs/10.1002/9781119815075.ch45

Freire, P. Ramos, M. Bergman., & Macedo, D. P. (2005). *Pedagogy of the oppressed* (p. 219). The Continuum International Publishing Group Inc.

Galguera, M. P. (2018). *Globalisation, Mass Education and Technical and Vocational Education and Training, The Influence of UNESCO in Botswana*. Springer International Publishing AG., https://www.springer.com/series/6969

Gandhi, N., Durth, S., Bérubé, V., Kedia, K., & Lim, R. (2025). The critical role of strategic workforce planning in the age of AI. *McKinsey & Company, February* 9–9.

GEM. (2024). *GEM 2024/2025 Global Report: Entrepreneurship Reality Check*. Global Entrepreneurship Research Association (GERA). http://www.witchwoodhouse.com

Getley, R. (1979). Entrepreneurial drive. *Industrial and Commercial Training*, *11*(1), 19–23. DOI: 10.1108/eb003711

ILO. (2023). *Improve Technical and Vocational Education and Training (TVET) to meet skills and labour mismatch*. https://www.ilo.org/resource/news/improve-technical-and-vocational-education-and-training-tvet-meet-skills

Jones, C. (2010). Entrepreneurship education: Revisiting our role and its purpose. *Journal of Small Business and Enterprise Development*, *17*(4), 500–513. DOI: 10.1108/14626001011088697

Kissi, E., Ahadzie, D. K., Debrah, C., & Adjei-Kumi, T. (2020). Underlying strategies for improving entrepreneurial skills development of technical and vocational students in developing countries: Using Ghana as a case study. *Education + Training*, *62*(5), 599–614. DOI: 10.1108/ET-11-2019-0264

Krueger, N., & Carsrud, A. L. (1993). Entrepreneurial intentions: Applying the theory of planned behaviour. *Entrepreneurship and Regional Development*, *5*(4), 315–330. DOI: 10.1080/08985629300000020

Kuratko, D. F. (2007). Entrepreneurial Leadership in the 21st Century. *Journal of Leadership & Organizational Studies*, *13*(4), 1–11. DOI: 10.1177/10717919070130040201

Lambrechts, W., Sinha, S., & Marwala, T. (2020). Decentralizing Emerging Markets to Prepare for Industry 4.0: Modernizing Policies and the Role of Higher Education. In Dorrsamy, W., Paul, B., & Marwala, T. (Eds.), *The Disruptive Fourth Industrial Revolution*. Springer., DOI: 10.1007/978-3-030-48230-5_6

Lans, T., Blok, V., & Wesselink, R. (2014). Learning apart and together: Towards an integrated competence framework for sustainable entrepreneurship in higher education. *Journal of Cleaner Production*, *62*, 37–47. DOI: 10.1016/j.jclepro.2013.03.036

Mack, A. J., White, D., & Senghor, O. (2019). An insight into entrepreneurship education practices in Technical and Vocational Education and Training institutions. *Journal of Global Entrepreneurship Reserch*. DOI: 10.1186/s40497-019-0169-z

Mahlobo, T. S. (2025). Linking TVET education with entrepreneurial and financial education, YouTube, Retrieved April 5, 2025, from https://www.youtube.com/watch?v=oGoei56y9kc. *New Economy Leadership Institute*. https://www.youtube.com/watch?v=oGoei56y9kc

Maritz, A., & Brown, C. R. (2013). Illuminating the black box of entrepreneurship education programs. *Education + Training*, *55*(3), 234–252. DOI: 10.1108/00400911311309305

Masoabi, C. S., & Alexander, G. (2021). Possible Merger, Entrepreneurship Education in TVET Engineering Studies: A Case for South Africa. *Journal of Entrepreneurship Education*, *24*(2).

McGrath, R. G., & MacMillan, I. (2000). *The Entrepreneurial Mindset: Strategies for Continuously Creating Opportunity in an Age of Uncertainty*. Harvard Business School Press., https://www.amazon.com/Entrepreneurial-Mindset-Continuously-Opportunity-Uncertainty/dp/0875848346

McGrath, S., & Powell, L. (2016). Skills for sustainable development: Transforming vocational education and training beyond 2015. *International Journal of Educational Development*, *50*, 12–19. DOI: 10.1016/j.ijedudev.2016.05.006

McKinsey. (2025). *Automation and adaptability: How Malaysia can navigate the future of work | McKinsey*. https://www.mckinsey.com/featured-insights/asia-pacific/automation-and-adaptability-how-malaysia-can-navigate-the-future-of-work

McKinsey & Company. (2014). *Unleashing Youth in Asia, Solving for the "Triple-E" challenge of youth: Education, Enployment and Engagement*. McKinsey Centre for Government.

McKinsey & Company. (2023). *The Skills Revolution and the Future of Learning and Earning, World Government Summit 2023*. McKinsey & Company.

MDEC. (2023). *Harnessing the Power of Technology: Building a Strong Digital Economy for Malaysia's Future*.

MIDA. (2022, October 29). TVET as a catalyst for economic growth. *MIDA | Malaysian Investment Development Authority*. https://www.mida.gov.my/mida-news/tvet-as-a-catalyst-for-economic-growth/

Morley, S. (2025). *Entrepreneurship and TVET_ Nurturing Tomorrow's Business Leaders*. https://www.worldoftvet.com/blog/entrepreneurship-and-tvet

Muridan, N. D., Rasul, M. S., Yasin, R. M., Nor, A. R. M., Rauf, R. A. A., & Jalaludin, N. A. (2023). Career Planning Indicators of Successful TVET Entrepreneurs. *Sustainability (Basel), 15*(8), 6629–6629. DOI: 10.3390/su15086629

Mwasalwiba, E. S. (2010). Entrepreneurship education: A review of its objectives, teaching methods, and impact indicators. *Education + Training*, *52*(1), 20–47. DOI: 10.1108/00400911011017663

Nabi, G., Liñán, F., Fayolle, A., Krueger, N., & Walmsley, A. (2017). The impact of entrepreneurship education in higher education: A systematic review and research agenda. *Academy of Management Learning & Education*, *16*(2), 277–299. DOI: 10.5465/amle.2015.0026

Ng, H. S., & Kee, D. M. H. (2018). *The Moderating Effect of Ethical Climate on Relationship between Personal Ethics and Ethical Attitudes*. International Conference on Technology and Humanities (IcoTECH), KDU Penang University College, Malaysia on 17-18 November 2018, UOWM Malaysia KDU Penang University College.

OECD. (2023). *A better future for rural youth*. OECD Development Centre. https://www.oecd.org/dev/G20-initiative-rural-youth-employment-brochure.pdf

OECD. (2024). *Education Policy Outlook 2024 Reshaping Teaching into a Thriving Profession from ABCs to AI*. https://www.oecd.org/en/publications/education-policy-outlook-2024_dd5140e4-en.html

Okoye, K. R. E., & Okoye, P. I. (2015). Enhancement and innovation in higher education in Nigeria. *Journal of Research and Development (Srinagar), 24*(1). https://www.researchgate.net/profile/Peter-Okoye-2/publication/280095798_ENHANCEMENT_AND_INNOVATION_IN_HIGHER_EDUCATION_IN_NIGERIA/links/55cb650308aeb975674c7894/ENHANCEMENT-AND-INNOVATION-IN-HIGHER-EDUCATION-IN-NIGERIA.pdf

Onweh, V. E., Akpan, N., & Emmanuel, C. (2022). Youth Empowerment and the Integration of Entrepreneurship Education into Technical Vocational Education and Training (TVET) in Nigeria. SSRN *Electronic Journal.* https://doi.org/DOI: 10.2139/SSRN.4166843

Padi, A., Dzisi, P. S., & Eshun, P. J. F. (2022). Entrepreneurship education in TVET institutions and entrepreneurial intentions of female students in Ghana: The social support factor. *Cogent Business & Management, 9*(1), 2137954. Advance online publication. DOI: 10.1080/23311975.2022.2137954

Parekh, S. S. (2020). Conquer the skills gap – and win the future – by rethinking talent: World Economic Forum 2020. *World Economic Forum,* 1–5.

Parua, R., & Yang, W. (2024). The driving logic of digital transformation in TVET. *Vocation. Technology & Education, 1*(2). Advance online publication. DOI: 10.54844/vte.2024.0590

Pittaway, L., & Cope, J. (2007). Entrepreneurship Education. *International Small Business Journal, 25*(5), 479–510. DOI: 10.1177/0266242607080656

Powell, L. (2012). Reimagining the purpose of VET – Expanding the capability to aspire in South African Further Education and Training students. *International Journal of Educational Development, 32*(5), 643–653. DOI: 10.1016/j.ijedudev.2012.01.008

Powell, L. (2014). *Reimagining the Purpose of Vocational Education and Training* [PhD Thesis]. University of Nottingham.

Raj, V. A., Jasrotia, S. S., & Rai, S. S. (2024). Mapping the research landscape of vocational education and entrepreneurship: Insights and future directions. *Higher Education. Skills and Work-Based Learning*, *14*(5), 992–1010. DOI: 10.1108/HESWBL-05-2023-0129

Sansone, G., Battaglia, D., Landoni, P., & Paolucci, E. (2019). Academic spinoffs: The role of entrepreneurship education. *The International Entrepreneurship and Management Journal*, *17*(1), 1. Advance online publication. DOI: 10.1007/s11365-019-00601-9

Sarasvathy, S. D., & Venkataraman, S. (2011). Entrepreneurship as Method: Open Questions for an Entrepreneurial Future. *Entrepreneurship Theory and Practice*, *35*(1), 113–135. https://journals.sagepub.com/doi/full/10.1111/j.1540-6520.2010.00425.x?casa_token=fMYF9GKhJhAAAAAA%3AINJJ0rkX8gKnLrh81a-KnvrjjJmltNrSpdZt6cgdh1f1X48XLgHrxe3OdNIH5xn1UAI2BRO0lo2Zvg. DOI: 10.1111/j.1540-6520.2010.00425.x

Shabbir, M. S., Arshad, M. A., Mahmood, A., & Sulaiman, M. A. B. A. (2019). 4th industrial revolution and TVET: The relevance of entrepreneurship education for development. *Opcion*, *35*(SpecialEdition24), 11–21.

Shah, N., Bano, S., Saraih, U. N., Abdelwahed, N. A. A., & Soomro, B. A. (2024). Boosting entrepreneurial intentions among potential TVET entrepreneurs of higher education institutes. *Education + Training*, *66*(7), 981–1006. DOI: 10.1108/ET-07-2023-0300

Shane, S., & Venkataraman, S. (2007). The promise of entrepreneurship as a field of research. In *Entrepreneurship* (pp. 171–184). Concepts, Theory and Perspective., DOI: 10.1007/978-3-540-48543-8_8

Shikalepo, E. E. (2019). Sustainability of entrepreneurship and innovation among TVET graduates in Namibia. *International Journal for Innovation Education and Research*, *7*(5), 133–145. DOI: 10.31686/ijier.vol7.iss5.1484

Suharno, S., Ihsan, F., Himawanto, D. A., Pambudi, N. A., & Rizkiana, R. (2025). Sustainability development in vocational education: A case study in Indonesia. *Higher Education, Skills and Work-Based Learning, ahead-of-print*(ahead-of-print). https://doi.org/DOI: 10.1108/HESWBL-01-2024-0018/FULL/XML

Teece, D. J. (2012). Dynamic Capabilities: Routines versus Entrepreneurial Action. *Journal of Management Studies, 49*(8), 1395–1401. DOI: 10.1111/j.1467-6486.2012.01080.x

UNESCO. (2025a). Quality TVET for all contributing to sustainable development, globally. *UNESCO.* https://unevoc.unesco.org

UNESCO. (2025b). *Strategy for Technical and Vocational Education and Training (TVET) (2016–2021).* UNESCO.

UNESCO-UNEVOC. (2013). TVET and entrepreneurial skills. In *Revisiting global trends in TVET: Refelction on theory and practice.* UNESCO-UNEVOC International Centre for Technical and Vocational Educaiton and Training.

UNESCO-UNEVOC. (2022). *Transforming Technical and Vocational Education and Training for successful and just transitions: UNESCO Strategy 2022-2029* (No. 9789231005527). https://www.unesco.org/open-access/terms-use-ccbysa-en

Valerio, A., Parton, B., & Robb, A. (2014). *Entrepreneurship education and training programs around the world: Dimensions for success.* https://books.google.com.my/books?hl=en&lr=&id=ypFtAwAAQBAJ&oi=fnd&pg=PP1&dq=Valerio,+A.,+Parton,+B.,+%26+Robb,+A.+(2014).+Entrepreneurship+education+and+training+programs+around+the+world:+Dimensions+for+success.+The+World+Bank.&ots=6UOGhV7HmM&sig=uiWONbBTKM3FkiqGSbqe8XjFQb4

Valiente, O. (2014). The OECD skills strategy and the education agenda for development. *International Journal of Educational Development, 39,* 40–48. DOI: 10.1016/j.ijedudev.2014.08.008

WEF. (2023). *The Future of Job Report 2023 Insight Report May 2023* (No. 9789811206818; World Economic Forum, pp. 296–296). World Economic Forum. DOI: 10.1142/11458

World Bank. (2023). *Building better formal TVET systems: Principles and Practice in Low-and Middle-Income Countries.*

Yusof, Z. N., Murad, N., & Yusof, B. (2022). Digital Skills and Entrepreneurial Education in Malaysia: Evidence from Experiential Learning. *Theorising Undergraduate Entrepreneurship Education: Reflections on the Development of the Entrepreneurial Mindset*, 311–332. DOI: 10.1007/978-3-030-87865-8_17

Compilation of References

Abbaszadeh, M., Abdavi, F., & Golmohammadi, H. (2023). *Improving the Validity of Mixed and Multi-Methods Through Triangulation in Sports Management Investigation.*, *4*(2), 16–27.

Abdelmagid, A. S., Jabli, N. M., Al-Mohaya, A. Y., & Teleb, A. A. (2025). Integrating interactive metaverse environments and generative artificial intelligence to promote the green digital economy and e-entrepreneurship in higher education. *Sustainability (Basel)*, *17*(12), 5594. DOI: 10.3390/su17125594

Abumdallala, S. M. (2019). The relationship between imports and inflation in Palestine: Toda and Yamamoto causality analysis. *International Journal of Business Administration*, *10*(2), 17–21. DOI: 10.5430/ijba.v10n2p17

Abun, D., Ranay, F. B., Encarnacion, M. J., & Magallanes, T. (2022). Investigation in Corporate & Social Science The Influence of Corporate Governance on the Individual Work Insight of Employees. *The Case of Private Higher Education.*, *11*(3), 82–98.

Abun, D., Ranay, F. B., Encarnacion, M. J., & Magallanes, T. (2022). The influence of corporate governance on the individual work performance of employees: The case of private higher education. *Journal of Corporate & Social Science*, *11*(3), 82–98.

Acheampong, R., Popovici, D.-M., Balan, T. C., Rekeraho, A., & Oprea, I.-A. (2025). A cybersecurity risk assessment for enhanced security in virtual reality. *Information (Basel)*, *16*(6), 430. DOI: 10.3390/info16060430

Affero, I., & Hassan, R. (2013). *Issues and Challenges of Technical and Vocational Education & Training in Malaysia for Knowledge Worker Driven. National Conference on Engineering Technology*. DOI: 10.13140/2.1.4555.2961

Ahmad, A., Ghazali, Z., Chang, V., & Nasir, M. H. (2022). Regulatory challenges in cross-border metaverse entrepreneurship: A review of jurisdictional implications. *International Journal of Digital Law*, *14*(1), 41–58.

Ajzen, I. (1991). The theory of planned behavior. *Organizational Behavior and Human Decision Processes*, *50*(2), 179–211. DOI: 10.1016/0749-5978(91)90020-T

Al-Maroof, R. S., Salloum, S. A., AlHamad, A. Q., & Shaalan, K. (2021). Understanding factors influencing adoption of metaverse applications in remote work settings. *Journal of Virtual Collaboration*, *9*(4), 211–228.

Alputra, F., & Saidin, S. (2025). *E-government: Digital transformation in government governance*. Cv. Eureka Media Aksara.

Alsafadi, Y., & Aljawarneh, N. (2020). Challenges and opportunities in integrating immersive technologies in emerging markets. *Journal of Business Research*, *117*, 456–467.

Amin, S. M., Ahmad Suhaimi, S. S., & Nazuri, N. S. (2023). The Present and Future of Malaysian Technical and Vocational Education and Training (TVET). *International Journal of Academic Research in Business & Social Sciences*, *13*(18). Advance online publication. DOI: 10.6007/IJARBSS/v13-i18/19952

Analysis, E. (2023). The Influence of Government Expenditure on Innovation in Nigeria. *An Empirical Analysis.*, (73), 1510–1521.

Andika, Y., Ekowati, S. H., Ismail, S., & Hierro, I. A. (2022). Need an analysis of virtual reality-based learning media for French listening skills of DELF A1. *KEMBARA: Jurnal Keilmuan Bahasa, Sastra, dan Pengajarannya*, *8*(1), 37–50. DOI: 10.22219/kembara.v8i1.20024

Arriaga, P., Clemente, F., Ortí, J. A., & Sánchez, A. (2021). Metaverse-based resources as strategic assets for competitive advantage. *Journal of Innovation & Knowledge*, *6*(3), 89–99.

Assad, F., Konstantinov, S., Patsavellas, J., & Salonitis, K. (2024). A framework for enabling metaverse for sustainable manufacturing. *Proceeding CIRP*, 128, 108–113. DOI: 10.1016/j.procir.2024.06.010

Audrezet, A., & Koles, B. (2023). Virtual influencer as a brand avatar in interactive marketing. In *The Palgrave handbook of interactive marketing* (pp. 353–376). Springer International Publishing. DOI: 10.1007/978-3-031-14961-0_16

Autor, D. (2022). *The Labor Market Impacts of Technological Change: From Unbridled Enthusiasm to Qualified Optimism to Vast Uncertainty* (No. Working Paper 30074). National Bureau of Economic Research. DOI: 10.3386/w30074

Avis, J. (2023). In pursuit of equity vocational education and training and social justice. *Research in Post-Compulsory Education*, *28*(3), 439–459. https://www.tandfonline.com/doi/abs/10.1080/13596748.2023.2221119. DOI: 10.1080/13596748.2023.2221119

Ayinaddis, S. G. (2023). The Influence of Innovation Orientation on Corporate Insight: Evidence from Micro and Small Manufacturing Corporates in Selected Towns of Awi Zone, Ethiopia. *Journal of Innovation and Entrepreneurship*, *12*(1). Advance online publication. DOI: 10.1186/s13731-023-00290-3

Azhar, S., Harris, R., Zaki, M., & Hafeez, M. (2023). Globalizing virtual enterprises: Lessons from metaverse-based entrepreneurship. *Technological Horizons in Education*, *20*(2), 115–132.

Bailenson, J. N., & Blascovich, J. (2004). Avatars. *Encyclopedia of human-computer interaction, 1*, 64-6.

Bakari, S., Mabrouki, M., & Othmani, A. (2018). The six linkages between foreign direct investment, domestic investment, exports, imports, labor force and economic growth: New empirical and policy analysis from Nigeria. *Journal of Smart Economic Growth*, *3*(1), 25–43.

Ba, L., Tangour, F., El Abbassi, I., & Absi, R. (2025). Analysis of digital twin applications in energy efficiency: A systematic review. *Sustainability (Basel)*, *17*(8), 3560. DOI: 10.3390/su17083560

Baltagi, B. H. (2021). Dynamic panel data models. In *Econometric analysis of panel data* (pp. 187–228). Springer International Publishing. DOI: 10.1007/978-3-030-53953-5_8

Bandura, A. (1997). Self-Efficacy: Toward a Unifying Theory of Behavioral Change. *Psychological Review*, *84*(2), 191–215. DOI: 10.1037/0033-295X.84.2.191 PMID: 847061

Barney, J. B. (1991). Firm resources and sustained competitive advantage. *Journal of Management*, *17*(1), 99–120. DOI: 10.1177/014920639101700108

Baškarada, S., & Koronios, A. (2018). A Philosophical Discussion of Qualitative, Quantitative, and Mixed Methods Investigation in Social Science. *Qualitative Research Journal*, *18*(1), 2–21. DOI: 10.1108/QRJ-D-17-00042

Baudrillard, J. (1994). *Simulacra and simulation*. The University of Michigan Press.

Beck, N., Piva, M., & Tether, B. (2021). Entrepreneurial innovativeness and organizational learning: A dynamic capability perspective. *Entrepreneurship Theory and Practice*, *45*(5), 1098–1123. DOI: 10.1177/1042258720945853

Bekos, G. S., Chari, S., Marikyan, D., & Papagiannidis, S. (2025). Metaverse adoption for competitive edge: The role of implementation capability & willingness to change. *Decision Support Systems*, *189*, 114385. DOI: 10.1016/j.dss.2024.114385

Beltramino, N. S., Valdez-juárez, L. E., Ingaramo, J. M., Gazzaniga, L. C., & Beltramino, N. A. (2023).. . *The Influences of Corporate Learning and Entrepreneurial Orientation on the Corporate Insight of Argentinean, Mexican, and Ecuadorian MSMEs.*, *7*, 1–21.

Bertot, J., Jaeger, P., Sarin, L., & Hansen, D. (2022). Digital transformation and the immersion economy: The promise of metaverse integration. *Government Information Quarterly*, *39*(3), 121–139.

Bhutoria, A. (2022). Personalized education and artificial intelligence in the United States, China, and India: A systematic review using a human-in-the-loop model. *Computers and Education: Artificial Intelligence*, *3*, 100068. DOI: 10.1016/j.caeai.2022.100068

Biocca, F. (1997). The cyborg's dilemma: Progressive embodiment in virtual environments. *Journal of Computer-Mediated Communication*, *3*(2), JCMC324. DOI: 10.1111/j.1083-6101.1997.tb00070.x

Biocca, F., Harms, C., & Burgoon, J. K. (2003). Toward a more robust theory and measure of social presence: Review and suggested criteria. *Presence (Cambridge, Mass.)*, *12*(5), 456–480. DOI: 10.1162/105474603322761270

Boellstorff, T. (2008). *Coming of age in Second Life: An anthropologist explores the virtually human*. Princeton University Press.

Branch, E., & Geneva, I. L. O. (2019). *Skills for trade and economic diversification in Ethiopia: A background paper for drafting of a sector skills strategy for the garment sector in Ethiopia*. International Labour Organization.

Brush, C. G., Greene, P. G., Hart, M. M., & Harold, S. H. (2001). From initial idea to unique advantage: The entrepreneurial challenge of constructing a resource base. *The Academy of Management Perspectives*, *15*(1), 64–78. DOI: 10.5465/ame.2001.4251394

Brynjolfsson, E., & McAfee, A. (2014). *The second machine age: Work, progress, and prosperity in a time of brilliant technologies*. W. W. Norton & Company.

Buchner, T., Kleinhans, M., Küpper, D., & Brown, J. (2025). *The transformative impact of the industrial metaverse*. Boston Consulting Group.

Budijaya, M., & Situmeang, M. (2025). Digital transformation in governance: Analysis of the effectiveness of application-based public services in the Society 5.0 era. *All Fields of Science Journal Liaison Academia and Society*, *5*, 1–13. DOI: 10.58939/afosj-las.v5i2.1024

Buli, B. M., & Yesuf, W. M. (2015). Determinants of entrepreneurial intentions: Technical-vocational education and training students in Ethiopia. *Education + Training*, *57*(8/9), 891–907. DOI: 10.1108/ET-10-2014-0129

Burina, E. V., & Dunaeva, L. A. (2022). ACQUIRING LISTENING COMPREHENSION SKILLS IN FRENCH IN VIRTUAL LINGUODIDACTIC ENVIRONMENT. *Мир науки, культуры, образования*, (4 (95)), 29-33.

Byrne, C., & Hall, R. A. (2013). Realising Australia's international education as public diplomacy. *Australian Journal of International Affairs*, *67*(4), 419–438. DOI: 10.1080/10357718.2013.806019

Caragliu, A., Del Bo, C., & Nijkamp, P. (2011). Smart cities in Europe. *Journal of Urban Technology*, *18*(2), 65–82. DOI: 10.1080/10630732.2011.601117

Carlson, J., Rahman, M., Taylor, A., & Varela, M. (2022). Social presence and flow in virtual environments: A model of consumer immersion. *Journal of Interactive Marketing*, *57*, 124–137.

Cavusgil, S. T., Knight, G., Riesenberger, J. R., & Yaprak, A. (2020). *International business: The new realities* (5th ed.). Pearson.

Central Statistics Agency. (2023). *DKI Jakarta in figures 2023*. https://jakarta.bps.go.id

Chang, C., Kao, H., Zheng, Z., & Zhao, L. (2022). Adoption and diffusion of metaverse innovations: A cross-cultural perspective. *Computers in Human Behavior*, *140*, 107571.

Chankseliani, M., & Anuar, A. M. (2019). Cross-country comparison of engagement in apprenticeships: A conceptual analysis of incentives for individuals and firms. *International Journal of Research in Vocational Education and Training*, *6*(3), 261–283. DOI: 10.13152/IJRVET.6.3.4

Chen, L.-T., & Liu, L. (2020). Methods to Analyze Likert-Type Data in Educational Technology Investigation. *Journal of Educational Technology Development and Exchange*, *13*(2), 39–60. DOI: 10.18785/jetde.1302.04

Chen, T., Wu, Q., He, J., & Chen, F. (2021). Pandemic-driven transformations in virtual business environments: A comprehensive analysis. *Journal of Business Analytics*, *4*(2), 63–79.

Chen, Y., Zhang, M., & Yu, S. (2021). Personalized learning pathways supported by artificial intelligence: A review of microlearning in higher education. *Computers & Education*, *172*, 104251. DOI: 10.1016/j.compedu.2021.104251

Chesbrough, H. (2003). *Open innovation: The new imperative for creating and profiting from technology*. Harvard Business Press.

Chung, K. W., Chan, F., Leung, L., & Yuen, S. (2022). Multidisciplinary approaches to metaverse organizational models. *Asia-Pacific Journal of Management Innovation*, *18*(4), 73–88.

Clark, J. R. (2025). Military strategy and the political dynamics of war. *Military Strategy Magazine*, *10*(1), 12–19. DOI: 10.64148/msm.v10i1.2

Cockburn, I. M., Henderson, R., & Stern, S. (2019). The impact of Artificial Intelligence on Innovation. An exploratory Analysis. In *The Economics of Artificial Intelligence: An Agenda* (Vol. 1–May, pp. 115–146). https://www.nber.org/system/files/chapters/c14006/c14006.pdf

Coleman, J. S. (1988). Social capital in the creation of human capital. *American Journal of Sociology*, *94*, S95–S120. DOI: 10.1086/228943

Croce, D., Castellucci, G., & Basili, R. (2020). GAN-BERT: Generative adversarial learning for robust text classification with a bunch of labeled examples. *Proceedings of the 58th Annual Meeting of the Association for Computational Linguistics*, 2114–2119. DOI: 10.18653/v1/2020.acl-main.191

Cull, N. J. (2008). Public diplomacy: Taxonomies and histories. *The Annals of the American Academy of Political and Social Science*, *616*(1), 31–54. DOI: 10.1177/0002716207311952

Da Costa, G. (2025, July 3). 2050 initiative deepens French-Indonesian strategic cooperation. Indo-Pacific Defense Forum. https://ipdefenseforum.com/2025/07/2050-initiative-deepens-french-indonesian-strategic-cooperation/

Desalegn, G., Tangl, A., & Boros, A. (2024). Ethiopian consumer's behavior towards purchasing locally produced apparel products: An extended model of the theory of planned behavior. *Complexity*, *2024*(1), 8745919. Advance online publication. DOI: 10.1155/2024/8745919

Deterding, S., Dixon, D., Khaled, R., & Nacke, L. (2011). From game design elements to gamefulness. *Proceedings of the 15th International Academic MindTrek Conference*, 9(7), 45-58.

Devi, G. A. (2024). Role of quality education for sustainable development goals (SDGs). *International Journal of Creative Research Thoughts*, *12*(6), 217–224. https://ijcrt.org/papers/IJCRT2506217.pdf

Devlin, J., Chang, M. W., Lee, K., & Toutanova, K. (2019, June). Bert: Pre-training of deep bidirectional transformers for language understanding. In *Proceedings of the 2019 conference of the North American chapter of the association for computational linguistics: human language technologies, volume 1 (long and short papers)* (pp. 4171-4186).

Di Pasquale, V., Cutolo, P., Esposito, C., Franco, B., Iannone, R., & Miranda, S. (2024). Virtual reality for training in assembly and disassembly tasks: A systematic literature review. *Machines (Basel)*, *12*(8), 528. DOI: 10.3390/machines12080528

Dionisio, J. D. N., Iii, W. G. B., & Gilbert, R. (2013). 3D virtual worlds and the metaverse: Current status and future possibilities. *ACM Computing Surveys*, *45*(3), 1–38. DOI: 10.1145/2480741.2480751

Dionisio, J., Lima, V., Bessa, M., & Vilarinho, H. (2021). The early stages of metaverse development: A review of immersive environments. *Virtual Reality & Intelligent Hardware*, *3*(4), 276–290.

Djafarova, E., & Rushworth, C. (2017). Exploring the credibility of online celebrities' Instagram profiles in influencing the purchase decisions of young female users. *Computers in Human Behavior*, *68*, 1–7. DOI: 10.1016/j.chb.2016.11.009

Djakaria, E. K., & Shlapai, H. (2022). Navigating Organizational Learning from Failure to Foster Innovation as a Process.

Dos Santos, S. C., Nobre, M. R. B., Varela, S. L. L., Figueroa, F., & Martins, D. E. (2024). Challenges in metaverse adoption on people, process, and technology perspectives: A review from the five past years. In *Proceedings of the 26th International Conference on Enterprise Information Systems* (pp. 485–496). DOI: 10.5220/0012617800003690

Du, C., Zhang, Y., & Li, J. (2017). LSTM-based model for ancient poetry generation. *Proceedings of the International Conference on Natural Language Processing*, 245-253.

Dwivedi, Y. K.. (2023). Metaverse Marketing: Strategies, Platforms, and Consumer Engagement. *Journal of Interactive Marketing*, *62*, 48–63.

Eichenbaum, M., Johannsen, B. K., & Rebelo, S. T. (2017). Monetary policy and the predictability of nominal exchange rates.

Eisenhardt, K. M. (1989). Building theories from case study research. *Academy of Management Review*, *14*(4), 532–550. DOI: 10.2307/258557

Ellis, J. L. (2020). Microlearning in second language acquisition: Theories, design, and practice. *Journal of Language Teaching and Research*, *11*(3), 345–356. DOI: 10.17507/jltr.1103.03

Fakhreddin, F., & Foroudi, P. (2022a). The Influence of Market Orientation on New Product Insight through Product Launch Quality : A Resource-Based View The Influence of Market Orientation on New Product Insight through Product Launch Quality : A. *Cogent Corporate & Management*, *9*(1). Advance online publication. DOI: 10.1080/23311975.2022.2108220

Fang, Y., Chen, S., Huang, C., & Tseng, T. (2022). Creating entrepreneurial value in the metaverse: Emergence of novel business models. *The Journal of Entrepreneurship*, *31*(3), 387–411.

Fathony, R., Muradi, M., & Sagita, N. I. (2021). Utilization of information technology in the provision of public services within the Bandung city government. *Jurnal Aggregasi: Action for Government Reform in Democracy*, *9*(2), 1–12. DOI: 10.34010/agregasi.v9i2.5581

Fauceglia, D. (2015). Credit constraints, firm exports and financial development: Evidence from developing countries. *The Quarterly Review of Economics and Finance*, *55*, 53–66. DOI: 10.1016/j.qref.2014.08.003

Fayolle, A., & Gailly, B. (2008). *From craft to science: Teaching models and learning processes in entrepreneurship education* (Vol. 32, Issue 7, p. 593). DOI: 10.1108/03090590810899838

Fayolle, A., & Linan, F. (2020). The future of research on entrepreneurial intentions. *Journal of Business Research*, *110*, 402–407. DOI: 10.1016/j.jbusres.2019.09.045

Fayolle, A., Liñán, F., & Moriano, J. A. (2014). Beyond entrepreneurial intentions: Values and motivations in entrepreneurship. *The International Entrepreneurship and Management Journal*, *10*(4), 679–689. DOI: 10.1007/s11365-014-0306-7

Flemming, P. L., Flemming, B., McLaughlin, G., & Faley, T. (2018). The Impact of Market Orientation, Mixed Method Research and Organizational Leadership: A research method proposition and implication for executive leadership. [IJBMM]. *International Journal of Business Marketing and Management*, *3*(7), 45–59.

Flemming, P. L., Flemming, B., McLaughlin, G., & Faley, T. (2018). The influence of market orientation, mixed method research and business leadership: A research method proposition and implication for executive leadership. *Journal of Leadership Studies*, *3*(7), 45–59.

Floridi, L., & Cowls, J. (2022). 22. A Unified Framework of Five Principles for AI in Society. In S. Carta (Ed.), *Machine Learning and the City*. Wiley Online Library. https://onlinelibrary.wiley.com/doi/abs/10.1002/9781119815075.ch45

Freire, P. Ramos, M. Bergman., & Macedo, D. P. (2005). *Pedagogy of the oppressed* (p. 219). The Continuum International Publishing Group Inc.

Galguera, M. P. (2018). *Globalisation, Mass Education and Technical and Vocational Education and Training, The Influence of UNESCO in Botswana*. Springer International Publishing AG., https://www.springer.com/series/6969

Gandhi, N., Durth, S., Bérubé, V., Kedia, K., & Lim, R. (2025). The critical role of strategic workforce planning in the age of AI. *McKinsey & Company, February* 9–9.

García, E. G., Magaña, E. C., & Ariza, A. C. (2020). Quality education as a Sustainable Development Goal in the context of the 2030 Agenda: A bibliometric approach. *Sustainability (Basel)*, *12*(15), 5884. DOI: 10.3390/su12155884

GEM. (2024). *GEM 2024/2025 Global Report: Entrepreneurship Reality Check*. Global Entrepreneurship Research Association (GERA). http://www.witchwoodhouse.com

Getley, R. (1979). Entrepreneurial drive. *Industrial and Commercial Training*, *11*(1), 19–23. DOI: 10.1108/eb003711

Ginting, G. (2017). *Pengaruh motivasi kerja, kompetensi, dan kompensasi terhadap kinerja karyawan. Scientific Journal of Reflection: Economic.* Accounting, Management and Business.

Gioia, D. A., Corley, K. G., & Hamilton, A. L. (2013). Seeking qualitative rigor in inductive research: Notes on the Gioia methodology. *Organizational Research Methods, 16*(1), 15–31. DOI: 10.1177/1094428112452151

Golan, G. J. (2013). An integrated approach to public diplomacy. *The American Behavioral Scientist, 57*(9), 1251–1255. DOI: 10.1177/0002764213487711

González, A., Santos, R., Barreto, L., & Guerra, F. (2022). Cross-sector collaborations in metaverse-based ventures: A systematic literature review. *European Management Journal, 40*(5), 821–833.

Grobler, S., & Dittrich, A. K. (2024). Envisioning quality education for sustainability transformation in teacher education: Perspectives from an international dialogue on SDG 4. *International Journal of Comparative Education and Development, 26*(3), 175–192. DOI: 10.1108/IJCED-06-2023-0048

Gu, Z., Guan, Y., & Zhang, S. (2024, August). A text restoration model for ancient texts based on pre-trained language model RoBERTa. In *Proceedings of the 2024 4th International Conference on Internet of Things and Machine Learning* (pp. 96-102). DOI: 10.1145/3697467.3697610

Hadi, R., Melumad, S., & Park, E. S. (2024). The Metaverse: A new digital frontier for consumer behaviour. *Journal of Consumer Psychology, 34*(1), 142–166. DOI: 10.1002/jcpy.1356

Ha, G., Park, J., Jung, J., & Yoo, S. (2022). Rethinking governance in the metaverse: Opportunities, risks, and policy recommendations. *Government Studies Review, 16*(2), 145–158.

Hailemariam, S. (2020). The effect of marketing strategy on micro and small enterprises sales performance: Evidence from service sector in Addis Ababa, in the case of Kirkos subcity (Doctoral dissertation, St. Mary's university).

Hamzeh, A., Hozarmoghadam, N., & Ghanbarzadeh, M. (2023). Investigating the level of satisfaction of policyholders with supplementary health insurance in Iran. *BMC Health Services Research*, *23*(1), 10134. Advance online publication. DOI: 10.1186/s12913-023-10134-1 PMID: 37951884

Han, T., Jiang, S., Wang, Q., & Feng, J. (2021). Architectural breakthroughs in virtual realism: A survey of immersive design and simulation. *IEEE Transactions on Visualization and Computer Graphics*, *27*(11), 4209–4220.

Harahap, F. R. (2013). The impact of urbanization on city development in Indonesia. *Society*, *1*(1), 35–45. DOI: 10.33019/society.v1i1.40

Harris, S., Daigle, M., Gleason, S., & Young, R. (2021). Virtual immersion, real impact: Corporate transformations in a post-pandemic metaverse. *Global Business and Organizational Excellence*, *40*(4), 31–44.

Harris, W., Katz, R., Shneiderman, A., & Thompson, E. (2023). Ethical frontiers in immersive environments: Reevaluating the role of corporate responsibility. *Journal of Virtual Societies*, *12*(1), 56–70.

Hasan, K. M. F., Mia, M. S., Rahman, M. M., Ahmed Ullah, A., & Shariat Ullah, M. S. (2016). Role of textile and clothing industries in the growth and development of trade and business strategies of Bangladesh in the global economy.

Hasan, M. M., Sharma, A., Johnson, F., Mariethoz, G., & Seed, A. (2016). Merging radar and in situ rainfall measurements: An assessment of different combination algorithms. *Water Resources Research*, *52*(10), 8384–8398. DOI: 10.1002/2015WR018441

Hess, T., Matt, C., Benlian, A., & Wiesböck, F. (2016). Options for formulating a digital transformation strategy. *MIS Quarterly Executive*, *15*(2), 103–119.

He, Z., Sang, W., Zhou, X., & Wang, J. (2020). Interactive realms: Charting the development of metaverse platforms. *IEEE Internet Computing*, *24*(6), 34–42.

Huang, A. Y., Lu, O. H., & Yang, S. J. (2023). Effects of artificial Intelligence–Enabled personalized recommendations on learners' learning engagement, motivation, and outcomes in a flipped classroom. *Computers & Education, 194*, 104684. DOI: 10.1016/j.compedu.2022.104684

Huang, Z., Li, T., Liu, Y., & Xu, F. (2022). Immersive learning in the metaverse: Pedagogical strategies and technological enablers. *Computers & Education, 180*, 104428.

ILO. (2023). *Improve Technical and Vocational Education and Training (TVET) to meet skills and labour mismatch*. https://www.ilo.org/resource/news/improve-technical-and-vocational-education-and-training-tvet-meet-skills

Indonesia Business Post. (2025, May 28). Macron's visit yields 21 strategic Indonesia–France agreements. https://indonesiabusinesspost.com/4403/capitol-influence-and-lobbying/macron-s-visit-yields-21-strategic-indonesia-france-agreements

Irawan, A., & Santoso, B. (2023). Fostering innovation culture in small and medium enterprises: Evidence from Indonesia. *Journal of Small Business Management, 61*(4), 1234–1256.

Jakarta Regional Disaster Management Agency. (2021). *Annual report on flood management in Jakarta*. https://bpbd.jakarta.go.id

Jakarta Smart City. (2022). *Citizen digital services performance and statistics report*. https://smartcity.jakarta.go.id

Jamilah, K. M., & Sari, D. S. (2024). Indonesia's defense diplomacy towards France in 2019–2023 from defense diplomacy motives perspective. Jurnal Pertahanan, 10(3), 383–396. https://jurnal.idu.ac.id/index.php/DefenseJournal/article/download/19647/pdf

Jones, C. (2010). Entrepreneurship education: Revisiting our role and its purpose. *Journal of Small Business and Enterprise Development, 17*(4), 500–513. DOI: 10.1108/14626001011088697

Kang, H., Yoon, Y., Bae, J., & Min, K. (2022). Governing virtual worlds: Policies, regulations, and codes of conduct in the metaverse era. *The Information Society*, *38*(1), 32–44.

Kaplan, A. M., & Haenlein, M. (2009). The fairyland of Second Life: Virtual social worlds and how to use them. *Business Horizons*, *52*(6), 563–572. DOI: 10.1016/j.bushor.2009.07.002

Kaplan, A. M., & Haenlein, M. (2019). Siri, Siri, in my hand: Who's the fairest in the land? On the interpretations, illustrations, and implications of artificial intelligence. *Business Horizons*, *62*(1), 15–25. DOI: 10.1016/j.bushor.2018.08.004

Kapoor, A., & Sindwani, R. (2025a). Artificial Intelligence as a Catalyst for Advancing Contactless Payments. AI Marketing and Ethical Considerations in Consumer Engagement, 321–338.

Kapoor, A., & Sindwani, R. (2025b). Navigating Inhibitors to Artificial Intelligence Adoption in Human Resource Management Practices: A Multi-criteria Decision-making Approach.

Kapoor, A., Sindwani, R., & Goel, M. (2022). Assessing Mobile Banking Service Quality Dimensions Using Multi-Criteria Decision Making. Future of Work and Business in Covid-19 Era, 131–147.

Kapoor, A., Sindwani, R., & Goel, M. (2021). Prioritising the key factors influencing the adoption of mobile wallets: An Indian perspective in covid-19 era. *Journal of Information Technology Management*, *13*(4), 161–182.

Kapoor, A., Sindwani, R., & Goel, M. (2023). Exploring quick commerce service experience: A moderated mediated investigation using SEM and fsQCA. Total Quality Management &amp. *Business Excellence*, *34*(13–14), 1896–1919.

Kapoor, A., Sindwani, R., & Goel, M. (2024a). Exploring the symmetric and asymmetric effects of mobile wallet service experience on brand loyalty in India: Evidence from SEM and fsQCA. *Journal of Financial Services Marketing*, *29*(4), 1524–1541. DOI: 10.1057/s41264-024-00280-w

Kapoor, A., Sindwani, R., & Goel, M. (2024b). A novel framework for understanding the interplay between the mobile wallet service quality dimensions and loyalty intention. *The TQM Journal*, *37*(6), 1716–1741. DOI: 10.1108/TQM-12-2023-0422

Kapoor, A., Sindwani, R., & Goel, M. (2024c). Assessing inhibitors to adoption of m-wallet: A BWM approach. *International Journal of Business Excellence*, *32*(4), 433–455.

Kapoor, A., Sindwani, R., & Goel, M. (2025a). Unlocking India's mobile wallet potential: Identifying and prioritising key sustainable growth catalysts using best worst method. *International Journal of Process Management and Benchmarking*, *21*(2), 218–230.

Kapoor, A., Sindwani, R., & Goel, M. (2025b). Assessing mobile wallet service quality using analytic hierarchy process and fuzzy evaluation method. *International Journal of Services and Operations Management*, *50*(2), 246–266. DOI: 10.1504/IJSOM.2025.144481

Karaev, F., & Mercan, M. (2023). Exploring the Influence of Market Orientation and Innovation on Corporate Insight in the Beverage Industry: The Mediating Role of Innovation. *Eurasian Journal of Economic and Corporate Investigations*, *1*(67), 139–155. DOI: 10.47703/ejebs.v1i67.256

Kattakinda, J. P., Dhananjaya, S., Mojžiš, S., Nadif, A., Hanna, M., Apsan, R., & Malavolta, I. (2024). Towards understanding the energy consumption of virtual reality applications in gaming, education, and entertainment. In *Proceedings of the 8th International Workshop on Games and Software Engineering* (pp. 50–57). Association for Computing Machinery. DOI: 10.1145/3643658.3643922

Kazu, İ. Y., & Kuvvetli, M. (2023). A triangulation method on the effectiveness of digital game-based language learning for vocabulary acquisition. *Education and Information Technologies*, *28*(10), 13541–13567. DOI: 10.1007/s10639-023-11756-y PMID: 37361816

Kementerian Pendidikan Tinggi. Sains, dan Teknologi Republik Indonesia. (2025). Laporan implementasi program riset dan pengabdian masyarakat 2025. https://kemdiktisaintek.go.id

Kero, C. A., & Sogbossi, B. B. (2017). Competitive strategy orientation and innovative success: Mediating market orientation a study of small-medium enterprises. *Global Journal of Management and Business Research*, *17*(3), 1–16.

Khaidar, M. F., Ardiansyah, M. N., & Permatasari, I. (2024). Development of a project management information system (PMIS) for monitoring and controlling systems at PT Telkom Indonesia. *Technologia: Scientific Journal*, *15*(4), 843. DOI: 10.31602/tji.v15i4.16401

Khan, W. A., Hassan, R. A., Arshad, M. Z., Arshad, M. A., Kashif, U., Aslam, F., & Wafa, S. A. (2020). The effect of entrepreneurial orientation and organisational culture on firm performance: The mediating role of innovation. International Journal of Innovation, Creativity and Change.

Khan, I., Ming, J., Ali, M., & Zhang, Z. (2022). Influence of Government Supports on Small and Medium Enterprises Progression: Case Investigation of Swat Valley. *Journal of Small Corporate Management*, *60*(6), 1484–1515. DOI: 10.1080/00472778.2020.1767487

Kissi, E., Ahadzie, D. K., Debrah, C., & Adjei-Kumi, T. (2020). Underlying strategies for improving entrepreneurial skills development of technical and vocational students in developing countries: Using Ghana as a case study. *Education + Training*, *62*(5), 599–614. DOI: 10.1108/ET-11-2019-0264

Knight, G. A., & Liesch, P. W. (2016). Internationalization: From incremental to born global. *Journal of World Business*, *51*(1), 93–102. DOI: 10.1016/j.jwb.2015.08.011

Koivumäki, T., Koivumäki, J., Hänninen, M., & Kuusijärvi, J. (2022). Legitimacy and control: Metaverse governance challenges for transnational enterprises. *International Journal of Technology Policy and Law*, *10*(2), 176–192.

Kolb, D. A. (2014). *Experiential learning: Experience as the source of learning and development*. FT press.

Krueger, N., & Carsrud, A. L. (1993). Entrepreneurial intentions: Applying the theory of planned behaviour. *Entrepreneurship and Regional Development*, *5*(4), 315–330. DOI: 10.1080/08985629300000020

Krugman, P. R. (1986). *Strategic trade policy and the new international economics. MIT Press. Rodrik, D. (2007). One economics, many recipes: Globalization, institutions, and economic growth.* Princeton University Press.

Krugman, P. R., Obstfeld, M., & Melitz, M. J. (2018). *International economics: Theory and policy* (11th ed.). Pearson Education.

Kumar, A., Shankar, A., Behl, A., Pereira, V., Kapoor, P., & Papa, A. (2025). Implementing enterprise metaverse as a means of enhancing growth hacking performance: Will adopting the metaverse be a success in organizations. *Journal of Business Research*, *188*, 115079. DOI: 10.1016/j.jbusres.2024.115079

Kuratko, D. F. (2007). Entrepreneurial Leadership in the 21st Century. *Journal of Leadership & Organizational Studies*, *13*(4), 1–11. DOI: 10.1177/10717919070130040201

Lambrechts, W., Sinha, S., & Marwala, T. (2020). Decentralizing Emerging Markets to Prepare for Industry 4.0: Modernizing Policies and the Role of Higher Education. In Dorrsamy, W., Paul, B., & Marwala, T. (Eds.), *The Disruptive Fourth Industrial Revolution*. Springer., DOI: 10.1007/978-3-030-48230-5_6

Lans, T., Blok, V., & Wesselink, R. (2014). Learning apart and together: Towards an integrated competence framework for sustainable entrepreneurship in higher education. *Journal of Cleaner Production*, *62*, 37–47. DOI: 10.1016/j.jclepro.2013.03.036

Laspro, M., Groysman, L., Verzella, A. N., Kimberly, L. L., & Flores, R. L. (2023). The use of virtual reality in surgical training: Implications for education, patient safety, and global health equity. *Surgeries*, *4*(4), 635–646. DOI: 10.3390/surgeries4040061

Lin, C., Ku, S., Huang, W., & Ho, L. (2023). Mixed-methods analysis of user engagement in immersive virtual environments. *Computers in Human Behavior*, *142*, 107814.

Liu, P., Zhang, X., & Mou, L. (2022). A character-level length-control algorithm for non-autoregressive sentence summarization. *Advances in Neural Information Processing Systems*, *35*, 29101–29112.

Li, X., Liang, Y., Chen, J., & Zhang, P. (2023). Learning from the metaverse: Organizational routines and adaptation in digital ecosystems. *Journal of Organizational Change Management*, *36*(3), 537–558.

Lo, J., Liu, F., Liao, T., & Tseng, M. (2021). Dynamic capabilities for metaverse-based strategies: Building resilience and competitive advantage. *Journal of Strategy and Management*, *29*(1), 115–129.

López, R., García, M., Acosta, J., & Delgado, L. (2020). The metaverse as a space for interaction for innovation and value generation. *Ibero-American Journal of Entrepreneurship*, *12*(4), 215–227.

Lucas, H. C.Jr, & Goh, J. M. (2009). Disruptive technology: How Kodak missed the digital photography revolution. *The Journal of Strategic Information Systems*, *18*(1), 46–55. DOI: 10.1016/j.jsis.2009.01.002

Mack, A. J., White, D., & Senghor, O. (2019). An insight into entrepreneurship education practices in Technical and Vocational Education and Training institutions. *Journal of Global Entrepreneurship Reserch*. DOI: 10.1186/s40497-019-0169-z

Mahlobo, T. S. (2025). Linking TVET education with entrepreneurial and financial education, YouTube, Retrieved April 5, 2025, from https://www.youtube.com/watch?v=oGoei56y9kc. *New Economy Leadership Institute*. https://www.youtube.com/watch?v=oGoei56y9kc

Mai, Q. H. (2023). Considering different aspects of digital and social media marketing to attract Generation Z and Alpha as the primary customer.

Malufti, M. F. (2025, February 7). Between opportunity and constraint: Recent developments in Indonesia–France security ties. The Diplomat. https://thediplomat.com/2025/02/between-opportunity-and-constraint-recent-developments-in-indonesia-france-security-ties/

Mankiw, N. G., & Reis, R. (2018). Friedman's presidential address in the evolution of macroeconomic thought. *The Journal of Economic Perspectives*, *32*(1), 81–96. DOI: 10.1257/jep.32.1.81

Maritz, A., & Brown, C. R. (2013). Illuminating the black box of entrepreneurship education programs. *Education + Training*, *55*(3), 234–252. DOI: 10.1108/00400911311309305

Martínez, L., Cruz, V., Rodríguez, T., & Paredes, P. (2022). Innovation and immersive marketing: New business models in the metaverse. *Latin American Journal of Digital Strategies*, *8*(2), 76–90.

Marwick, A. (2013). *Status Update: Celebrity, Publicity, and Branding in the Social Media Age*. Yale University Press.

Masoabi, C. S., & Alexander, G. (2021). Possible Merger, Entrepreneurship Education in TVET Engineering Studies: A Case for South Africa. *Journal of Entrepreneurship Education*, *24*(2).

Mavropoulou, E., & Arvanitis, P. (2023). CONTRIBUTION/IMPLICATIONS OF CHATBOT INTEGRATION ON TEACHING AND LEARNING A FOREIGN LANGUAGE. In *ICERI2023 Proceedings* (pp. 7596-7605). IATED.

McDonald, P. J., & Galambos, K. (2024). Trilateral politics in hierarchy, war, and state formation. *International Theory*, *16*(2), 178–210. DOI: 10.1017/S1752971923000209

McGrath, R. G., & MacMillan, I. (2000). *The Entrepreneurial Mindset: Strategies for Continuously Creating Opportunity in an Age of Uncertainty*. Harvard Business School Press., https://www.amazon.com/Entrepreneurial-Mindset-Continuously-Opportunity-Uncertainty/dp/0875848346

McGrath, S., & Powell, L. (2016). Skills for sustainable development: Transforming vocational education and training beyond 2015. *International Journal of Educational Development*, *50*, 12–19. DOI: 10.1016/j.ijedudev.2016.05.006

McKinsey & Company. (2014). *Unleashing Youth in Asia, Solving for the "Triple-E" challenge of youth: Education, Enployment and Engagement.* McKinsey Centre for Government.

McKinsey & Company. (2023). *The Skills Revolution and the Future of Learning and Earning, World Government Summit 2023*. McKinsey & Company.

McKinsey. (2025). *Automation and adaptability: How Malaysia can navigate the future of work | McKinsey*. https://www.mckinsey.com/featured-insights/asia-pacific/automation-and-adaptability-how-malaysia-can-navigate-the-future-of-work

MDEC. (2023). *Harnessing the Power of Technology: Building a Strong Digital Economy for Malaysia's Future*.

Mergel, I., Edelmann, N., & Haug, N. (2019). Defining digital transformation: Results of expert interviews. *Government Information Quarterly*, *36*(4), 101385. DOI: 10.1016/j.giq.2019.06.002

Metzgar, E. T. (2016). Institutions of higher education as public diplomacy tools: China-based university programs for the 21st century. *Journal of Studies in International Education*, *20*(3), 223–241. DOI: 10.1177/1028315315604718

Michael, D.G. (2020). "School of Graduate Investigations The Influence of Innovation on Manufacturing Corporates ' Insight in Ethiopia : Evidence from Garment Corporates ' in Addis Ababa The E Ffect of Innovation on Manufacturing Corporates ' Insight in Ethiopia : Evidence from Garment F Irms '."

MIDA. (2022, October 29). TVET as a catalyst for economic growth. *MIDA | Malaysian Investment Development Authority*. https://www.mida.gov.my/mida-news/tvet-as-a-catalyst-for-economic-growth/

Mikołajewski, D., Piszcz, A., Rojek, I., & Galas, K. (2024). Machine learning supporting virtual reality and brain–computer interface to assess work–life balance conditions for employees. *Electronics (Basel)*, *13*(22), 4489. DOI: 10.3390/electronics13224489

Miles, M. B., & Huberman, A. M. (1994). *Qualitative data analysis: An expanded sourcebook* (2nd ed.). Sage Publications.

Minbale, E., Bizuneh, B., Seife, W., Eyasu, A., Asfaw, T., & Sharew, S. (2024). Ethiopian Client's Behavior towards Purchasing Locally Produced Apparel Products: An Extended Model of the Theory of Planned Behavior. *Complexity*, (1), 8745919.

Ministry of Environment and Forestry [MoEF]. (2021). *Plastic policies in Indonesia: Landscape and strategic direction*. Jakarta: MoEF.

Ministry of National Development Planning [Bappenas]. (2021). *Circular economy Indonesia 2025–2045: National roadmap and action plan*. Jakarta: Bappenas.

Mohamed, A., Abdalla, G., Yusuf, H., & Rehman, M. (2022). Virtual marketing experiences: Strategies for consumer immersion in 3D digital worlds. *Journal of Marketing Trends*, *15*(2), 47–61.

Mohamed, A., Abdalla, S., Yusuf, A., & Rehman, M. (2022). Community building in metaverse branding: Insights from digital marketing research. *Journal of Digital Marketing Insights*, *5*(3), 201–215.

Morley, S. (2025). *Entrepreneurship and TVET_ Nurturing Tomorrow's Business Leaders*. https://www.worldoftvet.com/blog/entrepreneurship-and-tvet

Mukhlis, S., Awaliah, F., Usman Siam, N., & Karim, Z. A. (2023). Implementation of governance. *Journal of Social and Political Sciences*, *4*(2), 1069–1078.

Muridan, N. D., Rasul, M. S., Yasin, R. M., Nor, A. R. M., Rauf, R. A. A., & Jalaludin, N. A. (2023). Career Planning Indicators of Successful TVET Entrepreneurs. *Sustainability (Basel), 15*(8), 6629–6629. DOI: 10.3390/su15086629

Mursalim, S. W. (2017). Implementation of smart city policy in Bandung City. *Journal of Administrative Science: Media for the Development of Administrative Science and Practice, 14*(1), 126–138. DOI: 10.31113/jia.v14i1.1

Mwasalwiba, E. S. (2010). Entrepreneurship education: A review of its objectives, teaching methods, and impact indicators. *Education + Training, 52*(1), 20–47. DOI: 10.1108/00400911011017663

Mystakidis, S. (2022). Metaverse. *Encyclopedia, 2*(1), 486–497. DOI: 10.3390/encyclopedia2010031

Nabi, G., Liñán, F., Fayolle, A., Krueger, N., & Walmsley, A. (2017). The impact of entrepreneurship education in higher education: A systematic review and research agenda. *Academy of Management Learning & Education, 16*(2), 277–299. DOI: 10.5465/amle.2015.0026

Nakamura, L. (2009). Don't hate the player, hate the game: The racialization of labor in World of Warcraft. *Critical Studies in Media Communication, 26*(2), 128–144. DOI: 10.1080/15295030902860252

Nambisan, S. (2017). Digital entrepreneurship: Toward a digital technology perspective of entrepreneurship. *Entrepreneurship Theory and Practice, 41*(6), 1029–1055. DOI: 10.1111/etap.12254

Nasution, R. A., Lubis, F. R., & Hidayat, T. (2024). Overcoming digital divide in microlearning adoption: Evidence from Indonesian higher education. *Education and Information Technologies, 29*(2), 1805–1823. DOI: 10.1007/s10639-023-12015-6

National Development Planning Agency. (2021). *Study of the economic impact of traffic congestion in Greater Jakarta.* Ministry of National Development Planning/Bappenas.

Neergaard, H., & Ulhøi, J. P. (Eds.). (2007). *Handbook of qualitative research methods in entrepreneurship*. Edward Elgar Publishing. DOI: 10.4337/9781847204387

Ng, H. S., & Kee, D. M. H. (2018). *The Moderating Effect of Ethical Climate on Relationship between Personal Ethics and Ethical Attitudes*. International Conference on Technology and Humanities (IcoTECH), KDU Penang University College, Malaysia on 17-18 November 2018, UOWM Malaysia KDU Penang University College.

Nirwono Joga, D. (2017). *Sustainable smart cities*. November Issue.

Norman, D. (2013). *The design of everyday things: Revised and expanded edition*. Basic books.

Noroozinejad Farsangi, E., Shehata, A. O., Rashidi, M., Ghassempour, N., & Mirjalili, S. (2024). Transitioning from BIM to Digital Twin to Metaverse. *Frontiers in Built Environment*, *10*, 1486423. Advance online publication. DOI: 10.3389/fbuil.2024.1486423

Novikov, K., Hořejší, P., Kubr, J., Dvořák, M., Bednář, M., Krákora, D., Krňoul, M., & Šimon, M. (2024). Methodology for rationalization of pre-production processes using virtual reality based manufacturing instructions. *Machines (Basel)*, *12*(1), 2. DOI: 10.3390/machines12010002

Nowak, K. L., & Biocca, F. (2003). The effect of the agency and anthropomorphism on users' sense of telepresence, copresence, and social presence in virtual environments. *Presence (Cambridge, Mass.)*, *12*(5), 481–494. DOI: 10.1162/105474603322761289

Nowak, K. L., & Fox, J. (2018). Avatars and computer-mediated communication: A review of the definitions, uses, and effects of digital representations. *Review of Communication Research*, *6*, 30–53. DOI: 10.12840/issn.2255-4165.2018.06.01.015

Nowak, K. L., & Rauh, C. (2005). The influence of the avatar on online perceptions of anthropomorphism, androgyny, credibility, homophily, and attraction. *Journal of Computer-Mediated Communication*, *11*(1), 153–178. DOI: 10.1111/j.1083-6101.2006.tb00308.x

Nugroho, A., Putri, R. N., & Wicaksono, A. (2022). Digital infrastructure and urban resilience: A case study of Jakarta. *Indonesian Journal of Urban and Regional Planning*, *33*(1), 45–61.

Nyaribo, J., & Muturi, W. (2020). Consumer adoption of new technologies in emerging markets: A case study of VR in Ethiopian retail. *African Journal of Business Management*, *14*(10), 321–332.

Nye, J. S.Jr. (2008). Public diplomacy and soft power. *The Annals of the American Academy of Political and Social Science*, *616*(1), 94–109. DOI: 10.1177/0002716207311699

Odeleye, B., Loukas, G., Heartfield, R., Sakellari, G., Panaousis, E., & Spyridonis, F. (2022). Virtually secure: A taxonomic assessment of cybersecurity challenges in virtual reality environments. *Computers & Security*, *124*, 102951. DOI: 10.1016/j.cose.2022.102951

OECD. (2023). *A better future for rural youth.* OECD Development Centre. https://www.oecd.org/dev/G20-initiative-rural-youth-employment-brochure.pdf

OECD. (2024). *Education Policy Outlook 2024 Reshaping Teaching into a Thriving Profession from ABCs to AI.* https://www.oecd.org/en/publications/education-policy-outlook-2024_dd5140e4-en.html

Okoye, K. R. E., & Okoye, P. I. (2015). Enhancement and innovation in higher education in Nigeria. *Journal of Research and Development (Srinagar)*, *24*(1). https://www.researchgate.net/profile/Peter-Okoye-2/publication/280095798_ENHANCEMENT_AND_INNOVATION_IN_HIGHER_EDUCATION_IN_NIGERIA/links/55cb650308aeb975674c7894/ENHANCEMENT-AND-INNOVATION-IN-HIGHER-EDUCATION-IN-NIGERIA.pdf

Onweh, V. E., Akpan, N., & Emmanuel, C. (2022). Youth Empowerment and the Integration of Entrepreneurship Education into Technical Vocational Education and Training (TVET) in Nigeria. SSRN *Electronic Journal.* https://doi.org/DOI: 10.2139/SSRN.4166843

Ooms, W., Vanhaverbeke, W., Fini, R., & Golovic, E. (2023). Networks of innovation: Interorganizational collaboration in metaverse entrepreneurship. *Research Policy*, *52*(5), 104662.

Padi, A., Dzisi, P. S., & Eshun, P. J. F. (2022). Entrepreneurship education in TVET institutions and entrepreneurial intentions of female students in Ghana: The social support factor. *Cogent Business & Management*, *9*(1), 2137954. Advance online publication. DOI: 10.1080/23311975.2022.2137954

Palley, B., Poças Martins, J., Bernardo, H., & Rossetti, R. (2025). Integrating machine learning and digital twins for enhanced smart building operation and energy management: A systematic review. *Urban Science (Basel, Switzerland)*, *9*(6), 202. DOI: 10.3390/urbansci9060202

Pandey, P., & Kapoor, A. (2025). Cybercrime in the Digital Era: Impacts, Awareness, and Strategic Solutions for a Secure Future. *Sachetas*, *4*(1), 32–37.

Parekh, S. S. (2020). Conquer the skills gap – and win the future – by rethinking talent: World Economic Forum 2020. *World Economic Forum*, 1–5.

Parua, R., & Yang, W. (2024). The driving logic of digital transformation in TVET. *Vocation. Technology & Education*, *1*(2). Advance online publication. DOI: 10.54844/vte.2024.0590

Pegkas, P. (2015). The impact of FDI on economic growth in Eurozone countries. *Journal of Economic Asymmetries*, *12*(2), 124–132. DOI: 10.1016/j.jeca.2015.05.001

Peña, L., Benítez, H., Solórzano, R., & Montalvo, D. (2022). The influence of social capital on metaverse community development: Evidence from emerging platforms. *Journal of Interactive Learning Environments*, *30*(4), 574–591.

Perin, M. G. (2020). Entrepreneurial Orientation and Fi Rm Insight. *An Updated.*, *55*(2), 143–159. DOI: 10.1108/RAUSP-01-2019-0014

Pertiwi, N. (2021). *Implementation of sustainable development in Indonesia*. Pustaka Ramadhan.

Pittaway, L., & Cope, J. (2007). Entrepreneurship Education. *International Small Business Journal, 25*(5), 479–510. DOI: 10.1177/0266242607080656

Porter, M. (1980). *Competitive strategy: Techniques for analyzing industries and competitors*. Free Press.

Powell, L. (2014). *Reimagining the Purpose of Vocational Education and Training* [PhD Thesis]. University of Nottingham.

Powell, L. (2012). Reimagining the purpose of VET – Expanding the capability to aspire in South African Further Education and Training students. *International Journal of Educational Development, 32*(5), 643–653. DOI: 10.1016/j.ijedudev.2012.01.008

Prabowo, A., …. (2025). Determinants of export performance in Indonesia's plastic industry: A panel regression approach. Unpublished manuscript, EcoTrade Research Group.

Pramadi, Y., Fathy, R., & Arifa, S. H. (2023). Smart city based on smart communities in Bandung City: A social innovation. *Journal of Regional and Urban Development, 19*(3), 336–354. DOI: 10.14710/pwk.v19i3.43856

Puntoni, S., & Wertenbroch, K. (2024). Being Human in the Age of AI. *Journal of the Association for Consumer Research, 9*(3), 235–240. DOI: 10.1086/730788

Putra, A., & Nugroho, Y. (2019). Smart cities and the challenges of their implementation in Indonesia. *Journal of Public Administration, 13*(2), 125–138.

Qiao, F., Cheng, X., & Zhao, M. (2022). Building brand presence in the metaverse: A case study of Decentraland. *Journal of Virtual Studies, 10*(1), 45–61.

Rabener, N. (2023, June 12). Diversification versus hedging. CAIA Association. https://caia.org/blog/2023/06/12/diversification-versus-hedging

Radford, A., Wu, J., Child, R., Luan, D., Amodei, D., & Sutskever, I. (2019). Language models are unsupervised multitask learners. *OpenAI blog, 1*(8), 9.

Raes, L., Jain, A., Nguyen Ba, T., & Savels, R. (2022). *The economic impact of marine plastics, including ghost fishing, on fishing boats in Phư c Tinh and Loc An*. Ba Ria Vung Tau Province.

Rahman, M., Bhuiyan, A., Uddin, M., & Islam, S. (2022). Financial security and consumer protection in blockchain-based metaverse economies. *International Journal of Economic Policy in Emerging Economies*, *15*(2), 191–212.

Rahmawati, N., & Sarwono, J. (2020). The effectiveness of digital public reporting through the Qlue application in Jakarta. *Journal of Communication and Digital Society*, *8*(1), 70–82.

Raj, V. A., Jasrotia, S. S., & Rai, S. S. (2024). Mapping the research landscape of vocational education and entrepreneurship: Insights and future directions. *Higher Education. Skills and Work-Based Learning*, *14*(5), 992–1010. DOI: 10.1108/HESWBL-05-2023-0129

Raman, R., Kautish, P., Siddiqui, A., Siddiqui, M., & Nedungadi, P. (2025). The role of metaverse technologies in energy systems towards sustainable development goals. *Energy Reports*, *11*, 4459–4476. DOI: 10.1016/j.egyr.2025.04.012

Ramírez, A., Mena, F., Torrealba, R., & Guzmán, K. (2023). Value co-creation in metaverse marketplaces: A platform ecosystem approach. *International Journal of Market Research*, *65*(1), 47–64.

Ratan, R., Beyea, D., Li, B. J., & Graciano, L. (2020). Avatar characteristics induce users' behavioural conformity with small-to-medium effect sizes: A meta-analysis of the proteus effect. *Media Psychology*, *23*(5), 651–675. DOI: 10.1080/15213269.2019.1623698

Regan, D. B. (2021). The Influence of Small and Medium Enterprises in Employment Creation and Income Generation in Somali Regional State : A Case of Kebridahar Town. *Munich Personal RePEc Archive*, (105879), 32.

Renaud, K., van Biljon, J., Hearn, G., & Mathews, R. (2021). Early virtual worlds and the metaverse: An historical overview. *Virtual Reality Journal, 25*(2), 139–154.

Ribeiro, P., & Jardim Gonçalves, L. A. (2019). Urban resilience: A conceptual framework. *Sustainable Cities and Society, 50*, 101625. DOI: 10.1016/j.scs.2019.101625

Riva, G., & Wiederhold, B. K. (2022). What the metaverse is (really) and why we need to know about it. *Cyberpsychology, Behavior, and Social Networking, 25*(6), 355–359. DOI: 10.1089/cyber.2022.0124 PMID: 35696299

Rolofs, G., Wilking, F., Goetz, S., & Wartzack, S. (2024). Integrating digital twins and cyber physical systems for flexible energy management in manufacturing facilities: A conceptual framework. *Electronics (Basel), 13*(24), 4964. DOI: 10.3390/electronics13244964

Ruiz, M., Gil, S., Tabares, A., & Rangel, O. (2023). Managing organizational change for metaverse adoption: A case study of multinational corporations. *Journal of Change Management, 23*(2), 112–128.

Saint-Martin, L. (2025, April 9). France and Indonesia: Partners in economic sovereignty, creativity and innovation. The Jakarta Post. https://www.thejakartapost.com/opinion/2025/04/09/france-and-indonesia-partners-in-economic-sovereignty-creativity-and-innovation.html

Saleh, S., & Sumarsono, H. (2016). *Analisis penyerapan tenaga kerja sektor industri di Indonesia.* BIRCI Journal.

Sansone, G., Battaglia, D., Landoni, P., & Paolucci, E. (2019). Academic spinoffs: The role of entrepreneurship education. *The International Entrepreneurship and Management Journal, 17*(1), 1. Advance online publication. DOI: 10.1007/s11365-019-00601-9

Santoso Puji Ahmad, I. (2025). The role of digitalization in increasing government transparency and accountability. *Indonesian Journal of Public Administration Review, 2*(3), 1–10.

Sarasvathy, S. D., & Venkataraman, S. (2011). Entrepreneurship as Method: Open Questions for an Entrepreneurial Future. *Entrepreneurship Theory and Practice*, *35*(1), 113–135. https://journals.sagepub.com/doi/full/10.1111/j.1540-6520.2010.00425.x?casa_token=fMYF9GKhJhAAAAAA%3AINJJ0rkX8gKnLrh81a-KnvrjjJmltNrSpdZt6cgdh1f1X48XLgHrxe3OdNIH5xn1UAI2BRO0lo2Zvg. DOI: 10.1111/j.1540-6520.2010.00425.x

Sathisha, S. D. (2023). The effectiveness of risk management strategies in hedge funds. *International Journal of Research and Analytical Reviews*, *10*(3), 117–126. https://ijrar.org/papers/IJRAR23A3117.pdf

Scholl, H. J. (2015). *E-government: Information, technology, and transformation*. Routledge. DOI: 10.4324/9781315704906

Schumpeter, J. (1934). *The theory of economic development*. Harvard University Press.

SDGs Bappenas. (2023). *Roadmap SDGs 2023–2030*. https://sdgs.bappenas.go.id/product/roadmap-sdgs-2023-2030-eng/

Sedlmeir, J., Buhl, H. U., Fridgen, G., & Keller, R. (2021). The energy consumption of blockchain technology: Beyond myth. *Business & Information Systems Engineering*, *63*(2), 99–108.

Sekretariat Negara Republik Indonesia. (2025). RPJMN 2025–2029: Fondasi awal mewujudkan visi Indonesia Emas 2045. https://setneg.go.id

Setiawan, D., & Salamah, L. (2023). Interconnection of transportation modes in Jakarta's smart mobility system. *Journal of Transportation and Urban Studies*, *5*(1), 12–26.

Shabbir, M. S., Arshad, M. A., Mahmood, A., & Sulaiman, M. A. B. A. (2019). 4th industrial revolution and TVET: The relevance of entrepreneurship education for development. *Opcion, 35*(SpecialEdition24), 11–21.

Shah, N., Bano, S., Saraih, U. N., Abdelwahed, N. A. A., & Soomro, B. A. (2024). Boosting entrepreneurial intentions among potential TVET entrepreneurs of higher education institutes. *Education + Training*, *66*(7), 981–1006. DOI: 10.1108/ET-07-2023-0300

Shane, S., & Venkataraman, S. (2007). The promise of entrepreneurship as a field of research. In *Entrepreneurship* (pp. 171–184). Concepts, Theory and Perspective., DOI: 10.1007/978-3-540-48543-8_8

Sharma, V., Stephens, M., Khurshid, S., & Pereira, V. (2025). Metaverse governance in international business: A systematic literature review from 1990 to 2025. *Review of International Business and Strategy*, *35*(2), 210–235. DOI: 10.1108/RIBS-10-2024-0118

Shelton, T., Dexheimer, V., Gregorich, E., & Carter, C. (2021). Blockchain, NFTs, and the rise of digital assets in virtual economies. *Journal of Digital Asset Management*, *7*(4), 239–254.

Shikalepo, E. E. (2019). Sustainability of entrepreneurship and innovation among TVET graduates in Namibia. *International Journal for Innovation Education and Research*, *7*(5), 133–145. DOI: 10.31686/ijier.vol7.iss5.1484

Shin, D., Lee, H., Choi, M., & Kim, J. (2022). Protecting the metaverse: An integrative framework for cybersecurity in immersive environments. *Computers & Security*, *123*, 102903.

Shin, M., Park, J., Choi, S., & Sohn, J. (2023). Designing user experience in augmented virtuality: The interplay of presence, flow, and consumer satisfaction. *Journal of Retailing and Consumer Services*, *68*, 103019.

Sim, C., Lee, G., Lee, J., & Oh, S. (2022). Competitive strategies in the metaverse era: Opportunities for differentiated experiences. *Technological Forecasting and Social Change*, *180*, 121697.

Singh, A., Kumar, V., & Sharma, P. (2023). Artificial intelligence in microlearning: Enhancing engagement and adaptive learning for Generation Z students. *Education and Information Technologies*, *28*(6), 7895–7912. DOI: 10.1007/s10639-023-11867-2

Slater, M., Steed, A., McCall, R., & Pistrang, N. (2023). Realness in virtual environments: Investigating presence, embodiment, and immersion. *Computers in Human Behavior, 139*, 107477.

Šlogar, H., Morić Milovanović, B., & Hrvatin, S. (2023). Does the relationship between entrepreneurial orientation and subjective financial firm performance have an inverted U-shape? Evidence from Southeast European SMEs. *Administrative Sciences, 13*(2), 26.

Song, Y., Fang, J., Zhao, J., & Tang, S. (2023). Corporate communication in virtual realms: Stakeholder engagement through metaverse platforms. *Public Relations Review, 49*(1), 102243.

Son, T. H., Weedon, Z., Yigitcanlar, T., Sanchez, T., Corchado, J. M., & Mehmood, R. (2023). Algorithmic urban planning for smart and sustainable development: Systematic review of the literature. *Sustainable Cities and Society, 94*, 104562. DOI: 10.1016/j.scs.2023.104562

Sugiyono. (2017). Metode Penelitian Kuantitatif, Kualitatif, dan R&D. Bandung: Alfabeta.

Suharno, S., Ihsan, F., Himawanto, D. A., Pambudi, N. A., & Rizkiana, R. (2025). Sustainability development in vocational education: A case study in Indonesia. *Higher Education, Skills and Work-Based Learning, ahead-of-print*(ahead-of-print). https://doi.org/DOI: 10.1108/HESWBL-01-2024-0018/FULL/XML

Tai, T. Y., & Chen, H. H. J. (2021). The impact of immersive virtual reality on EFL learners' listening comprehension. *Journal of Educational Computing Research, 59*(7), 1272–1293. DOI: 10.1177/0735633121994291

Tang, X., Hu, F., Liu, M., & Shi, L. (2022). Driving open innovation in metaverse ecosystems: A framework for collaborative platform design. *Journal of Open Innovation, 8*(4), 182–199.

Teece, D. J. (2012). Dynamic Capabilities: Routines versus Entrepreneurial Action. *Journal of Management Studies, 49*(8), 1395–1401. DOI: 10.1111/j.1467-6486.2012.01080.x

Teece, D. J., Pisano, G., & Shuen, A. (1997). Dynamic capabilities and strategic management. *Strategic Management Journal*, *18*(7), 509–533. DOI: 10.1002/(SICI)1097-0266(199708)18:7<509::AID-SMJ882>3.0.CO;2-Z

Thomas, M., & Gardiner, C. (2020). *Digital learning and teaching: Microlearning in foreign language education.* Routledge., DOI: 10.4324/9780429341903

TomTom. (2022). *Traffic index: Measuring congestion around the world.* https://www.tomtom.com/en_gb/traffic-index

Toni, E., Toni, E., Fereidooni, M., & Ayatollahi, H. (2024). Acceptance and use of extended reality in surgical training: An umbrella review. *Systematic Reviews*, *13*(1), 299. DOI: 10.1186/s13643-024-02723-w PMID: 39633499

Topalidis, G. T., Kartalis, N. N., Velentzas, J. R., & Sidiropoulou, C. G. (2024). New developments in geopolitics: A reassessment of theories after 2023. *Social Sciences (Basel, Switzerland)*, *13*(2), 109. DOI: 10.3390/socsci13020109

Tran, T., Trinh, B., Nhung, N., & Thao, N. (2016). Finding economic structure and capital structure for a "greener" economy. *Journal of Economic Research*, *13*, 3153–3167.

Truong, Q., Linh, H., Vu, T., & Phan, K. (2023). Co-creation in architectural design: Virtual collaboration in metaverse-based projects. *Automation in Construction*, *148*, 104785.

Tsai, C., Chang, C., Chen, T., & Cheung, C. (2023). Gamification and user engagement in immersive environments: A meta-analytic review. *Information & Management*, *60*(4), 103722.

Turner, J., Brown, C., Holmes, P., & Wilson, S. (2023). Pathways to sustainable metaverse: Green computing and responsible innovation. *Environmental Innovation and Societal Transitions*, *46*, 126–139.

U.S. Congress. (2024, February 21). U.S. trade policy: Background and current issues. Congress.gov. https://www.congress.gov/crs-product/IF10156

Ui, F. E. (2010). *Evaluation of the policy.* Carolina Vivien Christianti, FE UI, 31–57.

UNESCO. (2025a). Quality TVET for all contributing to sustainable development, globally. *UNESCO.* https://unevoc.unesco.org

UNESCO. (2025b). *Strategy for Technical and Vocational Education and Training (TVET) (2016–2021).* UNESCO.

UNESCO-UNEVOC. (2013). TVET and entrepreneurial skills. In *Revisiting global trends in TVET: Refelction on theory and practice.* UNESCO-UNEVOC International Centre for Technical and Vocational Educaiton and Training.

UNESCO-UNEVOC. (2022). *Transforming Technical and Vocational Education and Training for successful and just transitions: UNESCO Strategy 2022-2029* (No. 9789231005527). https://www.unesco.org/open-access/terms-use-ccbysa-en

UN-Habitat. (2020). *World cities report 2020: The value of sustainable urbanization.* United Nations Human Settlements Programme. https://unhabitat.org/wcr/

United Nations Environment Programme [UNEP]. (2022). *Sustainable packaging and circularity: Trends and innovations in material use.* Nairobi: UNEP.

United Nations. (2015). Transforming our world: The 2030 Agenda for Sustainable Development. https://sdgs.un.org/2030agenda

Valerio, A., Parton, B., & Robb, A. (2014). *Entrepreneurship education and training programs around the world: Dimensions for success.* https://books.google.com.my/books?hl=en&lr=&id=ypFtAwAAQBAJ&oi=fnd&pg=PP1&dq=Valerio,+A.,+Parton,+B.,+%26+Robb,+A.+(2014).+Entrepreneurship+education+and+training+programs+around+the+world:+Dimensions+for+success.+The+World+Bank.&ots=6UOGhV7HmM&sig=uiWONbBTKM3FkiqGSbqe8XjFQb4

Valiente, O. (2014). The OECD skills strategy and the education agenda for development. *International Journal of Educational Development*, *39*, 40–48. DOI: 10.1016/j.ijedudev.2014.08.008

Vargo, S. L., & Lusch, R. F. (2004). Evolving to a new dominant logic for marketing. *Journal of Marketing*, *68*(1), 1–17. DOI: 10.1509/jmkg.68.1.1.24036

Verhoef, P. C., Lemon, K. N., Parasuraman, A., Roggeveen, A., Tsiros, M., & Schlesinger, L. A. (2009). Customer experience creation: Determinants, dynamics and management strategies. *Journal of Retailing*, *85*(1), 31–41. DOI: 10.1016/j.jretai.2008.11.001

Volery, T., & Müller, S. (2023). Digital skills, entrepreneurship education, and employability in the Fourth Industrial Revolution. *Journal of Small Business Management*, *61*(2), 345–367. DOI: 10.1080/00472778.2022.2041831

Wakjira, G. G. (2023). Partners Universal International Innovation Journal (PUIIJ) The Diagnostic Test Assumptions Model of Market Orientation on Corporate Insight the Mediating Role of Entrepre ... Partners Universal International Innovation Journal (PUIIJ). *The Di.*, (August). Advance online publication. DOI: 10.5281/zenodo.8265973

Wang, D. (2022). Sikubert and sikuroberta: Construction and application research of pre training models for digital humanities in the complete library of four branches. In *Lib. Forum*, *42*, 31–43.

Wang, Y., Gong, D., Xiao, R., Wu, X., & Zhang, H. (2024). A systematic review on extended reality mediated multi user social engagement. *Systems*, *12*(10), 396. DOI: 10.3390/systems12100396

WEF. (2023). *The Future of Job Report 2023 Insight Report May 2023* (No. 9789811206818; World Economic Forum, pp. 296–296). World Economic Forum. DOI: 10.1142/11458

White House. (2025, January 20). America First trade policy. https://www.whitehouse.gov/presidential-actions/2025/01/america-first-trade-policy/

Windhausen, A., Heller, J., Hilken, T., Mahr, D., Di Palma, R., & Quintens, L. (2024). Exploring the impact of augmented reality smart glasses on worker well-being in warehouse order picking. *Computers in Human Behavior, 155*, 108153. DOI: 10.1016/j.chb.2024.108153

Wirth, L. (1938). Urbanism as a way of life. *American Journal of Sociology, 44*(1), 1–24. DOI: 10.1086/217913

World Bank. (2020). The promise of education in Indonesia. https://www.worldbank.org/en/country/indonesia/publication/the-promise-of-education-in-indonesia

World Bank. (2022). *Global investment trends and development: Foreign direct investment and economic growth.* World Bank Publications.

World Bank. (2023). *Building better formal TVET systems: Principles and Practice in Low-and Middle-Income Countries.*

Xu, B., Lui, C., Li, D., & Li, C. (2023). Exploring the perceived ease of use and perceived value in enterprise metaverse applications. *Information Systems Journal, 33*(2), 214–233.

Xu, M., Zhu, Y., Chen, R., & Hao, C. (2022). Aesthetic experience and user satisfaction in metaverse spaces: Bridging design, presence, and emotion. *Journal of Computer-Mediated Communication, 27*(4), 431–448.

Xu, Q. (2024). Research on vocabulary sharing for machine translation from ancient chinese to modern Chinese based on UniLM Model. *Inf. Docum. Serv, 45*, 89–100.

Yee, N., & Bailenson, J. (2007). The Proteus effect: The effect of transformed self-representation on behaviour. *Human Communication Research, 33*(3), 271–290. DOI: 10.1111/j.1468-2958.2007.00299.x

Yee, N., Bailenson, J. N., Urbanek, M., & Chang, F. (2022). Avatars and identity exploration in the metaverse: Psychological findings and design implications. *ACM Transactions on Social Computing*, *5*(3), 17–29.

Ye, X., Hui, Y., Zhang, J., & Li, W. (2022). Strategies for digital transformation in the age of metaverse: A global enterprise perspective. *Journal of Global Information Technology Management*, *25*(4), 289–306.

Yuliati, E., Ramadhani, Y. C., & Wahyuni, D. U. (2022). Entrepreneurship Orientation and Market Orientation and on Corporate Insight Through Competitive Advantage. *International Journal of Academic Investigation in Corporate and Social Sciences*, *12*(6), 880–896. DOI: 10.6007/IJARBSS/v12-i6/13347

Yusof, Z. N., Murad, N., & Yusof, B. (2022). Digital Skills and Entrepreneurial Education in Malaysia: Evidence from Experiential Learning. *Theorising Undergraduate Entrepreneurship Education: Reflections on the Development of the Entrepreneurial Mindset*, 311–332. DOI: 10.1007/978-3-030-87865-8_17

Zahra, S. A., Neubaum, D. O., & Huse, M. (2022). International corporate entrepreneurship and the evolution of organizational competence. *Strategic Entrepreneurship Journal*, *16*(2), 145–167. DOI: 10.1002/sej.1456

Zefti Sulfatul Qoida, A. (2024). Regional development through smart city implementation in Sumenep Regency. *Journal of Public Sector Innovation*, *4*(3), 94–105.

Zhang, S., Lim, W. Y. B., Ng, W. C., Xiong, Z., & Niyato, D. (2022). Towards green metaverse networking technologies, advancements and future directions. arXiv preprint arXiv:2211.03057. https://doi.org//arXiv.2211.03057DOI: 10.48550

Zhang, Y., He, J., & Li, J. (2025). The role of flow experience in virtual influencer marketing: Insights into aesthetic, entertainment and parasocial influences on purchase intention. *Journal of Fashion Marketing and Management*. Advance online publication. DOI: 10.1108/JFMM-05-2024-0201

Zhu, Y., Cheng, G., Cheng, Y., & Zhang, M. (2022). Virtual brand communities: Corporate engagement strategies in metaverse contexts. *Journal of Brand Management*, *29*(6), 685–704.

About the Contributors

Syafiqah Bt Md Nayan is an experienced academician and researcher specializing in management and marketing. She earned her Ph.D. in Management from Universiti Kuala Lumpur (UniKL), focusing on the determinants of streamers' loyalty to live streaming platforms. With a strong academic background, including a Master's in Management and a Bachelor's in Business Administration, she has served as a Senior Lecturer at Management & Science University, teaching subjects such as Quality Management and Research Methodology. Dr. Syafiqah is also a published researcher, contributing to journals and international conferences on topics like service quality and customer satisfaction. Her global outlook, shaped by an international exchange program in Kazakhstan, complements her expertise in statistical tools like SPSS and Smart PLS. Dedicated to advancing education and management practices, she continues to inspire through teaching, mentoring, and research collaborations.

Azman Norhidayah is a lecturer in Faculties of Business Management and Professional Studies, Management and Science University, Shah Alam, Selangor, Malaysia. She holds a doctoral degree in Business Management "Consumer behavioural intention in healthy food product" from Management and Science University (MSU). With the strong 7 years industrial experience, her particular specialization is digital marketing, big data, management, human resources, consumer behavior and marketing. She also receives Certified Marketing Professional from American Industrial Certification Institute for completing marketing professional courses. She has participated and presented research papers in several International academic conferences.

Aeshah Mohd Ali is an experienced lecturer passionate about undergraduate and postgraduate education and applied research. She received her Doctor of Philosophy in Management from the University Kuala Lumpur. She is also an active researcher and reviewer for publications in business management studies.

Aisha Imtiaz is a distinguished academician and management professional with extensive experience in higher education and research. Currently serving as Assistant Professor and Incharge of the Department of Commerce at GC Women University, Faisalabad, she also holds key positions such as Deputy Director of Student Affairs and Manager of Innovation & Commercialization. Dr. Aisha earned her Ph.D. in Management from Universiti Kuala Lumpur, Malaysia, with a robust academic foundation including an MBA in Marketing and an MS in Management. Her research interests span diverse fields such as marketing, strategic management, and entrepreneurship, supported by a significant portfolio of publications in esteemed journals. Beyond academia, Dr. Aisha is an active contributor to industry-academia collaborations, serving as a Technical Expert on Industry-Academia Linkages at the Faisalabad Chamber of Commerce & Industry. Her leadership extends to managing student startup and business incubation centers, promoting innovation and entrepreneurship among young scholars. With multilingual proficiency in English, Urdu, Punjabi, and Malay, and a proven record of international engagement, she remains dedicated to advancing education, research, and business innovation.

***

Noman Arshed is a lecturer in the Department of Business Analytics, Sunway Business School, Sunway University. He has expertise in programming in R and Python and integrating advanced econometrics with machine learning. His research interests are exploring gains of AI integration in business and environment.

Dian Damayanti is a valued scholar member of the editorial board/ review committee/ European alliance for innovation, World Academy of Science, Engineering and Technology Economy and Management Engineering. They are also on an expert panel of AASE Chung Yuan Christian University research journals and conferences.

Johana Paola Davalos an engineering student in business management at the Fresnillo Higher Technological Institute in Mexico, with experience in academic and organizational research projects in the search to foster the growth of SMEs.

|Ninuk Lustyantie - Contributing Author|Lecturer Universitas Negeri Jakarta

Hee Song Ng is a lecturer at Sunway University. He holds a PhD and an MBA from Universiti Sains Malaysia (USM) and a Bachelor of Mechanical Engineering from Universiti Teknologi Malaysia (UTM). With over 37 years of combined experience spanning both industry and academia, Dr. Ng's research interests focus on entrepreneurship, leadership, and technology.

José De Jesús Reyes-Sánchez has a Ph.D. in senior management, has six master's degrees, in education, in management, professional soccer technique, in physical preparation, in professional soccer, in physical rehabilitation sciences, in sports sciences, as well as in coaching and integral well-being, who is a research professor at the TECNM Instituto Tecnológico Superior De Fresnillo, with more than 20 years of teaching experience, PRODEP profile and coordinator of the academic body with vast experience in conferences and workshops, currently novelist and writer.

Rajiv Sindwani holds PhD degree in the area of service quality management. Presently he is working in the Department of Management Studies at J C Bose University of Science and Technology, YMCA, Faridabad, India. He is having more than 15 years of experience in various sectors including consumer durables, banking and education. He has published many papers in reputed international journals and also presented papers in various international conferences.

Index

A

C

D

E

F

G

I

L

M

O

P

S

T

W

www.ingramcontent.com/pod-product-compliance
Lightning Source LLC
LaVergne TN
LVHW080857300926
849162LV00003B/446